Praise for *From Seed to Tree to Fruit*

"With great courage, emotional honesty and impeccable scholarship, the author embarks on a quest to learn the truth behind the mysterious death of her gentle scientist father in a psychiatric hospital when she was nine years old. Fearful of shattering a family imperative of silence, she finds unexpected joy in getting to know her youthful parents through a trove of letters written before her birth. *From Seed to Tree to Fruit* exemplifies the healing power of writing as a path through grief."

—Mindy Lewis, author of *Life Inside: A Memoir*

"While celebrating her seventy-third birthday in 2018, the author engaged the services of a street poet who had set up a makeshift sidewalk desk in Brooklyn. In preparation, the poet asked her to tell him about herself; Mlynarczyk surprised herself by discussing the death of her father when she was nine years old. The poignant verses the poet wrote for her, combined with the isolation of the subsequent Covid-19 lockdowns, prompted the author to write this memoir exploring grief, healing, and the power of love. By external appearances, Mlynarczyk's father, Bert C. Williams, had achieved the American dream, including a career as a botanist at the University of Alabama. . . . In March of 1954, Williams suffered a nervous breakdown (which seemed to come out of nowhere to the nine-year-old Mlynarczyk). . . . This remembrance is a poignant love letter to the father that Mlynarczyk has spent a lifetime grieving. While centering her own story of healing, the author also highlights the moments of joy her father brought her, from family car rides to the life lessons he continues to teach her beyond the grave. The book also offers a powerful depiction of mental illness. "Throughout his life," Mlynarczyk writes of her father, he "struggled toward the light, but darkness always lurked just a few steps behind." A professor emerita of English at the City University of New York, Mlynarczyk is a seasoned writer who offers readers a poignant, deeply personal portrait of a troubled father through a child's eyes. The book's gripping narrative is accompanied by a selection of family photos."

—*Kirkus Reviews*

"Through plain-speaking prose and forthright reflection, Rebecca Williams Mlynarczyk complicates the American idyll of a white, middle-class childhood as she recounts her early life in pre-Civil Rights Tuscaloosa, Alabama, and her father's mental illness and early death, a tragedy that derailed her childhood and haunted her adult life. Born to progressive, educated parents from the North, who were loving and attentive, the author also witnessed first-hand the violence of a segregated country. Through self-defining memories of girlhood and beyond, Mlynarczyk reveals facets of familial relations in a celebration of love and connection that belies simplicity and innocence. Such remembering comes with an ethical obligation to resist nostalgia and pursue understanding, but this most serious of endeavors is also remarkably entertaining as the author sifts through the past to offer vivid, local snapshots of fraught American history at a time when the hubris of technology deeply informed the zeitgeist of a post-war culture. Even as Mlynarczyk delves into the emotional puzzle of her father, a biology professor at the University of Alabama who both loved the world and yet struggled to be in it, the descriptions of his life and intellectual habits as well as explorations of the natural environment with his beloved daughter are both tender and enlightening. Entries from her father's journals, letters between her parents, photos, and other family artifacts punctuate the author's recollections like an anchor securing a boat in a strong tide, helping to fill in the child's partial memories and round out the adult's understandings of a father's death and a mother's struggles to raise her daughters in the aftermath of the unthinkable. *From Seed to Tree to Fruit* does what good memoirs must do: explain the present by helping us understand the past."

—Wendy Ryden, co-author of *Reading, Writing, and the Rhetorics of Whiteness*

"Haunted by her father's psychiatric crisis and his early and unexpected death, Mlynarczyk brings us on a poignant journey, exploring her father's violent breakdown and coming to terms with a past weighted with fear and silence."

—Julia Miele Rodas, author of *Autistic Disturbances: Theorizing Autism Poetics from the* DSM *to* Robinson Crusoe

"*From Seed to Tree to Fruit* is a quiet, compelling memoir of a daughter's lifelong struggle to come to terms with her brilliant father's mental illness and early death. Rebecca Mlynarczyk tells a poignant story of her father, Bert, and mother, Ruth, coming of age during the Great Depression, falling in love, and speeding into the nuclear age and the first use of the atom bomb in 1945, the year the author was born. Through the eyes of a six- or seven-year-old girl, Mlynarczyk describes a scary world outside her home in Tuscaloosa, Alabama, a world that penetrated those walls of love with strange ultraviolet machines, shoe-fitting fluoroscopes, and electroshock therapy. Idyllic walks in the woods with her father turn dark when he takes her along to the site of his research using radiation to study plant roots at the Oak Ridge National laboratory, secretly built during World War II as part of the Manhattan Project. As the tone shifts from something like a Norman Rockwell painting to a sense of hidden peril more akin to a David Lynch film, Mlynarczyk takes us on a journey of childhood trauma enshrouded in the silence of her mother's inability to grieve, the tumultuous historical backdrop of postwar technologies and radiation poisoning, and the deep love of a large extended family that gives her the courage to build her own life and continue to explore the tragedy at its core."

—Deborah Mutnick, author of *No Race, No Country: The Politics and Poetics of Richard Wright*

From Seed to Tree to Fruit
A Daughter's Memoir of Grief and Healing

Rebecca Williams Mlynarczyk

Purple Breeze
PRESS

Purple Breeze Press, LLC

purplebreezepress.com
From Seed to Tree to Fruit: A Daughter's Memoir of Grief and Healing
© 2025 Rebecca Williams Mlynarczyk

From Seed to Tree to Fruit: A Daughter's Memoir of Grief and Healing is a memoir. It reflects the author's recollections of experiences over time. Some names and descriptions have been changed. Events have been drawn from memory. Some dialogue has been recreated or reimagined.

Except in the case of brief quotations used in articles and reviews, no part of this book may be reproduced, stored in a retrieval system, or transmitted in any form without the author's permission.

Library of Congress Cataloguing in Publication Data

Names: Mlynarczyk, Rebecca Williams, author

Title: *From Seed to Tree to Fruit: A Daughter's Memoir of Grief and Healing*

Description: First edition. | Purple Breeze Press, 2025

Library of Congress Control Number: 2025905332

ISBN Paperback: 979-8-9918895-2-0

Excerpt from "After the Fall" from *Late Migrations: A Natural History of Love and Loss* (p. 218), by Margaret Renkl. Copyright © 2019 by Margaret Renkl. Reprinted with the permission of The Permissions Company, LLC, on behalf of Milkweed Editions, www.milkweed.org.

"Afterword: Lifelines" (pp. 236–237) from *Recollections Of My Nonexistence: A Memoir* by Rebecca Solnit, copyright © 2020 by Rebecca Solnit. Used by permission of Viking Books, an imprint of Penguin Publishing Group, a division of Penguin Random House LLC. All rights reserved.

Excerpt from *Naturalist* (pp. 103–104), by E.O. Wilson. Copyright © 1994 Island Press. Reproduced by permission of Island Press, Washington, D.C.

"Blessed," words and music by Lui Collins. Copyright © 1988 by Lui Collins.
Used by permission of Lui Collins.

Book designed and copy edited by Meg Vezzu / megvezzu.com

For my sister,
Carol June Williams

Contents

Prologue   i

PART I

1. Another World   1
2. The Fourth of July   8
3. The Spotted Men   17
4. Billy and Me   28
5. Tanglewood   34
6. Waiting for Justice   45
7. The Great Smoky Mountains   59
8. Oak Ridge   77
9. The Half-Life of Memory   87

PART II

10. There   101
11. July 6, 1954   109
12. Unanswered Questions   111
13. Crying   118
14. Summer on Alvord Boulevard   123
15. A Change of Scenery   135
16. Living on Tenterhooks   144
17. 2719 Short Marion   154

PART III

18. Opening the Book of the Past	173
19. Letters from the Psych Ward	190
20. Double Vision	214

PART IV

21. Holding the Gate Ajar	227
22. This Force We Call Love	247
23. The Burden Marriage Bears	269
24. Climbing Toward the Heights	283
25. The Romance of Being a Student	295
26. A Stake in the Future	312
27. From Seed to Tree to Fruit	330
28. Everything Endures	342
Epilogue	354
Acknowledgments	357
Notes	365
Photo Credits	375
About the Author	377

The basic human problems are eternal and the explications of science touch them but superficially and incompletely; the true solutions must be sought always in men's hearts, in an individual bravery, a personal courage, whether of the body, the mind, or the spirit.

—Geoffrey West, *Charles Darwin*

(My father copied this quotation into his diary on November 2, 1943.)

Prologue

It was the morning of my seventy-third birthday, May 3, 2018. The trees along Seventh Avenue in my Brooklyn neighborhood sparkled with fresh green leaves. Walking to the subway station at Ninth Street, I was purposeful as always, not wanting to waste a minute. Halfway across Third Street, I paused, turned around, and walked back to the corner I had just passed. Something unusual had caught my eye. There on the sidewalk, a young African-American man was sitting on a wooden chair behind a makeshift desk. A handmade sign next to the desk read, "Poems while you wait."

Looking into his eyes, I said, "It's my birthday today, and I would like a poem." Then, thinking practically, I added, "How much do you charge?"

This is so unlike me, I thought. I'm not the type to stop and talk to strangers on the street, and I've always felt guilty asking for things I want.

I was reassured when the man smiled up at me and answered. "The amount is totally up to you. I write it. You read it. And then you decide."

I smiled back. "That sounds great."

The poet, Lynn Gentry, explained that first we would talk for a few minutes. I could tell him what was on my mind, and then we would see what emerged from his portable typewriter, an Olympia just like the one I had treasured as a college student in the 1960s.

Lately, I explained, I had been thinking a lot about my early childhood in Alabama. My sister, my daughter, and I were considering taking a trip back there, a journey into the past. "Those were segregation days," I said. "I have never forgotten the inhumane way that Black people were treated under that system." There was also a painful personal side to my time there, I explained to him. "When I was nine years old, my father, a biology professor at the University of Alabama, had a psychotic break and had to be hospitalized. Three months later, he died in Bryce Hospital, the dilapidated state hospital in our town that was originally called the Alabama Insane Hospital."

Lynn nodded. Taking out a fresh sheet of paper, he began to type, pausing from time to time as he looked off into space. Then the keys began to click again. A few minutes later, he read over what he had written, stopped to correct a typo using Wite-Out tape, and handed me this poem.

> *Reflecting*
>   *as a child that has grown*
> *now steady on my path*
> *Living in a place long gone*
> *from the South of yesterday*
> *and in conversation passing*
> *I wonder if I should return*
> *To get beyond perception*
> *To see and learn*
>   *Understanding that to witness*
> *is to formulate a view*
> *and knowing the years that have passed*
> *perhaps I am ready to*
>
> *Knowing to not realize*
> *is to keep my eyes closed*
> *and I have chosen the path*
> *to be wise*

Reading these words, there on the corner of Seventh Avenue and Third Street, I was amazed. This man, a stranger whom I had met just a few minutes before, somehow intuited where I was at this time in my

PROLOGUE

life. He understood and put into words my feeling that I needed to go back to the past, to revisit the days of my childhood, to face the beauty and the pain.

In the months that followed, I kept telling myself I should start writing. I had so much material—all the letters, notebooks, and photographs my parents had saved over the years. I had been retired from full-time work for nearly ten years, yet sitting down to actually begin this project never seemed to happen. There were so many other things I needed to do. It was just so much easier not to write about the past.

And then the whole world ground to a halt. In 2019, a few cases of a strange new virus popped up in China. By March of 2020, it was clear that this highly contagious virus was becoming a global pandemic. Emergency rooms were filling up, and people were dying. *Many* people were dying. My Brooklyn neighborhood was becoming a hot spot. The wail of ambulances was almost constant, and no one was on the streets. Our vibrant city neighborhood began to feel like a ghost town.

On a weekend in the middle of March, my husband and I drove to our country house in Western Massachusetts, intending to spend one night there and return to Brooklyn the next day. We were actually in the car headed back to the city when my sister called in tears. She explained that she and her husband had been following the news all weekend, and the virus was spreading exponentially. "I don't think you should go back to the city," she said. It only took a few minutes for us to decide she was right. We turned around and drove back to Plainfield. We stayed there, with only occasional short trips back to the city, for the next two years.

During those months in the country, it was comforting to be surrounded by the beauty of nature while so much in our everyday lives seemed to be falling apart. And then, finally, I began to write.

The isolation and disruption of life's regular routines in 2020 enabled me to spend a lot of time in another year, 1954, the year my father had a nervous breakdown and had to be institutionalized. Part of me had remained stuck in that year, a nine-year-old self who never quite emerged from the pain and trauma of the seminal event of her childhood. Finally, when the whole world was traumatized and grieving, I found the time—and the courage—to examine the clues, to sift through the evidence, to face the fears that had haunted me for so long.

My mother had been a saver, and after her death in 2003, my sister and I gained possession of the countless photographs, newspaper articles, letters, postcards, and personal journals she had collected over her eighteen-year marriage to my father. Using these raw materials and my own memories as a guide, I have pieced together fragments of my interrupted childhood. The process has been arduous. For so many years my psychic energy had gone into repressing these memories. And now I was trying to dredge them back into awareness.

Something as simple as learning the exact date of my father's hospitalization and the hour of his death proved to be strangely reassuring. The obituary in his hometown newspaper, the *Greensburg* [Indiana] *Daily News* provides these details: "Ill since March 27, Dr. Williams died suddenly in a hospital at Tuscaloosa, Ala., at 6:45 a.m. on Tuesday, July 6." There it is in black and white, March 27, the day an ambulance came to our house and took him away, a Saturday as it turns out, exactly one week after his forty-fifth birthday. And the hour of his death three months later, 6:45 a.m. on an otherwise ordinary Tuesday in July. Both of these facts confirm the memories I have harbored for years.

Of course, I have other memories, happier memories. Going for walks in the woods with my father as my guide. Family car rides after supper, cruising along with all the windows down on nights when it was just too hot to stay inside. Sitting next to him in a movie theater watching a Western or a musical.

PROLOGUE

I try to keep these memories in mind as I sort through all the things my mother collected. Gradually, as I look back at the events of 1954, I have begun to understand that as painful as these experiences were for me, they actually happened in the real world, not just in my mind. Giving them a concrete existence by recording them in writing has lessened the fear and shame that used to weigh me down, especially in the month of March, the month when everything changed for our family.

PART I

Through writing, we revisit our past and review and revise it. What we thought happened, what we believed happened to us, shifts and changes as we discover deeper and more complex truths. It isn't that we use our writing to deny what we've experienced. Rather we use it to shift our perspective.

—Louise DeSalvo, *Writing as a Way of Healing*

1
Another World

IN THE SPRING of 1945, as the war in Europe neared its conclusion, my parents were about to begin a new life. Writing to my mother in April, my father said, "We both are getting exactly what we want and partly at the hands of a kind fate." He was at Indiana University working hard to finish his doctoral dissertation in botany so that he could start his new job as a professor of biology at the University of Alabama in Tuscaloosa. My thirty-three-year-old mother, who had worked full time since the age of eighteen, had recently resigned her job as director of child-care services in her hometown of Evansville, Indiana. Finally, after waiting so long to have a child, her dream was about to come true.

As he anticipated becoming a parent, my father wrote, "We shall give our children love, and security, and understanding, and try not to spoil them with too much attention or coddling, and try not to frustrate them by expecting too much in the way of scholastic achievement."

My mother, always so expansive, whether in speech or writing, described the kind of home she hoped to create for their children:

> If our home is as happy as the one I've conjured up in my imagination, life will really be glorious for us and our children. And I'm not thinking at all of the furnishings but a certain spirit—an atmosphere of love, congeniality, beauty, a home that is inviting, where people, young and old, love to come. In the summer we'll go on outings

with the children, teach them to swim, to know the trees and flowers, to become experts in the lore of the woods and fields. We'll play games together and laugh and sing together. And in winter on long Sunday afternoons, we'll pop corn and tell stories, read and act out plays. We'll study together and work together and everyone will have some chores to perform. We'll welcome our children's friends and make our home a center of activity and happiness. We'll have a garden and lots of trees and flowers. Just the mere thought sets my heart glowing. When two people love and understand each other as we do, it's so much fun to be together, and in one's own home one is never bored—or at least needn't be.

Many years later, as I try to recall the atmosphere of our home in Tuscaloosa, my mother's description rings true. For the first eight years of my life, I enjoyed a childhood filled with backyard birthday parties, walks in the woods with my biologist father, weekly trips to the public library, outings with my parents' friends, and quiet evenings at home with stories before bedtime. I was blessed to spend my early years in the kind of home Ruth and Bert had long dreamed of creating.

~

My father had never visited the University of Alabama when he accepted a job in the biology department. But he quickly came to love the university and the work he did there. Whenever a friend or relative visited us, he would always take them on a tour of the campus, and he often took me there as well. The visit I remember most clearly happened on an October weekend when I was six or seven years old.

As we got close to the campus, there was a lot of traffic, and we had to park a few blocks away. Walking with Daddy along University

Avenue, I could tell something special was going on. "Next week is Homecoming," he explained. "There's a big parade on Saturday afternoon, and the students compete to see who can make the best float."

A lot of flatbed trucks were parked next to the curb, and I could see groups of students stuffing colored paper into chicken wire to make the decorations for their floats.

"Can we come to the parade?" I asked.

"I think we might be able to arrange that," Daddy said. "I'll have to check with your mother."

Some of the floats had signs on them with big, colorful letters. "Roll Tide." "Go Bama!" "High Tide for the Crimson." I had been reading signs since I was five. Now that I was older, I loved to sit in Daddy's big chair in the living room and read chapter books. Recently, I had figured out that I didn't have to say the words out loud. I could just imagine them in my mind.

Daddy explained that the signs on the floats referred to a big football game that would be held at Denny Stadium next Saturday night. Alabama would be playing their archrival, Mississippi State. Our family didn't go to football games. My parents were not interested in sports. They got more excited about books than about ball games. But I knew that football was a big deal at the university. We had a red-and-white felt banner on the wall of our bedroom with "ALABAMA" spelled out in letters that got smaller toward the pointed end. That was the first word I learned how to spell: A-L-A-B-A-M-A. I loved it that every other letter was an "A."

We crossed a sidewalk and entered a huge open yard with lots of big trees around the edges. "This is the quad," Daddy said. "That's short for quadrangle, meaning it has four sides." The trees had lost most of their leaves since it was already October, and I could see the setting sun through the tree branches. Soon the campus would be dark.

"What's that?" I asked as we approached the middle of the quad. It was a big tepee-like thing made of crisscrossing pieces of wood. I went over to take a closer look. It was really tall, about twice as tall as my father, and he was six foot four.

"They're getting ready for the bonfire next week," he said. "Right before the big football game, they have a pep rally to get everyone excited. Then they take a torch and light the bonfire. It's huge. You can see the flames for miles. It's the university's way of celebrating Homecoming and the beginning of the cooler fall weather."

As we walked across the big lawn, I scuffled along, kicking up clouds of leaves. They smelled so good, sort of like the smoky smell in our fireplace at home. Every once in a while, the leather sole of my shoe would slide out from under me as my foot landed on an acorn.

Daddy pointed to the beautiful buildings arranged around the quad. "This is where I teach and where the students attend classes. The university is not just about parades and football games. It's really about learning." We headed over to one of the brick buildings with white columns in front. This was the biology department.

We climbed up some steps, and Daddy opened the big front door. I almost fainted! Just inside the door, I saw a full-grown black bear rearing up on its hind legs and baring its big yellowish teeth in a snarl. What a relief when I realized it wasn't alive. "Why did they put a bear here?" I asked.

"Biology is the study of life on earth," Daddy explained. "Not just human life, but animal and plant life, even tiny forms of life that you can't see except with a powerful microscope. We biologists like to collect specimens, small ones like ants as well as big ones like bears."

The entrance hall was beautiful and very quiet, like a church before the service begins. When I looked up, I saw that there was a balcony overlooking the hall. It reminded me of the choir loft in our church.

ANOTHER WORLD

"It's not usually this quiet," Daddy said. "On a school day, the place is humming with students and professors coming and going."

"I need to go upstairs to my lab," he said, "but first I want to show you the greenhouse." We walked through the hall, under the balcony, and out through a door at the back of the building. The greenhouse wasn't actually green. It was made out of clear glass and was bigger than I expected. Daddy had to use a key to open the door. The first thing I noticed was the smell. It was a good smell, like the soil in our back yard after a big rain. The air felt hot and heavy, and I knew the plants liked it. There were small trees growing in buckets on the floor and lots of plants of different sizes in pots on the benches. My favorites were the orchids. They had delicate-looking flowers in bright colors that reminded me of the names on my Crayola crayons—vermillion, goldenrod, blue-violet, burnt sienna.

"I thought you would like this place, Becky." I could tell Daddy was pleased. He even let me touch some of the plants, those with fuzzy leaves and others in the cactus section with spines and prickles. "I like to come in here at the end of my workday. I check on a few of the plants I'm growing. But I mainly just like to spend a few quiet moments here enjoying the beauty of nature."

When we left the greenhouse, we went back into the main hall and climbed up a narrow staircase to the third floor. We walked down a dark corridor past several doors with small glass windows near the top, and then Daddy stopped and opened a door on the left. "This is my lab," he said. "I teach my classes in a lecture hall, but this is where I work with the more advanced students and a few beginning students who just want to learn things they can't get from books and lectures." He flipped a switch near the door and turned on the fluorescent lamps over the lab benches.

The lab was a narrow room with a long wooden table running down the middle. There were microscopes on the table with wooden stools nearby. Arranged on shelves lining one of the long sides of the room were different-sized jars filled with a bright-yellow fluid. They contained all kinds of strange things. Daddy must have noticed that my eyes were riveted to these yellow bottles because he said, "Those are specimens that we've collected. Some of the jars contain internal organs from animals who were sick. Others contain preserved reptiles like snakes or lizards. The yellow stuff is formaldehyde. It keeps the tissues from decaying." I thought this was creepy, but I didn't say anything. I didn't want Daddy to think I was too young to understand. After he checked a few things with his microscope and made some notes in his notebook, he said, "I guess we'd better head on home. Your mother will be getting supper on the table."

ANOTHER WORLD

As we walked back across the quad, Daddy kept talking. This surprised me because he was usually such a quiet man. "When I was a boy growing up on the farm, I loved to walk in the woods and look at all the trees and plants. I thought if I ever got to college, that's what I would want to study, the beautiful plants that live all over the earth. I was lucky. I got a scholarship to DePauw University. And I quickly learned there was a lot more to plants than I knew when I was a boy. They depend on roots and huge underground networks. They send out pollen and seeds that travel for miles with help from insects and other animals. Over time, they keep changing, evolving to adapt to differences in their environment. The university opened up a whole other world for me, a world where I never stop learning."

I didn't say much after that. It was nice just to be with my father, holding his hand and walking across the campus on a fall afternoon. The floats, the bonfire, the bear, the greenhouse, the strange things in the yellow fluid. I was happy to get this glimpse of another world, Daddy's world.

2
The Fourth of July

My mother often told me about the time when I was just a tiny baby, and she and Daddy moved to Alabama to start a new life. He had recently completed his doctoral thesis at Indiana University, and she had just given birth to me, her first child. Although she had always loved children, she didn't know anything about taking care of a baby. As my parents packed the car to drive to their new home, her mother (my Granny Stamps) warned her to dress me warmly so I wouldn't catch cold on the long car trip. By the time they arrived in Tuscaloosa, I was covered in itchy, red welts. They drove straight to a pediatrician's office, where he quickly diagnosed the problem. "Take those woolen clothes off that baby. She is suffering from prickly heat. All she needs to wear is a diaper."

Feeling sheepish, they drove on to 89 Cedar Crest, the house where they would be living until they could afford to buy a home of their own. It was a modest house on a quiet street—perfect for families with young children. They had arranged to rent this house from another professor who was on a year's leave. In the end, he decided not to return, and they bought the little house where we lived for the next ten years.

That summer, Daddy taught two introductory biology classes. Meanwhile, Mother was adjusting to life as a full-time mom. For the first time in many years, she was not working outside the house, and since she couldn't drive, she spent almost all her time at home, marveling at her little daughter and fussing with the cooking and housework—tasks that had always been handled by her mother, who had lived with her even after her marriage in 1936.

A true extrovert, Mother needed to interact with other people, and she was quick to make friends with the neighbors, most of whom had been born and raised in the Deep South. That first summer, as July 4th approached, she was shocked to learn that people in the South didn't really celebrate Independence Day. There were no big parades or fireworks displays. As a student of U.S. history, she couldn't understand their failure to observe this day when the Founding Fathers declared their independence from Great Britain.

When she was a girl growing up in Indiana, July 4th had been one of the most wonderful days of the year. She loved to tell me about Fourth of July celebrations at Aunt Clara's farm surrounded by all her aunts, uncles, and cousins. These were all-day affairs with bratwurst, German potato salad, homemade ice cream, and—as soon as the sun went down—fireworks.

During Mother's first few years in Tuscaloosa, she was busy taking care of me, and then my sister, Carol, born in 1948, and she contented herself with celebrating the Fourth of July privately. Around the beginning of July, she would start singing her favorite patriotic songs, "My Country 'Tis of Thee," "I'm a Yankee Doodle Dandy," and my personal favorite, "You're a Grand Old Flag." All these years later, I can still hear her clear mezzo-soprano voice as she went about her chores, cooking and cleaning and singing—always singing. Every year she managed to have a few boxes of sparklers on hand for the Fourth of July, and on the evening of the holiday, I was allowed to hold a lighted sparkler if I was very careful not to burn myself on the hot wire.

But in 1951, when I was six years old and Carol was nearly three, Mother decided we needed more than a private celebration. She had taught elementary school for ten years before I was born, and she believed the neighborhood children needed to know something about their country's history. What better way to teach this lesson than a children's parade down our block on Cedar Crest to celebrate Independence Day?

Toward the end of June, she set out on her mission. Her first stop was the Bond house directly across the street. She explained to Mrs. Bond, mother of Billy and Mary Jane, that the children were invited to participate in a little neighborhood parade she was planning for the Fourth. She would put some music on the record player, and kids could ride their bicycles up and down the street. If they wanted to decorate their bikes, she would provide the supplies. There was hardly any automobile traffic on Cedar Crest, but she promised to watch carefully for cars and make the children pull over whenever a car turned onto our street.

After describing her plans to Mrs. Bond, she went next door to talk with Mrs. Gregory. Gretchen Gregory was about my age. She had a shiny slide in her front yard, and I often crossed the street to play with her. A few houses down was Mrs. Ridley, mother of Richard. My mother told me that if the poor little boy didn't produce a bowel movement by 10 a.m., he had to have an enema, but his mother did allow him to participate in the Fourth of July parade. Across the street from us and a couple of houses down lived the Nisbet family, whose twin girls, Judy and Jean, were my best friends. Surely, they would want to be in a neighborhood parade.

It's hard to know what the other mothers thought of this tall, take-charge Northerner proposing something that had never been done before on their street. She seemed to mean well. Surely, the children would enjoy it. Anything to relieve the monotony of an Alabama summer, when the heat drained all your energy, leaving the kids with little to do.

Mother had learned from her experience as an elementary school teacher and community organizer that a successful activity depended on advance planning. A trip to Woolworth's was called for. She asked Daddy to drive us downtown as soon as the store opened so that she could find what she needed for the neighborhood parade. She headed to the aisle with the art supplies and selected big rolls of red, white, and blue crepe paper. At the end of the aisle, she was pleased to find small American flags made of real cloth and mounted on little wooden sticks. She put ten flags in her basket. Next to the flags were boxes of giant sparklers decorated in red, white, and blue. On the outside of the box was a picture of the Statue of Liberty, but instead of holding a torch, she held a sparkler that was showering bright sparks all over the box. Mother stood there for a long time. "These are very expensive," she said. "Fifty cents a box." Finally, she reached out and took five boxes. "The children will love these," she said. "It wouldn't be the Fourth of July without fireworks."

At last, the big day arrived. One by one, the kids began to gather in our front yard, where they took long strips of crepe paper to decorate their bikes. Then we all lined up to start the parade. Billy insisted on going first on his shiny new bike. I rode behind him on my bright blue Schwinn. Carol was too young to balance on a two-wheeler, but she could go pretty fast on my old red tricycle with the chrome handlebars, which she had inherited. It was kind of scratched up, but even that old trike looked good with crepe-paper streamers flying in the breeze.

We rode up and down the block, pumping away. Whenever we passed our house, we could hear the march music on the record player Daddy had set up in the front yard, and we pedaled a little faster. But after a few trips back and forth, we were too tired and too hot to keep going.

"It's time for refreshments," Mother announced. She had made two large pitchers of Kool-Aid—orange and grape. A big watermelon was cooling in a galvanized washtub filled with ice and water. Daddy cut the melon into slices. The juice dripped down our faces, and we spat the seeds into the yard.

When we had eaten and drunk our fill, it was time for sparklers. Mother handed out one sparkler to each child. She also gave one to Daddy. He struck a match and lit his sparkler and held it very carefully so the children could light theirs. Soon the yard was filled with kids running and jumping as little stars shot into the air. I could feel a ping when a spark hit my arm, but it didn't really hurt. It just tickled. The children found all kinds of different things to do with their sparklers, whirling them in circles or figure eights or writing their names in the air. All too soon the sparkler would sputter out, and we would put the hot wire in a coffee can half-filled with water to snuff out any remaining sparks. I loved the sizzling sound it made as it hit the water. Daddy kept giving out fresh sparklers, but soon they were all gone.

Using her strong teacher voice, Mother gathered all the children together. "I imagine your parents will be expecting you home about now." Her lipstick was starting to fade, and a trickle of sweat ran down the side of her cheek, but her face was glowing as she said, "I hope you kids enjoyed our little parade."

THE FOURTH OF JULY

She walked over to the card table and picked up a shoebox containing the small American flags she had bought at Woolworth's. She handed a flag to each of the children and said, "Remember: the Fourth of July is about more than just parades and sparklers. It's about the birth of our country. On July 4, 1776, the Founding Fathers signed the Declaration of Independence. That was the beginning of the country we all live in, the United States of America."

Most of the kids remembered to say thank you to my parents, and then they walked back to their own houses. Mother just stood there looking across the street and smiling.

Once we were back in our own house, Carol and I realized we were pretty tired too. Daddy drew a warm bath, and we both hopped in the tub and washed the dirt of the day away. He dried each of us off with a towel. We quickly put on our pj's and climbed into bed. Mother came in to say goodnight.

"Well, girls, what did you think of our Fourth of July celebration this year?"

"It was really fun," Carol said.

"Mm-hmm," I agreed.

And then we fell asleep.

~

My mother never got over her love of the Fourth, as she always called it. In her elder years, she spent many of these holidays at "the farm." In 1972, four years after our marriage, my husband, Frank, and I bought an old house in the village of Plainfield, Massachusetts. We envisioned it as a refuge from our busy lives in New York City, and that is what, over the years, it has become.

Mother, who continued to live in Indiana, would visit for a week or two once a year, and after a few hectic visits to our city home in Brooklyn, she decided that she preferred the more relaxed atmosphere of the farm.

These visits usually took place in July, which presented a problem—and a possibility. It turned out that Plainfield, like Tuscaloosa, wasn't really into celebrating the Fourth. A few family picnics, perhaps. Sometimes, in the evening, we might see some stray fireworks above the hills beyond our house. This was definitely not enough to satisfy my mother.

After spending a few quiet Independence Days in town, she offered a suggestion. "Why don't we have a little party for the neighbors?" Mother's question created something of a dilemma for me. It has always been hard for me to approach people I don't know well. I had been spending summers in Plainfield for several years, but I still didn't really know most of my neighbors, and, on my own, I would not have had the gumption to organize a backyard celebration. From the earliest days of my childhood, I was used to following along behind my mother in social situations. She was so confident and assured, always reaching out to those around her. I was more inward, usually with my nose in a book. Outside the house, it was easy to let Mother take the lead, a role she relished. But I wasn't a child anymore, and remembering how much I had enjoyed our Fourth of July parades in Tuscaloosa, I took a deep breath and decided to host a celebration.

We invited the neighbors up and down Main Street. All of them said yes since nothing else was going on that day. The party was a success, and our Fourth of July celebration soon became a neighborhood tradition. As in the Tuscaloosa days, the highlight of the party was sparklers. These could not be legally sold in Massachusetts, but Mother always found a way to secure a sufficient cache before the holiday. Every year when she unpacked her suitcase, there they were—a few boxes of contraband.

Most years we couldn't wait until dark to light the sparklers. Our back yard, with its view of the surrounding hills, was the perfect place for this display, as the kids would run around leaping and spinning in circles. Even the adults managed to etch a few figure eights or write their names in the air while the sparks lasted.

After the sparklers were gone, the neighbors started drifting back to their homes. At the end of the day, I was almost as tired as I had been during my childhood celebrations in Alabama. Frank and I barely had enough energy to get our children, Susanna and Alex, bathed and into bed before we collapsed ourselves. Replaying the events of the day in my mind, the image that stood out was my mother. Now a woman in her seventies, she still had the energy and enthusiasm of a young child. And she still had a unique way of creating excitement and community wherever she went—especially on the Fourth of July.

Mother's last visit to the farm was for our daughter's wedding in July 2001. Five years earlier, when she was eighty-five, my sister and I could no longer deny that our strong, courageous mother was suffering from dementia, and we made arrangements for her to move to an assisted living community in Evansville. Although her mind had become unreliable, her enthusiasm and love of life were undiminished, and she was thrilled to be in Plainfield for her granddaughter's wedding. Sitting next to her in the church, I held her hand as Frank walked Susanna down the aisle. As our daughter stood with her six bridesmaids facing the altar, Mother kept whispering excitedly, "Which one is Susie?" I brushed away a tear as I answered, "She's the one in white."

My mother died peacefully two years later at the age of ninety-one.

3

The Spotted Men

When my little sister was three years old, she started having nightmares. The villains of these dreams were the Spotted Men. She had the same dream night after night, and she could describe the Spotted Men so clearly that I knew exactly what they looked like. They were made of wood and were even bigger than a grown man. All of them were painted white and covered with big, round spots in bright colors like red or yellow or blue. They were always on a train, prowling from car to car, chasing my little sister and scaring her to death.

One reason I could picture the Spotted Men so clearly was that they looked like a much bigger version of some toys Carol had gotten from Santa. They were called Bill Dings, and they were made of wood and about six inches tall. They came in many colors—red, green, yellow, blue, and white. None of them were spotted. They were intended for younger children, but I liked to play with them too even though I was six years old and had recently started first grade.

Bill Dings were like stick figures, only thicker, and they all looked exactly the same except for the color. Their legs were spread apart, and their arms were pressed straight down beside their bodies. They were flat, but they had clown faces painted on the front and wore rumpled-looking suits, also painted on. All of them, no matter what color, were men. There were no women or children Bill Dings. Maybe that's because they were all named Bill. Another reason for their name was that they were a building toy. You could stack them one on top of another to make a tower, like a block tower only made out of men. You could also balance them on each other's shoulders so that some of them stuck out to the side, sort of like acrobats in a circus. Maybe that's why they had clown faces. They were all smiling, but not in a nice way. Even though I liked to play with them, stacking them up in different ways until they all toppled over, I could see why Carol had nightmares about them. If you looked closely at their faces, they *were* scary.

Almost every night, Carol woke up crying. Mother would come into our bedroom, sit down on her bed, and hold her and talk to her in a soft voice. "Sweetheart, everything's okay. You just had a bad dream." But Carol was still frightened and whimpering. She could not fall back to sleep, so Mother would have to lie down next to her and stay there for a long time until she could finally tell from her breathing that she was asleep.

This went on for a long time. During the day Carol seemed fine, but every night at bedtime I could tell she was starting to get scared, afraid that the Spotted Men would be chasing her again that night.

A few days after Thanksgiving, something very scary happened for real. There was a terrible train wreck in the small town of Woodstock, Alabama, about twenty miles from Tuscaloosa, where we lived. A picture of the wreck was on the front page of the newspaper the next day. Two sleek new trains had crashed right into each other. Some of the cars had crumpled like pieces of aluminum foil. One car had fallen off the track and was lying on its side. It looked like it was about to topple over and roll down the hill.

I usually didn't read the newspaper; it was for grownups and pretty boring. But I read the whole article about the accident. It explained that the trains were going in opposite directions. One of them pulled over onto something called a "siding" to let the other train pass by. But then, for some reason, the engineer drove his train back onto the main track, and the two trains collided. The engineer was killed, and so were seventeen other people. Many people were injured.

I couldn't believe something this bad had happened so close to where we lived. We sometimes took the train all the way from Alabama to Indiana, where most of our relatives lived. I loved being on the train with our family all together. The sound of the wheels was so soothing, and I loved the rocking motion. I never thought anything bad could happen on a train. The picture in the paper was horrifying. We could have been on that train!

Then I had an idea. I called to Carol and asked her to come sit beside me on the couch. I showed her the picture and asked if she would like me to read the article to her. She nodded. I read most of the article just the way it was in the paper, but when I got to the part about the people who had died, I added, "The Spotted Men were traveling on one of the trains, and they were all killed." Carol didn't say anything.

Later that day, when I was alone with my father, I explained what I had told Carol and asked if he would drive us over to see the wreck. I said I thought she needed to see the trains for herself to really believe that the Spotted Men were dead. He agreed, and so before supper, the whole family got in the car and went to Woodstock. Many others were there too. They had already put up a sort of fence to keep people from getting too close to the trains. It was an awful thing to see—so much more real than just a picture in the newspaper. On the drive home, my parents went along with my story. They said it was terrible how many people had died in the crash, but they were glad that the Spotted Men had also been killed. And, in a way, they had.

Carol never dreamed about the Spotted Men again.

~

I cherish the memory of how I killed off the Spotted Men because it reveals the deep love and care I felt for my little sister, feelings that were carefully concealed beneath the petty acts of jealousy I perpetrated on a nearly daily basis.

Until the birth of Carol June on August 4, 1948, I had been the apple of my mother's eye. That metaphor springs to mind because I felt my mother's gaze upon me from the moment I woke up until she tucked me in for the night. She probably watched me when I was sleeping as well.

Childlike herself, Mother had always loved children and longed to have one of her own. In later years she often said, "I think I would have died if I couldn't have had children!" But she had to wait a long time before this dream could become a reality. For almost ten years after their marriage in 1936, my mother and father faithfully practiced birth control. It was the Depression, and they both had to work to support their families. Finally, in 1945, the stars aligned for my birth. The Depression was over, World War II was drawing to a close, and my father was putting the finishing touches on his dissertation at Indiana University. Soon he would be a professor. After all the years, they felt ready to start a family.

Although my mother had long yearned for a child, she was not the most confident of new mothers. Her anxiety was heightened when, three weeks after my birth, the newly expanded family moved to a small southern town four hundred miles from her home and extended family. My father was gone all day, putting in long hours at the university, and my mother, who started teaching when she was only eighteen, now found herself without a job. Without a job, that is, except for her new role as mother. She took this job very seriously and resolved to be the best mother any baby could have.

From the day I was born, she marveled at my every move, which she recorded meticulously in my baby book. Here is her record of my "Behavior Day" at eight weeks old, handwritten in her flowing schoolteacher script.

4:45 a.m.	Woke & cried to be fed
4:45 – 5:15	Nursed 15 min.
	5 ½ oz. Dextri maltose
	Drained bottle
5:15 a.m.	Heard Becky grunting. On tummy.
	Couldn't get left hand out
8:00 a.m.	Woke – fed her – took 4 oz. milk
8:30 a.m.	In buggy on porch
9:30 a.m.	Began fretting
9:50 a.m.	Asleep
10:30	Crying
10:45	Gave her a drink & played with her a little while
10:53	Crying
10:56	Stopped crying – resting
10:59	Fretting. Trying to crawl
11:20	Resting
11:23	Crying
11:35	Fed. Took 4 ½ oz.
12:13 p.m.	In bed. Began crying
12:45	Asleep
4:00	Awakened. Given cod liver oil & orange juice – bath – fed. Took 4 ½ oz.
8:20	Fed. Took 5 ½ oz.
	Cried 5 min. Asleep for the night

It wasn't easy, even for an infant, to be subjected to this kind of unrelenting surveillance. Poor little baby! She was always under her mother's watchful eye. Usually the gaze was one of amazement and adoration. But along with all that love, my mother experienced a fair amount of anxiety. "Why hasn't the baby rolled over yet?" "Is she late to get her first tooth?" "Why doesn't she smile more?"

Whenever Mother had a question, she turned to the experts. She was determined to raise her children by the book. For concerned mothers in the mid-1940s, that book was *Baby and Child Care* by Dr. Benjamin Spock. Usually, a quick consultation with Dr. Spock was enough to calm her down. But if the anxiety was intense, she would make an appointment with the pediatrician. After a thorough examination of little Becky, the doctor would reassure my mother: "Babies develop at different rates. Your little girl is completely normal." Most mothers would have been reassured by that comment, but normal wasn't good enough for my mother. She was determined that her first child would be extraordinary.

As I progressed through the milestones of the early years, learning to walk, talk, and use the potty, my days were spent almost entirely in the company of my mother. From morning to night, she talked and sang and played with me. I got used to having her undivided attention as we made our way through the long Alabama days. When Daddy came home from work, he would often shake his head and say, with a smile, "You two are quite a pair!"

But in the spring of 1948, with my mother visibly pregnant, things weren't going so smoothly. Mother began to wonder how she would cope once the new baby arrived. I must have sensed her anxiety, because I became very clingy. In an entry entitled "Behavior Problems, April 1, 1948 – almost 3," Mother noted in the baby book, "Very jealous of mother—too dependent. Won't go out & play with other children unless mother is along. When children come to play will not play with them. Aloof—follows mother into house."

By April 19, Mother had devised a solution: "Enrolled her in Northington Nursery School." I had other ideas. Mother recorded my rebellion in the baby book: "Threw a temper tantrum the first 2 times I left. Doesn't like it." A few days later, on April 23, even my body was rebelling: "Temperature. Kept her at home. Developed bad cold, croupy one night—out of school April 26 – 30." Having recovered sufficiently by May 3, my third birthday, I returned to school. Mother's assessment of my reaction? "Very unhappy."

On May 4, I actively questioned this new state of affairs, and Mother noted my queries: "Why do you want me to go to nursery school?" She must have explained that she needed time to do her own work, and I countered with another question: "Why do mommies need to work?" Clearly, in my three-year-old mind, this was not the way things should be in a perfect world.

By June 12, the battle of wills was over. Mother admitted defeat. "Attended nursery school 5 weeks in all. Never did really enjoy it. On June 8, neighbors started taking turns keeping children one day a week. Enjoyed the morning at Bonds; resisted going to Mitchells. Is playing outdoors much more—not nearly so dependent on Mother. Plays a lot with Faye Burtramm."

Things were clearly going in the right direction. I didn't have to leave the neighborhood. Even when another mother was in charge, I knew that my own mother was nearby, just a few houses away.

And then the unthinkable happened. On August 4, a new baby arrived in our family, and she absorbed almost all of my mother's prodigious energy. In later years, Mother often regaled us with stories of the first few weeks of Carol's life. "The baby cried every time I put her down." The pediatrician was quickly consulted, and he had a simple explanation for the baby's crying: "Colic."

Many different infant formulas were tried and abandoned. The crying continued. The only therapy that worked was simple but hard to accomplish. Mother had to hold the baby all day and most of the night. Often, in the middle of the night, when she was on the verge of collapse, Daddy would take over, holding and rocking Carol for hours. And then when she was about eight weeks old, as if by some miracle, the crying stopped. Almost overnight, she became a calm, charming infant. Mother, ever the optimist, found a positive side to these difficult early weeks. "Carol June is just the sweetest little thing! I think it's because she was held for the first eight weeks of her life. She got so much attention as a baby. She just got used to being loved."

But for me, the abandoned older sister, it was hard to see this intruder as sweet. She had arrived unexpectedly and taken my mother away. As she got older and even sweeter, my jealousy increased. I remember teasing her, pulling her hair to make her cry, and then when one of our parents arrived to take a photo, I would tickle her under her chin to make her smile for the camera.

Once, when she was a little older, I devised another trick. First, I had to get the pepper shaker, which sat on the shelf above the kitchen stove. It was made of white milk glass, with squared-off edges, and had a metal top painted red. Mother never actually used pepper in her bland Midwestern-style cooking, but the shaker was part of a matched set that came with our Magic Chef stove. I stood on a stool to reach it and hid it in the pocket of my shorts.

Carol was playing with her baby doll out in the front yard. I approached and explained that I had something special to show her. "But," I said, "first you have to close your eyes and stick out your tongue." She was so innocent. Never suspecting, she complied with my request. I pulled out the pepper shaker and sprinkled the dark-gray dust all over her tongue. She had never tasted pepper. When she opened her eyes and closed her mouth, she choked on the peppery ash and started to cry. I just laughed and said, "Surprise!"

After Carol's birth, my mother wasn't nearly as focused on me as she had been when I was her only child. The entries in my baby book, that meticulous archive of my early years, abruptly ceased in the summer of 1948. But my behavior toward my little sister did not go unnoticed. Mother often explained to friends or neighbors, "Becky is so mean to the baby. She is always teasing her or playing tricks on her. But Carol has such a sunny disposition. She just smiles and forgives."

Having gotten so much of my mother's attention in my first three years, I saw her as something like an all-powerful God. She had been the center of my world since I was born, and if she said something, it had to be true. After Carol's birth, Mother continued to sing my praises as she told her friends how smart I was, how capable, how pretty. I knew my mother loved me. There was never any doubt about that. But all the praise in the world could not offset her comments about how mean I was to Carol. I felt so guilty and ashamed. Still, I continued to torment my little sister. I just couldn't help it.

Which brings me back to the story of the Spotted Men. One reason I love this story is because it reveals my cleverness. I was only six years old, but I could read and understand the newspaper article, and I also had an innate understanding of child psychology. I thought I could help my sister get rid of her night terrors, but I knew that just hearing about the accident and seeing the picture in the newspaper would not be enough. Carol needed to see the train wreck with her own eyes, so I had to bring my father into the plan by asking him to drive us to the scene of the accident.

This story also reveals something about my personality. Not outgoing and ebullient like my mother, I prefer to work behind the scenes to solve problems, not calling attention to myself. Carol didn't know until much later that I, not the train accident, was responsible for killing the Spotted Men. But I knew, and that was what mattered. I felt so sorry for my little sister when she woke up screaming in the night, and I wanted to help her. When my plot succeeded, I did help her, and I helped myself as well since this act of kindness relieved me from some of my shame and guilt about being so mean to my sister. Despite the normal jealousy and sibling rivalry I felt toward Carol, I loved her deeply, and I was proud when my plot succeeded. The Spotted Men were gone forever, laid to rest by a clever six-year-old who wanted to free her little sister from her terrible nightmares.

More than seventy years after these events took place, the details are still clear in my mind: the creepy Bill Dings, the feel of that pepper shaker in my hand, the innocent look on Carol's face as she stuck out her tongue followed by her painful coughing and crying. Most of all, I remember the image of that terrible train disaster.

When I typed "Alabama train wreck 1950s" into my computer's search engine, several newspaper accounts of the accident appeared on Newspapers.com. Learning the exact date of the crash, November 25, 1951, was helpful since it revealed that my sister and I had been even younger than I thought; she was only three, and I was six and a half. I was also surprised by the extent of the devastation, seventeen people dead and more than sixty injured. The photos of the wreck that showed up online looked very familiar—the same shots that had appeared in the *Tuscaloosa News*, the same images of destruction engraved indelibly in my memory from my visit to the accident site.

A newspaper report that appeared more than a year after the accident on February 3, 1953, speculated on a possible cause of the disaster. It seems that a barge had damaged a bridge on one of the tracks, so the northbound train, an Alabama Great Southern Railroad streamliner, had to pull onto a siding to allow the southbound train to pass. But why did that same northbound train move out of the siding and back into the path of the oncoming train? An investigator from the Interstate Commerce Commission proposed a whimsical possibility: "Perhaps the engineer of the northbound train, who was killed, mistook a ray of sunlight for the signal to proceed."

Reading this report so many years later, I see the irony. Just as this sleek, modern train might have been derailed by a ray of sunlight, my peaceful childhood at the center of my mother's world was derailed by the unexpected arrival of a sunny-natured baby sister named Carol June. Little did I know at the time that she would become my best friend and lifelong companion.

4

Billy and Me

THE KITCHEN WAS STEAMY from the blackberries boiling on the stove, so I stepped outside to get some fresh air. Lantanas grew on either side of the kitchen door, flaunting their orange and yellow flowers. Even these hardy, heat-loving plants were starting to wilt today. Sitting on the step, I scuffled my bare feet around in the dust trying to see how many roly-polys I could count. It was fun to touch them with my toe and watch them roll into a ball.

Hearing voices on the street, I walked around to the front to see what was going on. A few of my friends were out there with Liberay, a young Black woman who worked for our neighbors. They were headed to the little store a few blocks away to buy some treats. After checking with Mother to see if I could go along, I joined the group. Counting me, there were six kids—Judy and Jean Nisbet, Gretchen Gregory, Billy Bond, and his little sister, Mary Jane.

Billy and I were both four, but he was a few months older and much bigger than me. He liked to dress up in the cowboy suit he got from Santa and strap on his Gene Autry six-shooter. It was shiny, with a handle that looked like ivory. When he felt like showing off, he would pull the gun out of its holster and twirl the cylinder. Then he would stretch out his arm, aim the pistol, and pull the trigger. It made a popping sound, and the younger kids would jump and cover their ears. Billy would just laugh and twirl the cylinder again.

The store was only about four blocks away, but we had to have a grownup with us to go there because it was on a big street with lots of cars whizzing back and forth. Liberay didn't look old enough to be an adult, but she worked full time for the Nisbet family, so I guess she counted as a grownup.

She made us hold hands as we crossed the busy street. Once inside the store, we forgot about how hot it was. There were so many exciting things on the shelves—all kinds of candy and even bubblegum. Mother didn't approve of chewing gum of any kind. I knew she would make me spit it out as soon as I got home, so I decided to buy a box of Cracker Jacks instead. I liked the sweet, sticky popcorn, and every box had a special surprise hidden inside. In the end, all the kids chose Cracker Jacks.

As soon as we were across the busy street and headed back home, Billy made an announcement. "Okay, everybody. Hand over your prizes."

The smaller children looked so sad, but they opened up their boxes and fished through the popcorn to find the prize. One by one, they gave their prizes to Billy. Even Judy and Jean, who were four years old like me, gave in to Billy's demand. But I just looked straight at him, holding my unopened Cracker Jack box.

"Hey, hand it over, Becky."

"No. It's my prize, and you can't have it." I stared at him as the other kids watched for what seemed like a long time.

Liberay knew better than to interfere in an argument between two White kids, so she just started walking toward Cedar Crest. Soon everyone else started walking as well, even Billy. But I could tell he was mad.

When I got home, I poured all my Cracker Jacks into a bowl and pulled out the small cellophane packet with the prize. It was a cheap ring made of green plastic. It didn't even have a fake jewel to make it look like a real ring. I was so disappointed.

Still, I was glad I had stood up to Billy instead of giving in to his bullying like all the other kids. He had fooled me before, and I was determined not to let it happen again. A few months ago, Billy and I had been in my back yard playing in the sandbox and swinging on the swings. After a while, he said, "I'm tired of this baby stuff. Let's go out to the ditch."

The ditch was my favorite place for adventures. About a year earlier, some big machines had come to dig a large trench behind our house. My parents explained that it was important to drain the water away so our yards wouldn't flood if we had a big storm. The workers never bothered to cart away all the dirt they dug out; they just piled it up on either side of the ditch. We kids liked to pretend we were mountain climbers scrambling up the big piles of red Alabama clay. When the ditch was filled with water, it was a great place to catch tadpoles.

On this day, the ditch was dry. Billy said, "Let's climb to the top." Once we were up there, I could see all the houses on the other side. "I've got an idea," he said. "Let's both pull our pants down while we're standing up high. You go first."

I don't know what it was about Billy. Whenever he told me to do something, I felt like I had to do it. So I grabbed the elastic of my shorts and pulled them down and then did the same with my underpants. All of a sudden, I felt so embarrassed. What if someone came out in one of the yards across the way? What would they think if they saw my bare bottom? And Billy standing there watching me?

I quickly pulled up my undies and shorts. Then I turned to Billy. "Now it's your turn."

"Hah! I fooled you!"

I was so mad. He had tricked me again!

Now, looking at the plastic ring in my bowl of Cracker Jacks, I felt a little better. Even though it was just a cheap piece of junk, I was glad I hadn't given in to his demand.

That night after supper, Mother came up to me looking concerned. "Becky, what did you do this afternoon to make Billy so upset?" She explained that Mrs. Bond had come over to talk to her. She said that when Billy got back from the store, he was crying and stomping around. He told his mother I had been mean to him.

"I don't think I was mean," I said. "It's just that I was the only one who wouldn't give him the prize from my Cracker Jacks. I paid for it with my allowance money, so it belonged to me." But when I heard what Mrs. Bond had said, I felt a little sorry for Billy. He always acted so tough, but inside he was just a big baby.

"Actually," I told my mother, "I don't even care about the stupid prize. You can tell his mother he can have it if he still wants it." I don't remember whether Billy ever decided to claim the prize.

~

A few years later, Billy's family moved to California, and I never saw him again. Judy and Jean's parents stayed in touch with the family through occasional letters and postcards. When Billy was twelve or thirteen years old, they learned that he had had a serious accident. He was out with some other boys playing with firecrackers. One of them went off unexpectedly and hit him in the eye. The accident left him blinded in that eye for the rest of his life.

When I heard about this, I wasn't too surprised. Billy was always showing off, trying to impress the other kids with how tough he was. Often, as in the Cracker Jack incident, he was the one who ended up getting hurt.

Looking back now, I wonder why, of all the kids on our block in Tuscaloosa, Billy Bond is the one I remember most clearly. Maybe it's because he was bigger and older than me. Or maybe he stood out as an alpha male in my mostly female childhood. I didn't even like him, but I couldn't help being fascinated by this boy who was so different from me. He was a bully and a braggart, and I was just a little girl who was afraid to leave her mother to go to nursery school. How did I manage to stand there on the side of the road and look the neighborhood bully in the eye, and say, in a strong voice, one simple word? "No."

~

There's a postscript to this story. While reading through a small notebook my father kept in 1949, one of the pocket-sized diaries where he recorded everything—plants he saw on his walks, reflections on his reading, comments related to our family's daily life—I recently came across a reference to the Cracker Jack episode. In his tiny, precise handwriting, he noted, "Becky makes up with Billy. She says, 'Now we will have joy in the street.'"

There is no doubt in my mind. My father is referring to the time I stood up to Billy on the way home from the neighborhood store. This quotation from my four-year-old self reflects my belated offer to give the worthless prize to Billy after he complained to his mother.

I treasure this childhood memory because it reflects a side of myself that I value. I wish I could be brave, but too often in threatening situations I remain silent, afraid to speak my mind. However, when I see a bully in action, I often find a way to swallow my fear and stand up for what is right. That is what happened between Billy and me so many years ago.

Perhaps this same type of persistence even in the face of fear is the quality that is enabling me to write this book. At last, I am forcing myself to take a long, hard look at my childhood, including all the fear and trauma related to my father's mental illness and unexpected death. I open the old notebooks and photo albums with trembling fingers. I dredge up memories that have haunted me for years. And sometimes, as with this little gem from 1949, I find a prize inside.

5

Tanglewood

"Hey, Becky," my father said as he walked into the living room, "would you like to come out to Tanglewood with me to see what we can find?"

Of course I wanted to go with him! I was five years old and had finished kindergarten about a month before. The summer stretched on and on with no end in sight. Today was a Sunday, so I'd have to skip Sunday school, but I knew my parents would be okay with that. I was pretty sure they believed it was easier to find God out in nature than sitting inside a church.

As far back as I can remember, I loved going on walks with Daddy. I understood that going to the wild places to look for things he wouldn't see in town was part of his work, but I also knew he loved it. It was in the woods that he was most alive. It was in the woods that he was most himself.

I had been to Tanglewood a couple of times before when he brought me along on walks with other professors and graduate students. Sometimes he even took some of the neighborhood kids on his walks. But today it would be just the two of us.

"You'd better put on your overalls," he said. Tanglewood was loaded with chiggers, and there were brambles and prickers everywhere. I didn't want to come home with itchy red chigger bites and scratches all over my body, so I ran into the bedroom to change.

TANGLEWOOD

Daddy didn't have to put on any special clothes. He dressed the same whether he was going to church, to the university, or out for a walk in the woods. Although he had grown up on a farm, you would never say he looked like a farmer. He always wore a neatly ironed white shirt, trousers, and leather shoes. Before he left home, he would put a pen and a small diary in his shirt pocket. He liked to make notes about plants or birds he saw on his walks or copy quotations from books he was reading. Sometimes he even wrote down the things Carol and I said.

As soon as I had changed, we went out through the front door. Daddy had me pose in the front yard while he took a picture of me with his Brownie camera, and then we climbed into the car and backed out onto Cedar Crest.

Tanglewood was a large plantation about thirty miles south of Tuscaloosa. A few years after we moved to Alabama, the old lady whose family had owned the property died. In her will, she gave the house and land to the university as a place where people could come to study nature. The house was all run down, and the fields were overgrown with native plants, so it was a perfect place for biology professors to come with their students to look for specimens to add to their collections.

It took almost an hour to get to Tanglewood, but we weren't in a hurry. With the windows rolled down, I could stick my hand out and feel the hot, humid air blowing through my fingers. Daddy didn't talk much in the car, but I could tell he liked this time too. As we got further away from town, I could see the lines on his forehead starting to smooth out. At Tanglewood, life always seemed simpler.

The roads kept getting smaller and smaller with trees and vines so close I could almost touch them. Finally, we turned onto a dirt road. I could see the old plantation house up ahead. As soon as Daddy parked the car, I jumped out. He went around to the trunk to get some things he would need for the hike. He pulled out a big stick he had found years ago and always took with him on long walks. Then he took out his vasculum, a big cylindrical container for storing plant specimens. It was shaped kind of like a hollow log but was made out of metal and painted olive green. To open it, you had to unlatch the metal fastener and lift the lid, which was attached with hinges. There was an adjustable strap on either end. Daddy would sling the strap over one shoulder so that it rested straight across his back. Nobody else I knew had a vasculum. Maybe that's why this battered metal object seemed magical to me—like Aladdin's lamp or a magician's top hat. I never knew what Daddy might bring home in his vasculum.

I didn't have any special equipment for the hike, just the pockets of my overalls, where I could save unusual rocks or nuts I found along the way or pieces of a bird's egg if I was lucky.

Leading away from the parking area was an old road that used to go through the cotton fields. Now it was really more like a path. Even though it was still morning, the air was already hot and heavy. Starting out, I walked as fast as I could, but soon Daddy was a few paces ahead of me. Then he noticed and adjusted his strides so he wouldn't leave me behind. As we walked, clouds of dust rose up from our shoes. Looking ahead through the bright sunshine, I could see dust motes, almost like a cloud of gnats. They danced in the air and tickled my nose. Dragonflies swooped across our path, disappearing into the woods on either side. Honeysuckle vines sprawled beside the road, their small yellowish-white flowers breathing a sweet fragrance into the summer air.

Without all the noise of city life, the air was alive with the sounds of nature. I could hear the click of grasshoppers and the steady metallic-sounding hum of cicadas. Birds were everywhere at Tanglewood. Even though Daddy was a botanist and studied plants, he was also very interested in birds and kept a list of all the different birds he saw in his little notebook. He could identify a lot of birds just by listening to their calls. On this day, we saw—or heard—mourning doves, cardinals, bluebirds, and a red-bellied woodpecker. The woodpecker had a bright red head and reddish feathers on its belly. Daddy wrote this one down in his notebook because he had never seen one of these before.

It felt so peaceful to be walking along this dusty road with Daddy even though we didn't talk much. Both of us were looking around, trying to see and hear as much as we could. But I do remember Daddy asking me, "Why do you think they decided to call this place Tanglewood?"

I kept walking and thinking. Finally, I said, "Maybe because once you go into the forest, things are all tangled together with roots and vines and fallen trees."

"Good thinking," he nodded. "I'm not sure about the name myself. I can imagine the old plantation with cotton planted in neat rows. But now the cotton is gone, and the land is overgrown with all kinds of vegetation. There are lots of native plant species here—even some that have never been identified and classified."

I liked it when Daddy talked to me like this, not like I was a little kid but like I was one of the students in his biology classes at the university.

"Speaking of the native plants," he said, "why don't we see what we can find in the woods?"

Daddy led the way as we walked off the path, poking around with his stick to keep from tripping on roots. "Alabama has more different kinds of trees than any other state in the country, so this is a great place to learn to identify trees."

I already knew a few things about trees. You could tell pine trees by their bright green spiky needles. Magnolias had big beautiful waxy leaves, dark green on top with a furry brown underside. In the summer, the magnolia trees were covered with beautiful white flowers.

At Tanglewood, there were lots of trees I didn't recognize. As we approached a tall tree, Daddy said, "Let's start with the oaks." He asked me to run my hands over the bark. It was rough with deep ridges, kind of like dry creek beds running down the trunk. One side was all green and mossy. "People like to say that the moss grows on the north side of the trunk," Daddy said, "and actually that's often true. It can be helpful to know that if you ever get lost in the woods."

"There are many different kinds of oak trees. To identify the species, you have to look at the leaves." He reached up and broke off a leaf and handed it to me. "What do you notice about this leaf?"

I twirled the stem around to look at both sides of the leaf. It was bigger than my hand and it had a line going down the middle. "It looks like a hand with fat fingers sticking out," I said.

"You're a good observer," Daddy said. "Those fingers are called lobes. This tree is a white oak. Their leaves always have rounded lobes like this."

Then he walked over to another tree. It was not quite as tall as the first one, and it had smoother bark. Daddy pulled off a twig with several leaves. These leaves were big like the white oak, but the lobes were pointy at the ends. This was a red oak.

Walking further into the woods, we came to a large fallen tree blocking our way forward. Daddy sat down on the log and patted it with his hand for me to sit too. The log made a nice seat, with my feet touching the ground.

Daddy took out the small pocketknife he always carried in his pants pocket and gently dug up a handful of soil, holding it in his left hand. "This might not look like much to you," he said, "but it contains everything you need to sustain life in a healthy forest."

He held it out for me to smell. I breathed deeply, inhaling the earthy scent of the forest floor. As he sifted the reddish-brown dirt through his long fingers, he explained that the forest soil is rich with tiny insects, plant roots, fungi, and fallen leaves that make new soil as they slowly decay. "Plants have their own communication system under the ground. That's why I'm so interested in roots. Although we don't usually see them or even think about them, life on earth would be impossible without these underground networks."

Looking up through the trees, we saw that the sun was higher in the sky. "It's getting late," he said. "We'd better get going." Walking out to the road, I had a special feeling. During those quiet moments in the woods, I felt that Daddy had given me a precious gift. I knew I would remember this day for a long time.

As we headed back to the car, we walked a little faster. All of a sudden, Daddy stopped in his tracks. Just a few feet ahead of us, a huge snake was slithering across the road. Lifting his big walking stick, he brought it down near the snake's head. He hit it three or four more times, and then everything was quiet. Daddy had moved so quickly that the snake was dead before I even had time to worry.

"I hated to kill such a beautiful animal." His voice sounded sad. "But this is a rattlesnake, and their venom can be deadly."

He had recognized the snake as an Eastern diamondback, the largest and most dangerous of all the rattlesnakes. Daddy took my hand as we moved closer to look at the snake. I had to admit that it was beautiful. It was about five feet long, stretching all the way across the road, with its tail end still concealed in the undergrowth on the roadside. Its scales were arranged in diamond-shaped patterns in muted shades of brownish-yellow and brownish-gray, outlined in light yellow. The scales on its head were light brown and a lighter shade of yellow.

Looking down at the snake, Daddy told me, "This will be an important addition to the specimens we have in the biology department. I'm going to take it back so that Ralph can preserve it for his collection." I remembered the specimens I had seen in Daddy's lab, lined up on a shelf in glass jars filled with yellow liquid, so I understood why this was important. Ralph was Dr. Chermock, the father of my friend Claudia. He was an entomologist, meaning he studied insects, but he was also very interested in snakes. Dr. Chermock had a huge collection of animal specimens.

Daddy took the vasculum off his back and set it down on the road. Then he knelt down and unlatched the metal lid. Very carefully, he pulled the tail end of the snake's body out of the bushes, showing me the rattles. Ever so gently, he began to coil it up until he had the whole snake wound up like a piece of rope. Then he carefully put it into the vasculum and fastened the lid.

On the way back to the car, I didn't notice very much. I just kept scanning the path, hoping we wouldn't find any more rattlesnakes.

~

When we got home, Mother was eager to hear about our hike.

"It was a very productive field trip," Daddy said. "I collected several plant specimens, and we saw a new bird, a red-bellied woodpecker." Then he took a deep breath and continued. "We were walking back toward the car when a rattlesnake crossed the path in front of us. It could have been a threat so I had to kill it."

Mother's eyes got bigger as she imagined what might have happened on this peaceful walk in the woods. She looked straight at Daddy.

"It will be a valuable addition to Ralph's herpetology collection, so I brought it back." He explained that if he left the snake in the vasculum overnight, it would not be a fit specimen in the morning when he took it in to the biology department. Looking at my mother for permission, he said, "I was hoping we could lay it out in the bathtub overnight."

She sighed and then she laughed. "I guess this is what I get for being married to a biologist."

Once he got the snake settled in the bathtub, Daddy sat down in his big armchair to read the Sunday paper, but before he opened it, he took out his pocket diary and made an entry dated June 11, 1950:

"To Tanglewood with Becky. Collected several plants. Killed Eastern Diamondback rattler and brought along for Ralph."

Mother was in the dining room setting the table. Then she went into the kitchen to check on the potatoes boiling on the stove. The next thing I heard was a squeak as she opened the bathroom door, followed by a scream. "It's alive!" she shrieked. "It's moving. I even heard it rattle."

Daddy rushed into the bathroom and confirmed that the snake was still alive. He quickly closed the bathroom door, ran to the garage, and grabbed the bottle of chloroform he kept on hand for killing insects for his collection. In large doses, chloroform could be lethal for a much larger animal, and that's how, on his second attempt, he killed the rattlesnake.

In the midst of this family drama, I wasn't worried, not really, even when the snake came back to life. I knew Daddy would know what to do. I knew that everything would be okay. Everything would always be okay as long as Daddy was there to keep us safe.

~

The rattlesnake episode is a good illustration of my parents' different views on nature. My mother, who had grown up in towns and cities, had been taught to fear the natural environment. Her mother, my Granny Stamps, was always warning her of the dangers that lurked outside the house. "If you swim in a lake, you might drown." "If you go into the forest, you might be attacked by a wild animal." "You're safer inside." Mother inherited these fears, but she made a conscious decision not to pass them along to her daughters. She made sure that Daddy took us on nature outings while she stayed home.

On the other hand, Daddy felt happiest and safest in the natural world. He had been born on a small farm in New Pennington, Indiana, on March 20, 1909. As the oldest of Jeff and Nora's six children, he spent his days wandering in the fields and forests surrounding his home. He swam in the pond—an old quarry hole near the family's orchard. He walked freely in the woods. If he encountered an animal, it was most likely a small, harmless creature like a rabbit or a groundhog. It's true there were snakes, but rather than fearing them, he studied them, learning about their habits and how to avoid their bites.

He enjoyed school and excelled in his class of seven students at New Point High School. Recognizing the boy's promise, the school's principal, Mr. Zuckerberg, nominated him for a prestigious Rector Scholarship. Edward Rector was born into a poor family, but through hard work, he eventually became a wealthy patent attorney in Chicago. He donated a large fund to DePauw University in Greencastle, Indiana, to enable students from modest backgrounds to get the kind of education he had been denied. In the words of Rector, these scholarships were "investments in humanity, in the men and women who are to carry on the work of our country and the world when you and I are gone."

In the fall of 1927, young Bert packed his belongings in a large trunk and set off by train for college in Greencastle, about a hundred miles away. Because of his love of the natural world, he chose to study biology at the university, but when he enrolled in a zoology class in his sophomore year, he was startled to learn of Darwin's theory of natural selection. This contradicted everything he had been taught in the fundamentalist Methodist church he attended as a boy, and he suffered what my mother described as a nervous breakdown, dropping all his courses and returning to the family farm. About a year later, he pulled himself together and returned to the university, graduating in 1933 with a major in mathematics and a minor in biology.

Although he had accepted Darwin, he had not given up on God. Believing there was something larger than our small selves, he spent the rest of his life searching for God. For him, God was not in a church, not in the Bible, not even in all the philosophy books he read after losing the faith of his childhood—faith in a God who created the world in six days and rested on the seventh. Listening to the call of a bird, feeling the forest floor under his feet, he understood that life and death and rebirth were all here and they all meant something. He struggled to put these thoughts into words, writing endlessly in his notebooks and journals. But only in the woods could he take a deep breath and know that it was true.

6

Waiting for Justice

Although I had been born in Evansville, Indiana, just north of the Mason Dixon line, my formative years were spent in the Deep South, the segregated South. As I grew into awareness, this was the only world I knew, but I always knew it wasn't home. When I learned to talk, I never spoke with an Alabama accent but with the same flat Midwestern speech of my parents. In our quiet middle-class neighborhood, it soon became clear that some of the neighbors were wary of our family, recent transplants from the North. Even as a young child, I felt their suspicion. Down the street at a neighbor's house, I was "the little damn Yankee." That's what my friend's father called me whenever I went over to their yard to play. He always chuckled as he said this under his breath, but I didn't think it was funny.

The fact that my mother intended to do her own housework was a sign of our strange, northern ways. The women on our block were scandalized, and eventually they persuaded her to hire a *girl* to come in and do ironing one day a week. One of our neighbors recommended a Black woman called Pinkie, and Mother hired her. I wasn't sure if Pinkie was her real first name, and I never knew her last name. To me, she was just Pinkie. A child who was taught to refer to her friend's parent as Mrs. Jones or Mr. Smith would never call a Black person Mr. or Mrs. That was just one of many unspoken rules in the segregated South.

Pinkie didn't look anything like a girl to me. She was a solid-looking woman in her forties with skin the color of mahogany. She always wore a bright bandanna to cover her hair, and she hummed spirituals as she sweated over the ironing. Although it was not her job to care for me, I spent a lot of time in her company. It was comforting just to be near her. I liked to watch her strong, graceful hands moving back and forth along the ironing board and listen to her gentle voice humming church songs, spirituals like "Deep River" and "Swing Low Sweet Chariot."

During the long summer days when it was too hot to play outside, I liked to sit on the dining room floor in front of the oscillating fan and watch Pinkie at her work. Something about this orderly process felt soothing to me. She would lift a piece of clothing out of the wicker ironing basket, dip her hand into a big bowl of water on the end of the ironing board, and flick her fingers, sprinkling the cloth with fine droplets. I loved it when a few stray drops of cool water fell on my face. Pinkie touched the fabric to see when it was damp enough, and then she would fold the edges in and roll the whole garment into a tight package and put it back in the basket. Once the clothes were sprinkled, the ironing could begin. She took pride in her work, fussing to make sure every wrinkle was smoothed out with the hot iron. Only then would she gently hang the shirt or dress on a wire hanger. We must have talked back and forth while I watched her iron, but I don't remember what we said.

Looking back on these years, I see Pinkie as one of the most important people in my childhood, so why didn't I know more about who she was as a person, as a human being? I was pretty sure she had children, but I didn't know their names or where they went to school. I assumed she went to church on Sundays, but I never knew the name of the church or where it was located. In the 1950s in the segregated South, little White children knew there were certain questions you didn't ask a Black woman, even one who worked for a nice White family like yours.

When I was six years old, one of my cousins, Patty Stamps, came to visit us in Tuscaloosa for about a month. She was fourteen years old at the time and seemed almost like a grownup to me. She stayed long enough to get to know Pinkie, and she became fond of her, as we all were. Patty was from a small town near Chicago, and she was not shy like me. She didn't hesitate to ask a question to learn whatever she wanted to know. One day she asked Pinkie, "You're here all day, from morning to night, but you never go to the bathroom. How come?"

"When I was much younger, my mother told me, 'You go to the bathroom before you leave the house in the morning to go work for the White people, and you don't go again until you get back home. You have to train yourself to wait.'"

Pat is now in her mid-eighties, but she never forgot what Pinkie told her so many years ago. Another thing she never forgot was how it felt to be discriminated against because of the color of her skin. One afternoon during her visit, Daddy dropped her off in downtown Tuscaloosa to go to a movie. When she went up to the window to buy her ticket, the attendant said, "I'm sorry, Miss, but you're not allowed in this theater." Patty had wandered over to the Black-owned Diamond Theater, which was located close to the White movie house. She was furious not to be allowed in and told all her friends about this when she got back to Illinois.

~

Both of my parents were ahead of their time in their attitudes about race. My father, the biologist, was in favor of interracial marriage partly because he thought it would lead to genomic diversity. My mother's views on race would also have been considered radical in our Southern town. I remember her telling me that the first step in eliminating racial prejudice was for Blacks and Whites to talk honestly and get to know one another on a personal level. In Tuscaloosa, she worked tirelessly as a volunteer organizer and activist to get voters to approve a large bond issue to finance a new high school for Black students to replace the decrepit Industrial City High School, which had opened in 1935. The bond issue was passed, and the new Druid High School opened in fall 1955.

Needless to say, our neighbors on Cedar Crest did not share my parents' progressive views on race. Mother's friends in the neighborhood were upset when they learned how much she was paying Pinkie—five dollars for a day's work. I was only six years old, but I was beginning to understand about money. One Friday I saw a friend's mother hand Eula Mae two quarters at the end of the day. She worked so hard! Cooking, taking care of the children, and doing all the housework. I wondered if the fifty cents was for one day or the whole week. I knew not to ask, but an image stayed with me—the white hand of my friend's mother reaching out and putting first one and then a second shiny quarter into the small hand of the young Black woman who did so much for their family. I already knew that a quarter didn't go very far when you went to the store.

One night I overheard my parents talking. My mother explained that the neighbors were afraid that when other Black housekeepers learned how much she was paying Pinkie, they would all want higher pay. Mother's voice got louder. "Pinkie has children to support. She has to make a living wage. I couldn't sleep at night if I didn't pay her fairly."

When my mother was a young girl living in Wabash, Indiana, in the 1920s, her own mother had to take in laundry to make ends meet as a single mother with three young children. I loved to hear Mother's stories about those early days. Doing the laundry was a complicated process. First, her mother, my granny, soaked the clothes in a big tub, then she scrubbed them on a washboard, dried them on a clothesline, and finally ironed them. Mother and her little brothers delivered the clean, folded clothes to their owners in a little wagon and collected the payment. Now, years later, Mother was living a comfortable, middle-class life. But she remembered what it felt like to be poor. While she could never understand most of the challenges Pinkie was facing as a Black woman in the segregated South, she could relate to the struggles of a single mother trying to make a living for her family.

Every Thursday, when Pinkie was finished with her work, she would sit on our screened-in porch resting her feet and waiting for Daddy to get back from his lab at the university. He always drove Pinkie home. In Alabama in the 1950s, it was unheard of for a White employer to do this. Black workers either had to walk miles back to their houses across town or wait, sometimes for hours, for the unreliable city bus. My parents were aware of this unwritten rule, but they persisted in breaking the social code.

I often went along when Daddy took Pinkie home. When we crossed the railroad tracks that divided the White and Black sections of Tuscaloosa, the paved street abruptly became a rutted dirt road. The neat white houses with green shutters and well-trimmed lawns were replaced by small unpainted houses with dusty front yards. There were no cars parked on the side of the road as there were in our neighborhood. Nearly every house had a front porch with chairs where people could sit and talk with their neighbors in the cool of the evening. On one porch I saw a red bicycle that looked just like the blue one I had at home, and there was a big dog sleeping on another porch.

As a child growing up in the segregated South, I wondered why people in our town seemed to live in two different worlds. The White people on my side of town lived comfortable, constrained lives, mostly staying inside their neat white houses. The Black people on the other side of the tracks didn't have much. They had to struggle for everything they got. When I saw them gathering on their front porches, I wondered what they talked about, what they laughed about, what they thought about. When Daddy parked the car outside Pinkie's house, I always wanted to go in, but we were never invited. Pinkie knew the code better than we did.

I don't recall ever talking with my parents about why Pinkie's neighborhood was so different from ours or why she had to leave her own children alone to come and work for White families. I don't think I ever mentioned being called a damn Yankee. I had seen the filthy water fountain at the Dairy Queen with its dirty, crudely lettered sign, Colored Only. Standing in the waiting rooms of bus and train stations, I glimpsed a few rows of benches off to the side where Black people were allowed to sit. I had seen the prisoners, all of them Black men, alongside rural highways as I rode by in the back seat of a car. As sweat poured from their bodies, they were hacking at the red Alabama clay with picks and shovels. If they tried to escape, they could easily be recognized by the prison-issued clothes they wore, banded with broad horizontal stripes, starkly divided into black and white like the world they were living in.

Even as a young child, I saw what was going on around me, and I knew that something was terribly wrong. I knew that my parents knew this too.

~

In the spring of 1954, everything changed for our family. Something happened to Daddy. It was like he became another person, acting strange and angry. At the end of March, he was taken by ambulance to the hospital, and he died three months later. As soon as the school year ended in 1955, our family moved to Evansville, Indiana, where Mother had accepted a job teaching history in a high school. After that, we only returned to Tuscaloosa once—in January 1956.

During that week, we spent a lot of time with the families who had been our neighbors on Cedar Crest. Mother visited some of her grownup friends and a few professors from the university and their wives. The specifics of these visits have vanished from my mind. Only one clear memory remains. Mother, Carol, and I went out to see Pinkie.

When we drove up in front of her house, I was sad to see how run-down it looked. A few years earlier, when we were still living in Tuscaloosa, her house had burned to the ground when a spark escaped from the wood stove used to heat the house in winter. Like all the other houses in the neighborhood, it was not insured, but friends from her church pitched in to build a new house for Pinkie and her family, and a few months later it was finished. The first time I saw it, I was struck by the natural beauty of the unpainted boards, so much prettier than the standard white clapboards on the other side of the tracks. But now I could hardly recognize the house. The freshly sawn wooden boards had turned gray and were starting to rot for lack of a coat of paint.

Our visit must have been arranged in advance because Pinkie was standing on the porch to greet us when we arrived. Then she did something we hadn't expected. She invited us to come in.

Inside, the house seemed a lot smaller than it looked from outside—basically just one large room. The raw pine boards lining the walls still looked fresh and new, dotted with knots where the branches had been. Pinkie insisted that the three of us sit on the sofa, the only comfortable seat in the room. Sinking into the well-worn cushions, I looked around. Family photographs hung on one of the walls, and a large framed picture of Jesus was on another wall. He wore a flowing white robe, and his head was encircled by a halo of wispy clouds. His hair was long and brown. His skin was white.

It was chilly outside on this January day, and cold air was seeping through the cracks between the boards. But the woodstove in the center of the room radiated heat and gave the room a fresh, woodsy smell. I remembered how careful Pinkie had been when she was ironing our clothes, and I could see that she took this same kind of care in her own home. The wood floor looked like it had just been scrubbed, and the simple furniture was polished to a shine.

Two of Pinkie's children were home, a girl about my age and a teenaged boy. The girl stood across from me, looking down at the floor as she shifted her weight from one foot to the other. This might have been the first time she had seen a White person inside her home. I hoped she would speak, but she never said a word. The boy stood in the doorway with a blank look on his face. I wondered if he was embarrassed to have this White family inside his house. What would his friends say? Our visit took place just a few weeks after Rosa Parks had refused to move to the back of the bus in Montgomery, a hundred miles south of here. How did this boy feel about standing there in the doorway while these White folks were sitting on the best seat in the house?

If Pinkie was aware of the Montgomery bus boycott, she didn't mention it. This was not something she would ever discuss with a White woman. Instead, she and Mother chatted away like old friends, which is what they were. At the time, I sensed a closeness between the two women that went beyond the assigned roles of White employer and Black employee, though this was an inescapable part of their relationship.

It wasn't until many years later that I learned about the special circumstances that bound them together. A few months after my parents moved to Alabama in 1945, my granny came to live with us—helping with the cooking, cleaning, and child care. Shortly after Carol was born in the summer of 1948, she moved back to Indiana to help care for her sister, Pauline, who had recently had surgery. Mother told me that she felt abandoned by her mother just when she needed her most. Here she was miles away from her home state, trying to recover from childbirth and take care of a colicky baby while also managing all the housework and cooking. Things began to look up when she hired "a wonderful woman named Pinkie," as she told me, to help with the ironing and heavy work around the house. Not only did Pinkie help my mother learn how to run a household, but she also provided a warmth and acceptance that she had never felt from her own mother. With this support, Mother finally gained the confidence that she could cope with all the tasks of caring for children and managing a home. She was eternally grateful to Pinkie for her wisdom and generosity in a difficult period of her life.

Knowing what I know now, I realize that our visit to see Pinkie in January 1956 was more than just a social call. The two women had had a meaningful connection, and they wanted to make a statement: friendship and mutual respect can transcend racial barriers. During the years we lived in Tuscaloosa, my parents showed me what it means to honor a person's humanity regardless of race. When Pinkie invited a White mother and her two young daughters into her home, she was honoring this truth as well. With this gesture of friendship across racial lines both women were defying the social code that regulated every aspect of life in the South.

I was not aware of any of this as we drove away from Pinkie's house on that chilly day in 1956. I just had that warm, comfortable feeling I always had after spending time with Pinkie.

~

Once we were back in Indiana, a fight for freedom exploded across the South. Watching scenes of the violence on television, I wondered where the protestors found the courage to stand up against police who attacked them with dogs and water hoses. How did they manage to sing and march and pray when I would have run away? How did they feel when time after time they had to defer their dream of freedom for another day?

Although I didn't know about it at the time, one of these incidents took place in Tuscaloosa only days after we returned to Evansville in 1956. On February 3, a twenty-six-year-old Black woman, Autherine Lucy, the daughter of sharecroppers, tried to enroll in graduate education courses after having been officially admitted to the University of Alabama. This was nearly two years after Brown v. Board of Education, in which the U.S. Supreme Court ruled that racial segregation in all public schools and colleges was illegal. But that didn't stop the protests when Lucy showed up and tried to attend classes. The admissions committee hadn't realized she was Black.

Wanting to learn more about what had happened, I searched the archives of the University of Alabama libraries. There I discovered a collection of twenty-two photographs taken during these protests by a student named James William Oakley, Jr. Looking at the pictures, I could hardly believe this was the same peaceful quad I had walked across with my father on visits to his lab in the biology department. In one photo, hordes of well-dressed White male students congregated on the steps of the Union Building in a midnight rally to protest Autherine Lucy's enrollment. I could almost hear their hate-fueled screams as a Confederate flag waved in the breeze above their heads. Another showed three policemen, one with a riot gun at his side, staring blankly at events unfolding across the street. In the most horrifying picture of all, a group of Ku Klux Klan members in full regalia gathered under a tree on the dark campus as they prepared to protest against Autherine Lucy's enrollment.

I clicked on James Oakley's photographs again and again as I tried to imagine the emotions lurking just below the surface on this idyllic-looking college campus. Thinking of my gentle, sensitive father, the professor who insisted on driving Pinkie home at the end of her workday, the biologist who was in favor of interracial marriage, I felt grateful that he wasn't there to see the quiet campus he loved disfigured by the racial hatred that had been simmering under the surface for so long. He would have felt so angry—and so helpless—in the face of this senseless violence.

Of course, the riots didn't go on forever. After three days, the university's board of trustees temporarily barred Lucy from attending classes, saying it was necessary to ensure the safety of students and faculty. That night, she was permanently expelled by the board of trustees, who claimed she had made "false, defamatory, impertinent, and scandalous charges" against university officials in a lawsuit filed by the NAACP Legal Defense and Educational Fund (Thurgood Marshall was one of her lawyers). The court battles continued, but the ban against Lucy's enrollment persisted for many years.

Looking at these photos of violence and mayhem taken in 1956, I remember how happy I felt as a teenager graduating from high school in Indiana when I learned that the University of Alabama had finally been integrated. In 1963, seven years after Autherine Lucy was refused admission, two brave students, Vivian Malone and James Hood, registered for classes at the university. Governor George Wallace stood in the doorway of Foster Auditorium refusing to admit the students. It took reinforcements from the National Guard, ordered by President John F. Kennedy, but at last the University of Alabama was no longer an all-White institution.

Years later, when I discovered the story of Autherine Lucy, I couldn't stop thinking about her. All she wanted was a good education, the kind of education that White students could easily get at this public university. What she got instead were mobs of White students throwing eggs and rotten vegetables and threatening her life. And then she got expelled. In an interview with the New York Times in 1992, thirty-six years after she first tried to register for classes, Lucy described her experience during the violent protests of 1956:

> It felt somewhat like you were not really a human being. . . . I did expect to find isolation. I thought I could survive that. But I did not expect it to go as far as it did. There were students behind me saying, "Let's kill her! Let's kill her!"

In 1988, twenty-two years after Autherine Lucy first tried to attend, the university ended the ban on her enrollment. She registered for a master's program in elementary education, receiving her M.A. in 1992.

Eventually, a scholarship and a clock tower at the university were named for her, and she was awarded an honorary doctorate. But these belated tributes by university officials could never atone for the terrible ways she suffered as a young woman in the struggle for basic civil rights. In 2022, a building on the Tuscaloosa campus was dedicated to Autherine Lucy. It had previously been known as the David Bibb Graves Building in honor of a former Alabama governor and Grand Cyclops of the Montgomery Klavern of the Ku Klux Klan. The original plan was to rename the building the Lucy-Graves Hall. But after protests against the idea that Lucy's name would be linked with that of a Klan leader, the trustees settled on calling it the Autherine Lucy Hall.

At the naming ceremony on February 25, 2022, just a few days before she died on March 2, at age ninety-two, Autherine Lucy returned to the place where her life had been threatened sixty-six years earlier. I wonder what she thought as she sat there in her wheelchair listening to all these White people praising her courage in the fight for educational opportunity. After the speeches, they presented her with a certificate from the state of Alabama declaring her a "master teacher." This was her response:

> If I am a master teacher, what I hope I'm teaching you is that love will take care of everything in our world, don't

you think? It does not depend on what color we are, that's what I want to teach. It's not your color. It's not how bright you are. It's how you feel about those you deal with.

Then she waved and said, "Love you, and so long." As she sat there smiling and listening to the applause, maybe she remembered what her mother taught her so long ago: "You have to train yourself to wait."

7

The Great Smoky Mountains

"Hurry up, Becky," Mother called out. "We need to leave by 8:30 if we're going to make it all the way to Chattanooga in one day." Stepping closer to my bedroom, she reminded me, "Don't forget to pack your bathing suit. Some of the motels might have a swimming pool."

Our whole family was going on a vacation to the Smoky Mountains. Grabbing my suitcase, I ran out to the driveway. Carol was already there with her security blanket thrown over her shoulder and Jimmy, her pink teddy bear, nestled under her arm. Granny was standing beside the car with a small suitcase and her sewing kit, filled with quilt patches she could baste together at night in the motel.

Daddy opened the trunk and stowed the luggage inside. He was so proud of our car, a dark blue 1950 Ford sedan. This was the first brand-new car he had ever been able to afford, and he wanted it to look perfect for the trip. The day before we left, he washed it with soapy water and rinsed it with the hose. Then he coated it all over with carnauba wax and polished it to a shine. The front bumper was made of chrome and shone like sterling silver. Above the bumper, right in the center of the hood, was a decoration that looked like a royal crest. It was divided into red, blue, and silver triangles with a small silver lion in each segment and the word FORD spelled out at the top in capital letters. When he was finished with everything else, he rubbed that hood ornament until it gleamed.

Now everything was ready and it was time to go. I opened the door to the back seat and crawled in. The seat was covered with a gray fabric that felt smooth and soft, kind of like I imagined the fur of a little gray mouse would feel. Carol went over to the other side and got in. All three grownups sat in the front, with Mother in the middle.

The tires crunched over the gravel as Daddy backed the car out of the driveway. "We're off on a great adventure," he announced. For the past few summers, he had spent several weeks doing research at a place called Oak Ridge. To get there, he had to drive through the Smoky Mountains, and he had fallen in love with these rolling hills. Now he wanted to take the whole family to see the mountains he loved so much.

It felt special to have everyone, even Granny, packed into the car together. I rolled down my window and felt the hot air drying the sweat on my body. From where I was sitting, I could see Daddy at the wheel. He was so tall, and he had beautiful black hair. The steering wheel looked like a toy in his big, strong hands. When he stuck his arm out the window to signal a turn, he could almost touch the cars going the other way with his long, graceful fingers.

About two hours into the trip, things started to get rowdy. These were the days before seat belts, so Carol and I had slid off the seat and were rolling around on the floor, hanging on to the back of the front seat and kicking each other. "Girls," Mother said as she twisted her head around to look at us, "get back up on the seat." We both knew not to argue with her when she spoke in her teacher voice.

"If you're feeling so bored," she said, "I have an idea. You know how much Granny loves music. Why don't we sing some of our favorite songs?" She asked Carol to choose a song.

She didn't have to think long before she said, "Oh, Susanna." She liked this song because it was about somebody from Alabama, like us.

Mother, Carol, and I started to sing. Granny and Daddy didn't sing along, but they nodded their heads in time to the music.

When we finished the last verse, Mother looked at me. "Becky, what would you like to sing?" I knew more songs than Carol, who was only four and a half. The first one that came to my mind was one of Mother's favorites, "Carolina in the Morning." Her voice was strong and sweet as she sang about meeting her sweetie when she got to Carolina in the morning. Maybe she was thinking back to the time when she and Daddy were first married. It was during the Depression, and they were working as schoolteachers in different towns, so about once a month one of them had to travel a few hours by car or bus to spend the weekend together. In between visits, they wrote letters to each other almost every day, but nothing could substitute for actually being together. I knew this song about Carolina was a special one for Mother and Daddy. Carol and I didn't know all the words, but we followed along the best we could.

We sang a few more songs, and then Mother turned to Daddy and said, "Bert, we should be looking for a place to have lunch. The girls are getting hungry, and we could all use a break."

One of the best things about vacations was eating in restaurants. Soon we pulled over to a little place on the side of the road. I ordered a grilled cheese sandwich and French fries. Even though it wasn't a weekend, Mother let Carol and me order soft drinks. My Coke came in a little bottle with a glass full of ice and a straw on the side. All three grownups ordered iced tea. Once everyone had finished their meals and used the bathroom, we got back in the car.

"The pause that refreshes!" Mother said as we were getting settled. She always said that after we stopped to have a bite to eat or go to the bathroom. "Even if you don't feel tired, you should stop every so often just to stretch your legs."

Carol didn't have to take a nap after lunch any more, but as the car sped down the road, she stroked her blanket and cuddled Jimmy. Her eyelids began to droop, and pretty soon she was asleep.

"Look at that!" Daddy said. "We must be getting close." He pointed to a big barn near the side of the road with See Rock City painted on its roof in huge white letters. He explained that the man who ran Rock City had hired a sign painter to paint this message on lots of roofs along the road as a way to advertise his park. It was just a few miles east of Chattanooga, and we would be going there tomorrow.

After seeing that first barn, we started a competition to count how many of these big signs we could spot. Daddy and I took the left side of the road, and Mother and Granny looked for signs on the right. Granny was very good at this game, and her team was leading. At some point, I must have fallen asleep like Carol because the next thing I knew we were pulling into a motel in Chattanooga.

Right after breakfast the next morning, we piled into the car again and arrived at Rock City about half an hour later. After Daddy parked the car, he turned to Granny. "Mom, it's pretty steep and rocky. I'm not sure if you'd feel comfortable on the paths here." Granny was dressed as she usually was—in a printed house dress. She was wearing black leather lace-up shoes with two-inch heels. Unlike my mother, she never wore socks, even inside the house. Instead, she wore nylon stockings rolled above her knees and held up with rubber garters. Always concerned about the needs of others, Daddy continued, "Do you want to come with us? Or just wait here in the car?"

Back home Granny hardly ever left the house, so her answer surprised me. "We're on a vacation, and I want to see all the sights."

When we got to a rest area, Daddy snapped a photo. Later, when I saw the picture, I was surprised to see Granny standing next to Carol and looking straight into the camera. In every other photograph of my grandmother, she was turned to the side so that only the left side of her face was visible. Granny was very self-conscious about what she called her "bad eye." When she was about twelve years old, she had a serious injury. She was bringing the family's cows home from the pasture, and when she flicked the whip, it flew back and hit her in her right eye. It was very painful, but her parents didn't even take her to the doctor. A few weeks later, she lost all vision in that eye. To me, the eye didn't really look that bad, just kind of cloudy and unfocused, but she thought it looked terrible, and she never wanted it to be seen in a photo. Maybe being on vacation, she was so relaxed that for once she didn't worry about how that eye might look.

After Mother and Granny saw the steep path up to Lover's Leap, the highest point at Rock City, they decided to go to the gift shop instead. Daddy, Carol, and I were determined to make it to the top. The twisting, narrow trail led around giant rock formations. When we reached the summit, the view of the hills seemed to stretch on and on. People liked to say that on a clear day you could see seven states from here, but Daddy said no one could actually prove that.

We took a different trail on the way down. As we walked along, Daddy pointed out some delicate wildflowers growing beside the path. Suddenly we came to a long bridge that went across a deep ravine. As people walked, the bridge swayed back and forth, making a creaking sound. Looking across, Carol started to cry. I didn't cry, but I was scared too. "I can't do it," she sobbed. Daddy knelt down and put his arms around her. "The Indians who used to live here built bridges like this. They knew how to use all the materials they had from nature to make what they needed. These bridges are very strong."

She was still whimpering when Daddy said, "I know you can do this." He explained that I should go first. Then he said to Carol, "All you have to do is keep your eyes on your sister and follow her. Whatever you do, don't look down." He promised that he would be right behind her. "If you should slip or fall, I will catch you."

Very slowly, I walked onto the bridge. Holding onto the flexible railing with my right hand, I kept walking. About halfway across, I began to feel more secure and even started to enjoy the rhythmic swaying of the bridge. The next thing I knew, I was stepping onto solid ground. I looked back at Carol. She was smiling.

The rest of the trail back down the mountain seemed easy after that. It was paved with stones and had stone walls on each side that were almost as tall as Carol. When we got down, we found Mother and Granny waiting outside the gift shop. "How was it?" Mother asked.

Carol spoke first. "I walked across a long scary bridge over a deep valley. But I wasn't scared. I just pretended I was an Indian."

"Did you know that you might actually be part Indian?" Mother asked. "My father, Bill Stamps, was born in Oklahoma. He told me that his mother was half-Chocktaw, so you girls may have some Indian blood. But we can't be sure because not everything he told me was true."

THE GREAT SMOKY MOUNTAINS

As soon as Mother mentioned Bill Stamps, Granny started walking as fast as she could toward the parking lot. She couldn't stand to hear anything connected with her ex-husband. I knew never to mention his name. He was my grandfather, but I never got to meet him. Granny gave up on her marriage and left him before I was born.

The next day was a Saturday—June 6, 1953. It was only one day, but it seemed to have a whole year's worth of adventures packed into it.

Our first stop was the Ocanaluftee Indian Village, just outside the town of Cherokee, North Carolina. Daddy explained that all the land in this part of the country used to belong to several different Indian tribes, but after the White settlers came, they moved them off their land and sent many of them to reservations far away from their homes. Now, some of the Cherokees who still lived here had created this village to show outsiders what their lives had been like before they were forced to leave.

When we got to the visitor center, a Cherokee woman in a long dress said that she would be our guide. She showed us all around the village. We saw a man and a woman weaving baskets out of long strips of wood that were soaked for days to make them flexible. We also saw how they made canoes by slowly burning the insides out of a big log. Some of the women used their fingers to weave colorful scarves and belts. I was surprised that the Cherokees didn't live in tepees like they did in our picture books. Instead, they built homes using wood and clay, sort of like log cabins. To me, they looked cozy, with all family members living together in a big open space. In the middle, there was a circle of stones surrounding the fire they used for cooking and heating.

Before we left the village, our parents told Carol and me that we could use our allowance money to buy something at the gift shop. There was a lot to choose from, and it was hard to decide. Finally, I bought a necklace that looked like it was made of real turquoise, and Carol chose a doll dressed in traditional Cherokee clothes. She was about six inches tall and wore pants and an apron with geometric designs painted on it. She had long black hair and wore a red headband, like the ones we saw being woven in the village.

We had only been back on the road for a few minutes when we came to a big sign that said Welcome to Great Smoky Mountains National Park. "I hope all of you will love these hills as much as I do," Daddy said as we entered the park.

Driving along the winding road, Daddy had to shift gears as we climbed higher. "Gott im Himmel!" Granny yelled from the front seat. I didn't know exactly what those words meant, but Granny only said them when she was upset. The car window on her side looked out on a big drop-off. She was twisting a handkerchief around and around her fingers, and sometimes, when we got close to the edge, she closed her eyes. I could understand why she was scared, but I also understood why Daddy loved this place so much. The Smokies weren't really mountains like the Rocky Mountains out West that I had seen in our Compton's Pictured Encyclopedia. Daddy stopped at an overlook so we could see them better. Carol and I stood on the very edge looking out over the soft, green hills that rolled on and on, one after another, into the distance.

After about an hour, the grownups decided we needed to stop for lunch. Mother had packed some fruit and sandwiches before we left Chattanooga, and there were picnic tables where you could eat while looking out at the hillsides.

Once we were back in the car, the road got even steeper. A sign said we were approaching Newfound Gap, the highest point on the road. The car kept switching back and forth as the road zigzagged over the mountain range. Pretty soon Carol said, "My tummy doesn't feel good." Mother was also subject to motion sickness—she couldn't even stand beside us on a merry-go-round—and she too was feeling queasy. Once we got over the pass and started down the other side of the mountain, the road straightened out, and they both began to feel better.

We didn't talk much as we rode along. We just looked out the windows at the beautiful scenery. We passed some rushing waterfalls tumbling over rocks as they splashed down the hill. Daddy said that June was the peak season for the rhododendrons that grew wild in the park. As we drove along, the roadside was lined with their pink blossoms and waxy green leaves, and beyond them the lush green hillsides, one after another, becoming blue and then a hazy kind of slate gray as they faded off into the distance. After a while, Daddy turned to Mother and Granny. "I'd really like to take the girls on a short walk. Would you ladies like to come along?" They both shook their heads and said they'd just rest in the car.

At the next overlook, Daddy pulled over to the side of the road. There was a sign showing a trail map. Once we got away from the road, it was so quiet. All we could hear was the wind rustling through the trees and birds calling high above. As we walked along, Daddy told us the names of the wildflowers beside the trail: painted trillium, foamflower, speckled wood lily. I loved these names. They made it seem as if the flowers had their own personalities. Daddy reached up to look closely at the branch of an evergreen tree. "This is Tsuga canadensis," he told us. "The common name is hemlock. We don't have these trees in Tuscaloosa. It's too hot for them." Gently, he broke off a twig, including some tiny seed cones, and put it in his pocket. "This will be a nice addition to the department's collections."

Soon Daddy looked at his watch and said we'd better get back to the car. On the way down, I hadn't realized the trail was so steep. Walking back up, we had to stop every once in a while to catch our breath. On one of these stops, we heard a thin, high-pitched bird song. Daddy pointed to a nearby tree. All three of us looked up and saw a bright orange splash of color surrounded by the dark green of the evergreen tree where a tiny bird was perched. We stood there in silence, looking and listening. Then, with a flick of its wings, it flew off into the distance. "That was a treat," Daddy said. "It was a male Blackburnian warbler. They're quite common here in the Smokies. He was singing to attract a mate."

When we got back to the car, Daddy took his little notebook out of his shirt pocket and made some notes about what we had seen on the walk. I remember thinking how lucky he was to have a job where he could study so many different, beautiful things. To me, his job didn't seem like work. It seemed like play.

After the hike, Carol and I were both pretty tired. I was almost asleep when the car stopped suddenly. Looking out the front windshield, I could see a long line of cars. "There's been a bear sighting," Daddy said. We crept along until we came to a parking area, and he parked the car. Grabbing the camera, he opened the door and climbed out. "Does anyone want to come with me?" We all shook our heads.

We could see him and a few other people walking along the side of the road, and then we saw the bear. It was huge, with matted, dark brown fur. It turned toward our father, who was holding out the camera to take a picture. The bear did not look happy. Slowly, Daddy backed away. The bear just stood there staring at him.

We were practically shaking when he got back to the car. "These bears are not likely to attack a person," he said, sounding calm. He just sat there in the driver's seat for a few minutes, and then he took out his notebook and began to write.

> Took picture of bear coming close to the camera. Someone took a picture of me taking a picture of the bear. He was very close. Ruth, her mother, and the girls would not get out of the car.

Then he dated the entry: June 6, 1953.

As he put the car in gear and drove on, I wondered what Mother would say. She looked over at him, shaking her head, "Honestly, Bert," she said in a serious voice, "sometimes I think you're going to give me a heart attack with your biological research!" He just kept driving.

As we got close to Gatlinburg, the town where we would be spending the night, the sun began to fade. Now the mountains were covered with clouds that looked like pillows of smoke—not charcoal gray like the smoke pouring out of a factory but a soft bluish gray that blended with the brighter blue of the sky—almost like a mirage, something I might see in a dream. Looking into the distance as far as I could see, it was almost like listening to music.

Once we got to Gatlinburg, there were lots of motels, and Mother and Daddy chose one with a swimming pool. But Carol and I were too tired to use it. After dinner, when we got back to the motel, we went straight to our room. We took out the things we had bought at the Cherokee Village and laid them on the bed. I could tell that my necklace wasn't real turquoise. It was made out of plastic dyed to look like turquoise. Carol took the clothes off her small Indian doll. The decorated apron looked like it was made of leather, but it too was just plastic. The doll's skin was dark, but her features looked like any other White doll. When Carol turned her over, stamped on the doll's back I saw the words Made in Japan.

Soon we put our new toys on the bedside table and crawled into bed. It was so much cooler here than back home in Tuscaloosa. Snuggled next to my sister in this cozy bed, I thought about all that had happened that day—the long drive through the Smoky Mountains, the beautiful flowers and birds and then the bear. Lying here with the covers pulled up to my neck, what I remembered most clearly was the Cherokee Village we visited at the beginning of the day. I imagined that I was an Indian girl living in one of the houses we saw at the village. Everyone slept in one room and ate together around the fire. They didn't have a lot of furniture or even toys, but it seemed like a peaceful way to live. And then the White men came and drove them off their land. I knew how sad I would be if strangers forced me to leave my home and move far away from everything that was familiar. I felt so sorry for the Indians. And I hoped this would never, ever happen to me.

Mother woke us up early the next morning. "Rise and shine," she sang out as she pulled open the drapes. "We need to be on the road soon because we have to get all the way back to Chattanooga by evening."

After a quick breakfast at a restaurant near the motel, we packed our luggage and got into the car. Daddy had decided to drive back on the same route we took yesterday. It was the only road that went through the national park and the quickest and most direct way to get home.

The mountains were just as beautiful on the way back, but we didn't make many stops. About an hour into the trip, I said, in a whiny voice, "I'm bored." There weren't any signs or painted barns inside the park, and we had seen these same things yesterday.

THE GREAT SMOKY MOUNTAINS

Mother had lots of strategies for dealing with kids who were bored. "I have an idea," she said. "Yesterday you learned about how the Indians lived a long time ago. But how much do you know about your own grandmother's life when she was a girl? I know a game called Twenty Questions. We can all take turns asking Granny questions about growing up on the family farm in Darmstadt, Indiana."

I asked the first question. "Did you have to do chores like I do?"

"Them days kids had to do a lot of work," she said. "I was in charge of baking all the bread for my family from the time I was ten or twelve years old." She had to bake bread twice a week, and every Saturday she baked twelve or thirteen kuchens. I knew Granny's kuchens because she always made them for our family at Christmas time. They were delicious, sprinkled with brown sugar and drizzled with vanilla icing when they were still warm from the oven.

"Were you a good baker even when you were a girl?" I asked.

She sounded proud when she answered this question. "Whenever I cooked, it was cooked right. You kids have no idea how much work we had to do on the farm."

"What was your school like?" Carol asked.

"We were only allowed to speak German at school, so I didn't learn much English until I was a teenager." She explained that her school only went up to sixth grade. "I took that grade twice and then dropped out. There was no higher grade for me to go to."

Granny sounded sad when she said this. I knew how smart she was. She loved to listen to operas on the radio, and she was good at solving math problems that came up when she was piecing a quilt. I thought it was terrible that she had to stop going to school when she was only twelve or thirteen years old.

"What do you remember about your teachers?" Mother asked.

Granny told us that there was only one teacher for all six grades—Preacher Zimmerman, who was also the minister of the Lutheran church they attended in Darmstadt. "How did he enforce discipline?" As a teacher, Mother knew this was an important question.

"With the hand!" Granny said in a loud voice. "As you know, I'm left-handed, but Preacher Zimmerman forced me to write with my right hand. If he caught me using my left hand, he smacked it with his ruler."

Once, when she didn't get the right answer to the preacher's question, he got so mad that he scratched the answer into her slate with his thumbnail. "We didn't have pencils and paper like you girls do," she explained. "That was too expensive. We had to use small slates, like little blackboards, and we wrote the answers in chalk. I can still hear the horrible screeching sound of his nail biting into my slate. Preacher Zimmerman wasn't very patient with kids."

I think it upset Daddy to hear these stories about Preacher Zimmerman. He was a teacher himself, and he often told me that teaching was based on mutual respect between students and teachers. He asked another question to change the subject. "What was farming like when you were a girl?"

"Well," Granny began, "almost everything had to be done by hand. At the end of the growing season, we had to cut the corn with a three-foot-long knife, and then we made it into big shocks. But I couldn't do that. I wasn't strong enough. The men had to do that."

"I remember on our farm in New Pennington," Daddy said, "threshing time was always a busy time of year. What was it like for you?"

"Father didn't have the strength to do it by himself, so we kids had to help. We would pick up the bundles of wheat and lay six this way and six that way. Sometimes it took us a whole week." Then, she said, they rented a threshing machine that would be set up in their yard to separate the wheat kernels from the chaff. Even with the help of this steam-powered invention, threshing was an exhausting operation for the whole family. "I used to be wet down to my knees from the sweat," Granny remembered.

I began to wonder if there was anything except work in my grandmother's childhood. "Did you ever do anything just for fun when you were a girl?" I asked.

"It wasn't like today when you can just go to a movie or watch something on television," she said. "We had to make our own fun." About once a month, someone in the neighborhood would have a corn husking or dance party in their granary or kitchen. I was happy to hear this because I loved dancing. I had started taking ballet lessons when I was six and hoped to get my first pair of toe shoes soon. In Granny's day, people didn't take dance classes or buy special shoes. "The family would slick up the floor and get some neighbor boys to play the music." Honestly, I couldn't imagine my grandmother ever dancing, even when she was young. But I knew she liked listening to the music, and she must have enjoyed watching other people dance.

I couldn't help thinking about how different Granny's childhood was from my own—how she had to stop going to school after sixth grade and how hard she had to work on the farm. Things got even worse when she had to leave home at sixteen or seventeen to work at Schmidt's Greenhouse in Darmstadt. She sent her wages of about a dollar a week back home to her family. She and another girl, Myrtle Stork, worked under a long shed, washing beets and carrots in a tub of water and making them into bundles. "Nasty, dirty work, I'll tell you that!"

When I looked over at Carol, I could see tears rolling down her cheeks. Carol was such a tender-hearted little girl. It made her sad to learn about all that Granny went through in her life. I felt like crying too but held back my tears.

Looking out at the hillsides, I remembered something Mother told me a few months ago. I had asked her why Granny sometimes yelled at her over silly things like how long to cook green beans or whether the roast was done. She said Granny had had a very hard life, and that sometimes made her grouchy. When Granny was in her early twenties, her mother made her travel all the way to Colorado to take care of a sick relative. While she was out there, she fell in love with a man named Ed Schnute. But the love affair didn't last. According to Mother, a friend visiting from Indiana flirted with Ed and succeeded in breaking them up. This woman had such a silly name—Hulda Harrell. Ed later dated Hulda, but he didn't marry her. That was no consolation for Granny. Ed's betrayal had broken her heart. I had read sad stories like this in some of the books I checked out from the library, but I never imagined my own grandmother had gone through such terrible times when she was young.

Suddenly, Mother's voice broke into my thoughts. She never liked to dwell on sad things for too long. "Bert, we need to be thinking about where to stop for lunch."

Granny seemed relieved. "That's all I have to say," she said. "You'd better remember it because I'm not gonna talk about them days again!" The car was quiet after she said that. Then, a few miles after we left the national park, we stopped at a little restaurant for lunch. Once we were back on the road, we didn't stop again until we got to the Shamrock Motel in Chattanooga. We chose this place because it had a swimming pool and a TV in every room.

Granny shared a room with us kids, and Mother and Daddy had the room right next door. Carol and I put on our swimsuits and ran out to the pool. Nobody else was there. I jumped into the middle and dog-paddled over to the edge. Carol was standing by the shallow end. I stood up to show her how deep it was. "Don't worry. It's nice and warm," I said. "I'll hold you up if it's too deep for you." She sat down on the edge and dangled her feet in the water. Then, all at once, she slid in. After all those days cooped up in the car, it felt so good to move our arms and legs freely and splash around in the pool.

A little while later, Daddy came out with his suit on and walked over to the edge of the pool. "Would you girls mind if I joined you?"

"Come on in," Carol said. "The water's nice and warm."

He slipped his long legs into the water and swam a few laps back and forth across the pool. Then he came over to the shallow end, where Carol and I were playing. Back home in Tuscaloosa, he had been trying to teach us to swim. "The most important thing," he always said, "is to learn to trust the water." Now, in the motel pool in Chattanooga, he took turns holding us as we tried to float on our backs. "Don't worry," he said. "The water will hold you up if you just relax." I closed my eyes, tilted my head back, and arched my back, and as he moved his hands away, I understood that what he said was true. I really did stay on top of the water without sinking for a few seconds before my legs started to curve downward toward the bottom of the pool. After this short lesson, we just splashed around, acting silly. We could have stayed there for hours, but soon Mother came out to remind us, "Time to change into dry clothes for supper."

The restaurant was right next to the motel, so we didn't have to get in the car again. After dinner, we all went back to Mother and Daddy's room. Granny sat in a chair, basting her quilt patches together. She was making a flower garden quilt with scraps left over from other sewing projects. I recognized some of my favorite dresses in those quilt patches. Mother propped up all the pillows against the headboard, and the rest of us climbed onto the bed to watch TV. Carol was nestled close to Mother, and I snuggled up next to Daddy. I was excited when *I Love Lucy* came on. That was one of my favorite shows. At home I often went over to the twins' house to watch it with my friends. It was even better to be watching it in a motel room with my whole family. We couldn't keep from laughing at Lucy's crazy antics. After a few minutes, Granny put down her quilt patches and started watching too. I think I even heard her giggle once or twice.

I don't know what came on the screen after Lucy because I must have fallen asleep. The next thing I knew, Daddy had picked me up and carried me next door to our room. He tucked me into bed next to Carol, who was already sound asleep. My body had that great feeling I always had after being in the water. As I lay there in that big bed, I thought about all that had happened on our vacation. This last day hadn't been as exciting as the ones that came before, but it was my favorite day of the whole trip. All five of us in one small motel room after a nice dinner watching a silly program on TV—not talking, just being together. Listening to the steady hum of cars and trucks whizzing by on the road outside, I hoped this feeling would never end.

8

Oak Ridge

OAK RIDGE. These words always had an almost magical sound to my ears. I couldn't imagine what my father found so fascinating about this place. More fascinating than nature walks at Tanglewood. More fascinating than teaching biology at the university. So fascinating that he would give up the chance to spend the summer months with his family in Tuscaloosa in order to do research at this mysterious place in Tennessee. Finally, we were actually going to visit him there.

It was August of 1953, and Daddy had been at Oak Ridge since the middle of June while Mother, Granny, Carol, and I stayed in Tuscaloosa. Summers in Alabama were always fun—lazy days with no school, delicious home-cooked meals, swimming lessons at the beautiful pool in Queen City Park. But after two months in a home without a husband and father, we were lonely. Sometime in July, my parents indulged in the rare luxury of a long-distance phone call. Then Daddy checked the bus schedule and purchased three round-trip tickets to Tennessee.

On the morning of Friday, August 21, Mother, Carol, and I boarded a Greyhound bus in Tuscaloosa, and more than twelve hours later, Daddy picked us up at the bus station in Knoxville. We were all exhausted, so he took us directly to our motel. He had reserved a "twin bedroom with bath and cots" for $7.50 a night, as noted in his small memo book for 1953. Six days later, on August 27, he delivered us back to the bus station for the trip home: "Girls on bus in K'ville. 11:10 AM."

It's too bad that, as an eight-year-old, I didn't keep a diary of my own that summer because I remember so little from the August trip to Oak Ridge. All that remains are a few disconnected fragments, like scenes glimpsed while surfing channels on TV.

In the first scene, we are in the motel room in Knoxville, and Daddy is asking me a question. "Hey, Kiddo, would you like to see my lab at Oak Ridge?" Of course, I wanted to see his lab! All summer I had been trying to picture the place he found so compelling that he wanted to spend the whole summer there—away from us!

Security procedures at the lab were tight, he explained, because some of the materials they used in their research could be dangerous. Children under six were not allowed to enter the facility, so Carol would have to stay with Mother in Knoxville while the two of us drove the twenty-five miles to Oak Ridge.

A shutter in my mind clicks to the next fragment. I see a big sign announcing Welcome to the Oak Ridge National Laboratory. Daddy showed his identification papers to the guard at the gate, and we drove through. Once inside, I was shocked to see a landscape that looked like the surface of the moon. This vast place, so different from the lush hills surrounding it, was a flat, lifeless wasteland. Nothing remained of what had flourished here before, when the spot was called Bear Creek Valley. Now it was just bare dirt, paved parking lots, and faceless rectangular buildings, punctuated by towering smokestacks. Instead of names, these buildings had letters and numbers: K-25, X-10, Y-12.

In the next scene, I am inside Y-12—a huge, air-conditioned, sterile-looking space with high ceilings and cinderblock walls painted white. There were men in the room dressed in white coveralls and wearing funny white caps to cover their hair. This cavernous space contained strange-looking machines reminding me of a scene from *Frankenstein*, a movie I had watched on TV. What kind of monster, I wondered, had they created here in Oak Ridge?

One of the men in white was holding a thing that looked like a gun. Attached to it was a long, black cord plugged into a small box-like machine with lots of dials. Daddy said the machine was a Geiger counter. Once we went through the metal door, we would be exposed to something called radiation. He explained that we all have a small amount of radiation in our bodies, but if too much gets in, it might make us sick. The man in charge of the Geiger counter had to check us before and after we visited the lab to make sure we hadn't absorbed too much while we were inside. He checked Daddy first, waving the gun-like thing all over his body. This caused a clicking sound to come from the machine. Then he checked me, and I heard the same kind of clicking—sort of like static on a radio when the signal wasn't coming through clearly. It scared me to think that I already had some of this dangerous stuff inside me. I wondered if my body was always sending out this staticky sound, and my ears just weren't sharp enough to hear it. What other sounds might be coming from my body without me knowing?

It wasn't just our bodies that might pick up radiation in the lab, Daddy said, but also our clothing. Another man gave Daddy a clean white coat to protect him from the radiation. For me, he chose the smallest coat he could find, hoping that it would fit my eight-year-old body. It was much too big and almost touched the floor, but he wrapped me up the best he could and tied a cotton strap around my waist to hold the coat in place. Then he gave me a white cap to cover my hair. I had to take off my shoes and put on some floppy slippers made of white cloth. They were way too big for me and skidded around on the shiny linoleum floor.

By this time, I wasn't so sure I wanted to see the lab. But Daddy said it was safe to go in now, so I did. The man in charge had to press some special buttons so that the heavy metal door would open, and we walked through. When the door clanged shut, I had a creepy feeling. What if we needed to leave in a hurry, and there was no one on the other side to let us out? What if there was a fire or an explosion, and we couldn't get out?

By now I was really frightened. Maybe that's why I don't remember much about what the lab was like. Men in white coats were fiddling with the dials and controls of machines mounted on the walls. Daddy held my hand as we walked over to his workstation. It was at a bench, sort of like the bench in his lab at the university, only this one was not made of wood; it was covered with a hard, black slate-like material. Daddy sat down and reached out to adjust the microscope he used. "This is a very powerful machine," he said. "Much stronger than the one I use in Tuscaloosa."

"Why do you need such a powerful microscope?"

He explained that the research he was doing was intended to improve how farmers grow our food. "I use something called radioactive phosphorous to trace how nutrients from the soil get into the roots of plants." He motioned to a tray set up under a bright light. There were dozens of tiny seeds sprouting on thick, wet sheets of paper in the tray. He put on a pair of rubber gloves and picked up one of the sprouts with a pair of tweezers. I could see its tiny white roots dangling down. "I water these little plants with a solution that contains radioactive phosphorous, and then use this special microscope to see where the radioactivity has traveled inside the root."

He removed the lid of a black box about the size of a thick notebook. It contained rows of glass slides. He took one out, placed it on the microscope, and lowered the lens down onto it. "Here's a sample I prepared yesterday. This one wasn't treated with radioactive phosphorous, so it's safe for you to look at it." I climbed up on his lap and looked through the eyepiece of the microscope. I thought I could see some squiggly looking things that might have been root cells, but I wasn't sure.

Daddy carefully removed a few more of the slides from the black box and checked them under the microscope. "I never get tired of seeing the way a plant's root is made up of different kinds of cells," he said. "I love the way they're neatly organized in a circular pattern. It's really very beautiful."

After he wrote some notes in the notebook he kept in a drawer under the bench, we walked back to the metal door. He punched some numbers into a keypad attached to the wall, and soon a buzzer sounded and the door opened.

I was relieved to be back in the big room, even though it was cold and had a strange smell. Daddy and I took off our protective clothing—the white coats, hats, and slippers—and put our own shoes back on. Then we were checked by the man with the Geiger counter. When he waved the wand over our bodies, we heard the same clicking sounds as before. I thought the clicking was a little faster than it had been the first time. Everything must have been okay though because the man said we were free to go.

As we drove through the gate and into the mountains surrounding Oak Ridge, I took a deep breath. It was good to be back in our car with the windows down. I hoped the air blowing through my hair might also be blowing away any extra radiation I had picked up in the lab. I could almost imagine the clicks on the Geiger counter getting slower and softer as we drove along the winding mountain road.

Looking out the window at the green hills and valleys, I asked my father why Oak Ridge looked so different from everything around it. I don't remember the words he used, but he explained that during World War II, our country's government needed to find a place to do some important research so that we could help to defeat the Germans. It was important to pick a place that was completely isolated from the outside world because this research was top secret.

Daddy hardly ever mentioned the word *war*. I knew there had been a big war before I was born, and I also knew he hated all wars. He always said he was glad he wasn't drafted into the army like his brother Dwight. I couldn't imagine him being able to carry a gun and shoot another person.

"Why did everything have to be top secret?" I thought only kids had secrets, not our country's government.

"It's very complicated," he said, looking over at me. "Hitler, the leader of Germany during the war, was a very bad man. He wanted to conquer the whole world and destroy our democracy." Daddy explained that in the early years of the war, some brilliant scientists were working on a very powerful bomb. They called it the atomic bomb. And if we developed it before the Germans did, it would help us and our allies win the war and defeat Hitler once and for all. But the Germans were trying to develop this same kind of bomb, and they would love to steal the work of our scientists. So everything had to be done in total secrecy, and for that reason, they had to build a big, new lab in the middle of nowhere. "Oak Ridge just fit the bill."

"What happened to the people who already lived there?"

"That's a very sad part of this story," he said. He explained that more than a thousand families, people who had lived here for generations, were paid a little money by the government and told they had to leave their homes. Many of them couldn't even read the signs that were posted on their cabins telling them they had to leave. Most of them had about sixty days to get out, but some only had two weeks. Many didn't receive any payment until they had moved out completely.

"Can you imagine," he said, "if someone knocked on our door in Tuscaloosa and told us we had two months to pack up everything and move somewhere else?" What made things even worse was that the people in Tennessee didn't have cars to help with the move or money to rent a new place to live. "I really don't know how they did it," he said, "but by the time the big machines arrived to bulldoze the land for the new buildings, everyone who lived there before was gone. They had no choice."

He sounded upset when he talked about these people being forced off their land, and I started to think about how the same thing had happened to the Indians on the other side of these mountains when the White settlers decided to take over the land where their tribes had always lived. I had read about this on a sign at the Cherokee village our family visited on our way to the Smoky Mountains in June. About a hundred years ago, our government passed a law forcing the people who lived there to move out West to a place called Indian Territory. It wasn't even a state yet, just a dry prairie that later became Oklahoma.

Thousands of Native people died on the long trip. Later, the route they took became known as the Trail of Tears.

The year before, when I was in second grade at Northington School, we had a class called social studies, where we studied the history of our country. We learned about the Pilgrims, who came to America on the Mayflower so they could practice their own religion, and about George Washington, the father of our country, who fought a lot of battles so we wouldn't have to be ruled by the English king. But they never taught us about the Indians. It didn't make sense. Why didn't they teach us about the people who used to live in the very place where we live today, people who were forced by the government to move far away?

For a while, neither of us spoke. Then Daddy broke the silence. "Pretty pensive over there. What are you thinking?"

It took me a while to answer. "I was wondering. If we live in such a great country, why does the government keep forcing people to leave their homes so other people can take over their land?"

"That's a good question." He thought for a minute. "It's important to remember that there are two sides to every issue. Take Oak Ridge. I feel for those people who had to leave their homes, but a lot of good has come from the work done at Oak Ridge."

He explained that by 1945, the year I was born, the scientists at Oak Ridge and out west in New Mexico had succeeded in developing an atomic bomb. President Truman decided that if we used this bomb, we could end the war sooner and save thousands of lives and protect our democracy. In August, he gave the order to drop atomic bombs on two cities in Japan, and by the middle of that month the war finally ended when the Japanese surrendered.

"I've never been sure if that was the right decision," he admitted, "but now that the war is over, the scientists at Oak Ridge are working hard to make the world a safer place and to develop good ways to use atomic energy. I have met so many outstanding scientists working here at Oak Ridge, and I think you will live to see the benefits of the work we're doing."

As I sat in the car watching the graceful hills in the distance, I realized something important, though I couldn't yet put it into words. I sensed that my father lived in two different worlds. One was the world of nature, a world of sights and sounds and scents, a world that had existed even before there were people to observe it, a world he had loved since his boyhood on the family farm in Indiana. The other world was man-made, a world of machines and the men who designed and operated them, men whose goal was not just to understand nature but to control it, to shape it to their own desires.

FROM SEED TO TREE TO FRUIT

My father was a man of few words, but you could tell he was always thinking. I wonder how he felt, deep down. It must have been hard, kind of like walking a tightrope, trying to keep his balance while living and working in two such different worlds.

9

The Half-Life of Memory

Basking in the unconditional love of my exuberant mother and my thoughtful, gentle father, I was a fortunate child. But there was another side to my early years, a secret side, the stuff of nightmares—glimpsed in dimly lighted corners, rarely seen and never spoken about. Trying to reconstruct these memories so many years later, I'm reminded of the way radiation slowly decays, reaching its half-life, not as dangerous as it once was but still there, just waiting to erupt if something should go wrong.

Odd as it may sound, one of the most intimidating of these secret fears was inspired by a piece of furniture—the love seat. That's how Mother always referred to it. It sat in the front hall of our little house at 89 Cedar Crest, and though it was called a seat, no one ever sat on it because it was so hard and uncomfortable. Perhaps this Victorian monstrosity was a hand-me-down from Mother's Aunt Pauline, who was always redecorating. It was upholstered in a maroon velvet that had seen better days. What captured my child's imagination were the identical carved wooden dragons that served as supports on either end. The mouth of each of these creatures gaped open in a snarling grin, and its scaly body ended in a powerful tail, ready to lash out and grab an unsuspecting child and squeeze her to death. Coming through the front door, I always walked as fast as I could, just in case. I never mentioned this fear to my parents, and once I got past the dragons into the living room, the feeling subsided. But sometimes, before I fell asleep at night, I had visions of these creatures coming to life and destroying our family.

The next item in my childhood cabinet of curiosities was the ultraviolet light machine. This strange device was stored in a heavy black case made of imitation leather and kept safely out of a child's reach on the top shelf of the living room closet. I don't know if my parents rented or purchased this piece of medical equipment, but I do know that it frightened me. My father only got it out when I had a sore throat or fever, which happened often before I had my tonsils removed.

Daddy explained that the machine emitted ultraviolet light, similar to sunlight but under man's control. Exposure to this light would help to heal my sore throat, but it was so powerful that it might damage my vision if I were to look at it directly. Before every treatment, he would remove a pair of dark goggles from the velvet-lined case and fasten the strap around the back of my head. I also had to take off my shirt and undershirt so that more of my body would be exposed to this artificial sunlight. Even through the goggles, I was aware that the machine cast an unnatural purple-blue glow. But the color of this strange light didn't look anything like the purplish-blue violets that grew just outside our screened-in porch—the first flowers to bloom in the spring. The machine also exuded a sickly sweet smell that I cannot describe or compare to anything else. If I ever smelled it again, I would recognize it instantly.

I knew my parents were smart and loved me beyond measure, but I was afraid of this machine, which they said would be good for me. I didn't like the wires dangling from it or the dark goggles. I didn't like that unpleasant medicinal smell. I didn't like taking my clothes off to expose my bare body to the eerie glow coming from the machine. I was almost relieved when they gave up on this treatment and scheduled me for a tonsillectomy at the hospital when I was seven years old.

In recent years, I have found myself thinking about this machine and the dread it inspired in me. I checked with my sister, who also had sore throats as a child, and she has no memories of it. However, a quick computer search for "ultraviolet light, sore throat, 1950s" confirmed its reality. For most children, these light treatments took place in a medical facility, but my father's job in a university biology department affiliated with a medical school must have given him access to this machine and enabled him to treat me at home. Although Daddy was always careful to explain the rationale for these treatments, I never fully understood why I was being subjected to this bright light, with its unnatural glow and strange smell, when the brilliant Alabama sunlight was so readily available just outside our front door.

Today, every well-informed person is wary of too much UV exposure, but in the 1950s, physicians and parents were less aware of this danger. Many people who had these treatments as children have developed skin cancer later in life. I myself have had three bouts of skin cancer on my face. Whether this was caused by exposure to ultraviolet light in my childhood, sunburns acquired from baking in the sun as a teenager, or a combination of the two is impossible to know. Still, it seems that my fear of the mysterious machine, with its pungent odor and spectral glow, was justified.

I was exposed to another disconcerting machine whenever I needed a new pair of shoes. Mother, who had always suffered from foot trouble, believed that wearing sturdy, properly fitted shoes was essential for a growing child. Whenever I needed new shoes, we headed to the Buster Brown shoe store in downtown Tuscaloosa.

Once inside the store, she made it clear that she was interested only in shoes of the highest quality. "Nothing but the best for my children." The shoes had to be made of genuine leather with sturdy leather soles. While I sat on the edge of a chair, a serious salesman knelt on the floor in front of my sock-clad feet. He measured each of them, for length and width, with a carefully calibrated metal tool and then brought several pairs of shoes for me to try on. The choices were so disappointing—leather lace-ups with hard leather soles, never glamorous ballet flats like the ones my friend Gretchen wore with her frilly dresses. Mother usually selected the sturdiest and ugliest pair. After putting them on and tying the laces, I had to stand up and walk over to the X-ray machine to check the fit. Putting my feet through a slot at the bottom of a large wooden cabinet, I could peer through an opening on top and actually see the bones of my feet inside the shadowy outlines of the shoes. Both my mother and the salesman were able to check the fit by looking through two larger openings atop the machine, sized to accommodate an adult's face. Mother, who was always impressed by the wonders of modern technology, would exclaim, "Isn't this marvelous?" But I had my doubts. How could this machine actually see the bones inside my body? The long, skinny bones of my feet reminded me of the plastic skeletons our neighbors used to decorate their houses for Halloween. I thought the X-ray machine was creepy.

It turns out I was right to be scared. These shoe-fitting machines, known as fluoroscopes, delivered a high dose of radiation—the same dangerous radiation that Daddy was exposed to in his lab at Oak Ridge, the same kind of radiation that necessitated all the safety precautions when I visited the lab in the summer of 1953. Fortunately, no children were terribly injured by these machines in shoe stores, but a number of salespeople, who were exposed on a daily basis, later developed serious illnesses such as dermatitis or cancer, in some cases leading to amputations or even death. Like the ultraviolet light machine in my parents' closet, the fluoroscopes in shoe stores were actually endangering the children they were supposed to be protecting.

Even more disturbing than the love seat, the ultraviolet light machine, or the X-ray machine at the shoe store was something I discovered at my grade school, Northington Elementary.

In the early 1950s, children were not closely guarded as they are today. Once the recess bell rang, we were free to roam about the school and grounds with no adult supervision. I usually followed the other kids out to the play area—a large, undefined space between several plain brick buildings that looked like army barracks.

The pavement was cracked, with weeds forcing their way up through the asphalt, but that didn't stop our gang of girls from playing jump rope on the warped surface. Even today, if I close my eyes, I can hear the rope whipping through the air and hitting the pavement with a snap. Two of the bigger kids turned the rope while the rest of us took turns running in and jumping until we stumbled or ran out of breath. Often, standing in line waiting for my turn to jump, I caught a whiff of a strong ammonia-like odor. When this happened, I knew that Trudy was nearby. She was in my same grade but bigger than the other girls. She never jumped rope but just stood on the side watching. Something of an outsider myself, I felt sorry for Trudy. I couldn't imagine how embarrassing it must be to come to school every day in the same wrinkled brown dress, smelling of urine. But I never spoke to her or asked her to join our games. Something held me back.

One day I got tired of jumping rope and wandered away from where the other kids were playing. Scattered on the ground in a distant part of the schoolyard, I saw hypodermic needles like the ones the doctor used to give me a shot, except these were all rusty and bent. I knew not to touch them, but I also knew not to mention them to my teacher or even to my parents.

Another day—I must have been in second or third grade—when it was time for recess, I decided to stay inside. I had always wondered what was behind the double doors at the end of the hall. Standing on tiptoes, I looked through one of the glass panels near the top and saw another long hallway. When I pushed on one of the doors, it swung open and I walked through. This dusty, unused corridor seemed to go on and on. There were rooms on either side, some of them labeled with numbers or words. I tried one of the doors and found it unlocked. Inside, against the far wall, were wooden wheelchairs, piled up helter-skelter, at odd angles with wheels askew, jumbled up in a heap as if a tornado had swept through years ago and no one had ever bothered to clean up the mess. Staring at this chaos, I backed out of the room, closed the door, and walked back through the double doors to my own classroom. No one was there. I sat down at my desk and waited until my classmates and teacher returned from recess. I never mentioned what I saw in the unused corridor to my teacher, my parents, or anyone else.

Years later, recalling the abandoned hypodermic needles and damaged wheelchairs, I wondered if I had really seen these things or they were just scenes from a recurring nightmare. Why would a school building intended for the education of young children contain these medical relics?

The answer to my questions was a simple web search away. While I hadn't known it at the time, my school, Northington Elementary, was a small part of what had been an enormous medical complex. Begun in 1942 and completed a year later, the U.S. Army Northington General Hospital sprawled over 140 acres and contained beds for more than two thousand soldiers wounded during World War II. The hospital had been named in honor of Dr. Eugene Garland Northington, an Alabama native who studied at the University of Alabama and started his medical practice in Birmingham. He owned the first X-ray machine in the state and carried out extensive experiments with this powerful new technology. Sadly, his frequent exposure to X-rays established, for the first time, the dangers of these rays. Dr. Northington developed extensive cancers on his hands and arms, leading to many surgeries and eventually to the amputation of both arms. He died at age fifty-three on June 19, 1933, a medical martyr for his unwitting discovery of the dangers of radiation.

Radiation seemed to be everywhere in my childhood—from the weird light my parents hoped would cure my sore throat, to the X-ray machines at the shoe store, to my father's lab at Oak Ridge. It even led to the untimely death of the doctor for whom my elementary school was named.

The men treated at Northington Hospital in the 1940s were not suffering from radiation exposure but from the physical and psychological wounds of war. The hospital was considered a state-of-the-art facility and prided itself on reconditioning the men as quickly as possible so they could be sent back to the front. When I came across a 1943 photo of wounded veterans in wheelchairs at the hospital, I recognized the chairs instantly. They were the same wooden wheelchairs I had seen at my school so long ago—chairs that were more broken than the wounded soldiers who once needed them for transportation around the sprawling hospital complex.

Less than a year after the war ended, Northington Hospital was declared surplus property by the U.S. government. The University of Alabama gained control of the site, and a number of the hospital barracks were used to house Northington Elementary School. My shadowy images of abandoned medical equipment were not just snippets of a bad dream but part of the pre-history of my own elementary school.

~

I can't help wondering why these disturbing scenes from my childhood have remained with me while other, happier memories have vanished. Like radioactive isotopes, they seem to have a kind of half-life, getting fainter with time but lingering in the depths of my consciousness.

Perhaps they served as a kind of early warning system, reminding me that damaging light rays could be lurking in the living room closet, rusty hypodermics could be scattered on the school playground, a pile of broken wheelchairs could be just down the hall from my cheerful classroom. I knew there had been a big war before I was born, and a smaller war was going on now in a place called Korea, but these were not topics of conversation in our house. My parents observed an unspoken rule: Never talk about disturbing things in front of the children. Although such things were not discussed, I could see that they were all around me. And if the grownups in my life could not protect me from these dangers, I might never be entirely safe.

When I think back on my childhood in Alabama, the people and places that shaped my life so long ago, one memory haunts me. In the normal times, before Daddy got sick, he would often turn to Carol and me after supper and say, "It's so stuffy here in the house. What say we go for a little drive?"

We always said yes. It was a nice way to end the day, being alone in the car with our father, the windows down, the breeze riffling our hair. Daddy knew all the roads, over by the Black Warrior River where the chemical smell of the Gulf States paper mill tickled our noses, out in the country where he pointed out the different trees and flowering plants depending on the season. Sometimes, on the way home, he would drive past the state mental hospital. It was near the university and had a large, beautiful campus with huge old trees—Southern magnolias, sycamores, pines, and oaks.

One evening, I must have been six or seven, as we went past the hospital, I heard Daddy say in a low voice, as if he was speaking just to himself, "I hope I never end up there."

THE HALF-LIFE OF MEMORY

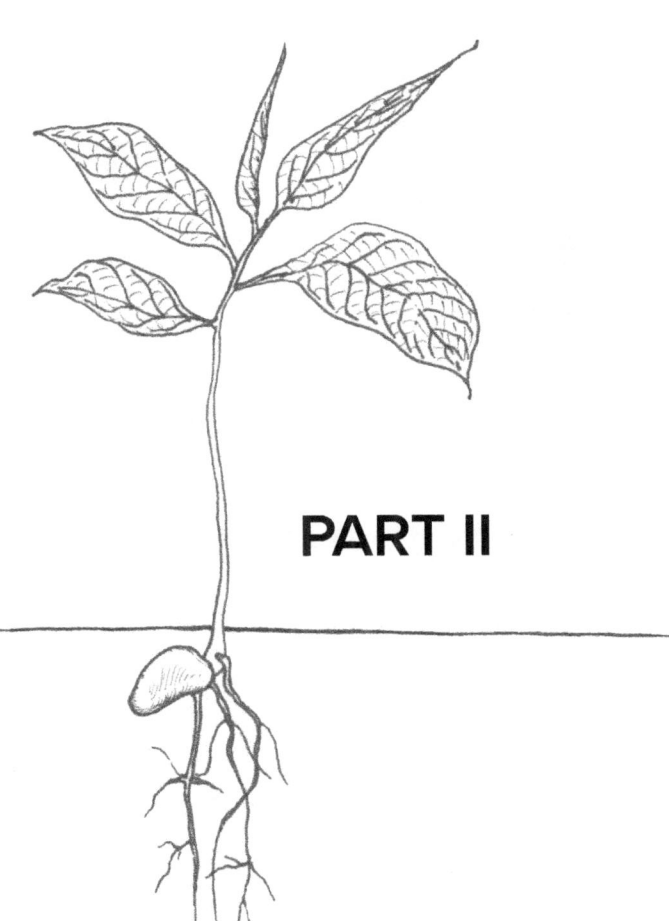

PART II

You are waking into a new shape. You are waking into an old self. What I mean is, time offers your old self a new shape. What I mean is, you are the old, ungrieving you, and you are also the new, ruined you.
You are both, and you will always be both.

—Margaret Renkl, *Late Migrations*

10

There

"Your father was in *Bryce*?"

There was shock in her voice. Laurie is an artist who cuts hair for a living. Like me, she grew up in Alabama and now lives in Brooklyn. As she removed the cape around my shoulders and stood back to admire her work, I mentioned that for years I had been wanting to write about my childhood in Alabama but just couldn't seem to get started. The subject was emotionally fraught, I explained, because my father had had a nervous breakdown, and after a few months in a private hospital in Birmingham, where Laurie was born and raised, he ended up in Bryce, the state mental hospital located in Tuscaloosa, the university town where I spent my first ten years.

I had never seen Laurie rattled before. Sitting in her swivel chair, I can say things I don't say to anybody else. After confiding in her about my father's mental illness, I was in a hurry to leave. Standing up, I grabbed my purse and cell phone and prepared to pay the cashier. Laurie wasn't quite ready to let me go. Looking deep into my eyes, she said with kindness and conviction, "But you turned out great, Rebecca."

The shock in Laurie's voice and the look in her eyes confirmed what I had always suspected and feared: Being in Bryce was a terrible thing. My father had been there. My father had died there.

~

I clearly remember the day when some men came to our house and took my father away. It was March 27, 1954. He had been acting strange for a few weeks, smoking cigarettes and talking a lot in a very loud voice. That wasn't like him at all. My father had stopped smoking years ago. He was a man of few words, and when he did talk, he spoke quietly.

These changes in my father were terrifying to me. He had taught me that it was wrong to let out your anger. You should just keep smiling no matter how angry you might feel inside. Now he was no longer holding in his anger, and I was afraid of what he might do. He was so big and strong. I just tried to stay away from him, hiding in my room or going over to the twins' house across the street.

Mother explained that he was under a lot of pressure because of an important committee meeting at the university at the end of March. He would be representing the biology department on the university's Committee on Nuclear Studies. Once this meeting was over, she told me, he would get back to normal. He would be gentle and calm like he always used to be. His forty-fifth birthday was coming up on March 20, but I remember Mother telling me that we wouldn't celebrate it until after this big meeting was over. He was too distracted now to enjoy the celebration.

But things didn't get better after the meeting. They got a lot worse. When he got home from the meeting, he was more upset than I had ever seen him, pacing around the house and chain-smoking cigarettes. Mother told me he had started saying crazy things at the meeting and even tried to attack the dean. They had to send for the campus police to remove him from the meeting and take him home. Carol and I felt like we were in the middle of a nightmare, but we were still awake and this was really happening.

Fortunately, the mind has a way of protecting children by blocking out trauma that is just too frightening to remember. Many years later, when I was trying to learn more about what had happened to my father in 1954, Mother described a terrifying scene that occurred the day after the committee meeting. Neither my sister nor I have any conscious memories of it, but in my mother's telling, it was so vivid that I can see it clearly in my imagination.

The whole family was together in our small dining room between the kitchen and the living room. Daddy was agitated, talking about the events of the day before and railing about how his behavior at the meeting would bring disgrace on the whole family. "This will be in all the newspapers," he said. "I will never be able to go back to teaching at the university after this. It would be better if we were all dead." Suddenly, he grabbed a butcher knife from the kitchen and waved it toward Carol and me.

And then something happened that I find hard to believe, although I know it is true. Granny—my small, shy sixty-eight-year-old grandmother, who suffered from anxiety and usually seemed afraid of her own shadow—picked up one of the heavy mahogany dining room chairs and pointed its legs toward my father, all 6 feet, 4 inches of him, like a lion tamer in the middle of a circus ring. She spoke in a strong voice we had never heard before. "If you even touch those girls, I will kill you."

It was like flipping a switch inside my father. His shoulders dropped, he slumped and laid the knife down on the dining room table. This was when Mother decided to call the ambulance. It was no longer safe for Daddy to remain at home with the family.

I was looking out the front window when the ambulance pulled up in front of our house. Three men came inside. They told Daddy that he needed to go to the hospital. He refused and started striking out with his long arms. It took all three of them to get him down our front steps and out to the curb. Standing at the window, I watched as they forced him into a strange-looking linen jacket that kept his arms from moving.

Finally, they got him into the ambulance. I stood in silence as I watched the ambulance drive away.

Mother did her best to explain what had happened. "Your daddy is sick, and he needs to go to the hospital so he can rest and get better." She tried to be reassuring. "He will get the best of care. They're taking him to a big, new hospital in Birmingham. He will be treated by a special doctor called a psychiatrist. He will know how to help your daddy."

But as it turned out, no one really knew how to help my father. Friends, relatives, and his students from the university sent him cheerful get well cards. His brother Dwight flew all the way from Indiana to visit him at Jefferson-Hillman Hospital in Birmingham. In a postcard he sent to their parents back on the farm, written just a few days after Daddy was hospitalized, Dwight wrote, "This is an impressive place. I think Bert will be fine in a few weeks. He just needs to rest."

His psychiatrist wasn't so certain. When Mother talked to Dr. Elmore on the phone, he said Daddy had a serious illness called paranoid schizophrenia. They didn't have any medicines for this condition. All they could do, the doctor said, was to hook him up to a machine and give him an electric shock. This might shake up his brain enough to make it start working better. I was scared when I heard that because I had seen what happened to my little sister when she got a shock. Mother was bathing Carol in the bathroom sink, and she stuck her finger in an empty light socket next to the medicine cabinet. The electricity shot through her little body, and she cried and cried. It took hours for her to get back to normal.

For the first few weeks that Daddy was in the hospital, we couldn't see or talk to him. Birmingham was sixty miles away. Mother had just gotten her driver's license a few months earlier, and she didn't trust herself to drive all the way to Birmingham. Besides, the doctor said he needed to rest, no outside distractions. Our house felt sad and lonely without him. I sent letters to try to cheer him up, and Carol, who was only five years old, drew a picture of Daddy in his hospital room and made up a poem that Mother copied out at the bottom of the picture.

Seven lonely days make one lonely year.
Seven lonely days I cried and cried for you.
Oh, my darling, I'm crying–boo–hoo–hoo.
Oh, my darling, I'm crying–crying for you.

About a week before my ninth birthday on May 3rd, Mother, Carol, and I got to visit him at the hospital in Birmingham. Dr. Walker, Daddy's boss at the university, drove us there. When we got out of the car in front of the hospital, I looked up. I had never seen such a big building. It was about fifteen stories tall, made of bricks with a white tower on top, like they took the steeple off a church somewhere and put it on top of this huge, brick hospital.

The lady at the front desk told us how to get to Daddy's room. We had to walk down a long hall and then take an elevator. Once we stepped off the elevator, I just wanted to go back home. What would he be like? Would he be acting scary like the day they took him away? I walked slower and slower, lagging behind my mother and sister. The long hallway was painted a sickly shade of green that reminded me of my school bathroom, and the smell . . . I can't describe it. All I can say is that it smelled like sick people. My lifelong fear of hospitals began on that day.

Even as an eight-year-old child, I never had any doubts about whether my father was mentally ill. The man who walked back in the house after that meeting at the university was another person, not the kind and gentle Daddy I had known my whole life. I was terrified of what we might find when we entered his hospital room. But here we saw a different man, so meek and unsure of himself, not the competent father who took me for walks in the woods and taught me how to use a microscope. He looked so helpless sitting up in bed, dressed in flimsy pajamas that were too small on his big body. He didn't talk much, but when he did, he was quiet and polite, like always. He said he couldn't wait to be back home, living with us again. He hoped he might even be home before my birthday if his doctor agreed. And then we said goodbye. I didn't lag behind when we walked back down the hall to the elevator. I couldn't wait to get back outside and smell the fresh air.

A few weeks later, Daddy convinced his doctor he was well enough to come home to Tuscaloosa for the weekend. Dr. Walker drove our 1950 Ford to Birmingham with Carol and me in the back seat and Mother in the front. When we got to Daddy's floor of the hospital, he was dressed and ready to go. I only remember one thing about the trip back to Tuscaloosa. Carol and I had to use the bathroom, so we stopped at a gas station. Everyone got out to stretch their legs. Suddenly, we saw the car pulling away. Daddy had gotten in and started driving. My heart sank. I thought I might never see him again. Then we all breathed a sigh of relief. He just drove over to the gas pump so he could fill up the tank. Maybe he just wanted to be back in the driver's seat for a few seconds with his hands on the wheel.

After that scene, my mind goes blank. I don't remember the rest of the trip to Tuscaloosa or how the weekend went. Soon it was time for Dr. Walker and Mother to take Daddy back to the hospital. Carol and I didn't go along this time. We stayed home with Granny. As they drove away, the three of us stood on the front steps waving goodbye.

That was the last time I saw my father.

~

The next week, Mother had a long talk with Daddy's psychiatrist, Dr. John Elmore. She told me that he was a real expert. He had gone to the best medical schools and had trained in famous hospitals in New York City. Now he was on the staff of the Kay Clinic in Birmingham. He had been Daddy's doctor ever since he went to Jefferson-Hillman at the end of March, but now, in May, he told my mother something that was hard to hear.

"Your husband will never recover. He will not be able to go back to his job as a professor at the university, and he will not be able to live at home with the family."

When Mother heard this news, she had to make a big decision. The private hospital in Birmingham was very expensive, and the family was running out of money. If Daddy wasn't going to get better, what was the use of paying all those hospital bills? Especially when the state hospital was right in Tuscaloosa. It wouldn't cost us anything, and it would be so much easier for Mother to visit him there. Dr. Elmore assured her that he would prescribe the same type of care he was getting in Birmingham, including regular shock treatments. In the middle of June, 1954, my father was committed to Bryce Hospital.

I didn't go to see him there. Maybe it wasn't permitted, maybe Mother thought it would be too upsetting, maybe I was just too afraid to go. But I still remember two things my mother told me about his short stay at Bryce. One of Daddy's friends saw him walking on the hospital grounds. They said he looked almost normal except that his shirt wasn't buttoned up quite right. The other thing she told me was that while Daddy was at Bryce, one of his biology students from the university, a pre-med student who was doing an internship there, saw him on one of the wards. According to Mother, "Your daddy was so ashamed to have his student see him as a mental patient. That was just too much for him to bear."

11

July 6, 1954

IT WAS EARLY, but I was already awake. Carol was asleep in the bed next to me. The windows were open as always at this time of year, and the scent of honeysuckle wafted into the room. A few weeks ago, Granny had set up her quilt frame over my bed. A section of the quilt lay exposed above my head—a rectangle a little bigger than my twin bed. As I lay there looking up at the quilt, I pretended I was a princess lying under a canopy. Thinking of what I might want to do on this lazy summer day, I felt calm and protected.

Then I heard a knock on the front door. And another knock. My mother, who had been working in the kitchen, opened the door. I heard a man's voice. As they talked, I could tell that something was wrong. This wasn't just a neighbor stopping by to ask a favor. Mother was asking questions, and the man was answering them. Neither of them had much to say. Then I heard the door close, and all was still.

My body stiffened as I lay there waiting. When Mother came into our bedroom, she went over to Carol's bed and shook her gently. Then she sat down on the end of her bed and spoke to both of us in a strong, quiet voice. "Girls, I have something sad to tell you." She paused, and I held my breath, waiting. "Your father died early this morning."

She explained that the man at the door was Dr. Walker, the head of the biology department at the university. He had been helping our family ever since Daddy got sick and had to go to the hospital in Birmingham.

Someone at Bryce had called and asked him to come over and tell Mother what had happened.

During the months that Daddy was away, my Sunday school teacher kept telling me that everything would be okay if I prayed hard enough. God would heal my father. But I didn't believe her. Everything in our family had changed so quickly, and I had been so unprepared. I was a smart girl. I would start fourth grade in the fall. I couldn't understand why I hadn't sensed that things were not as good as they seemed. Why hadn't I done something to prevent this tragedy? On this morning in July when Dr. Walker came to the door, I really wasn't surprised. I knew bad things would just keep happening to me and my family.

When Mother told us this news, she didn't cry, and neither did I. We just sat there in the bedroom looking down at our hands. Then she hugged each of us and explained, "Your daddy didn't suffer. He died in an instant. His heart just stopped beating. The doctors called it a coronary occlusion."

I don't remember anything else from that day. But those few minutes, lying in bed on that hot July morning, thinking about what I might do that day and then hearing the knock on the door and the man's voice in the living room, that scene plays over and over in my head like a movie I've watched hundreds of times. That memory never fades.

12

Unanswered Questions

WHEN WE DROVE UP in front of the Walkers' house, the first thing I noticed was the row of spirea bushes in full bloom. Mother had taught me that the common name for this shrub was bridal wreath. I always remembered this because in the summer its branches were covered with tiny white flowers that swept down in a graceful arc like a bride's veil.

Mrs. Walker greeted us at the front door. "Hello, girls," she said. "I was so sorry to learn about your daddy. Please come in. Dr. Walker and I hope you will feel welcome in our home."

She led us into the front hallway.

It was Wednesday, July 7, the day after Daddy died. Mother was on a train to Indiana, where his funeral would be held on Friday. The grownups had decided that the Walkers' house would be the best place for Carol and me to stay while she was gone.

Mrs. Walker's husband was not the Dr. Walker who came to our house yesterday to break the news of Daddy's death. This Dr. Walker was a well-known physician in Tuscaloosa and the grandfather of my best friends, Judy and Jean Nisbet. Although we spent lots of time at the Nisbets' house across the street from us on Cedar Crest, before today we had never been to the Walkers' house on Forest Lake Drive.

The maid took our overnight bags and followed Mrs. Walker as she showed us the room where we would be sleeping. Then she led us through the big house and out to their screened-in porch on the shore of a lake. I knew this lake. Every weekend, after Daddy picked us up from Sunday school, he would take us to the drug store next to Forest Lake for ice cream. There were tables outside, and it was so peaceful to sit there with Daddy, eating ice cream and looking out over the water.

Now, sitting on the Walkers' porch, the lake looked different, so big and black with waves slapping at the shore. Motioning us toward a card table covered with a pretty cloth, Mrs. Walker said, "You girls must be hungry." The maid brought out two plates with sandwiches and potato chips. I tried to eat, but it was hard to swallow. I was afraid they'd think I didn't like the food their cook had prepared, but I couldn't eat more than a few bites.

After supper, we watched TV in the living room. When it was time for bed, Mrs. Walker took Carol and me down the hall to the bedroom. She gave us each a hug, tucked us in, and turned out the light on the dresser. It was still light outside, so I wasn't too scared. Then it got dark.

All night long, I lay there listening. I could hear the soft sounds of my little sister breathing. She was only five years old, too young to be as scared as I was. Outside, I could hear the clicking sounds of insects and the leaves rustling on the trees whenever the wind blew over the lake. Inside, the house was quiet except for the ticking of the grandfather clock in the front hall. Every fifteen minutes throughout that long night I heard the clock's loud chime. Echoing through the large, quiet house, it felt like an unanswered question as I lay there in the strange bed wondering what would happen to us, two little girls all alone in the world.

~

Thinking back on events from the summer of 1954, so much has vanished completely while other memories are preserved forever, flooded in the harsh light of childhood trauma. I can still hear that knock on our front door on July 6 followed by the serious voices in the living room. I see

UNANSWERED QUESTIONS

Mother coming into the bedroom, sitting down on Carol's bed and saying, in a soft voice, "Girls, I have some sad news." I empathize with my nine-year-old self sitting in a strange house, looking out over that big lake, unable to swallow even a few bites of my supper. I remember a soft bed in the guest room and the chintz curtains rustling in the breeze. And—clearest of all—I hear the sounds of that tall grandfather clock, its steady ticking followed by the loud chime, announcing that another quarter hour had passed in a seemingly endless night.

Once the sun rose on a new day, I recall nothing. Not a single image or memory of what happened after my father's death. I can't remember how Carol and I were reunited with Mother after the funeral or where we spent the rest of the summer. And I have no recollection of where Granny was in all of this. Like Daddy, she simply disappeared.

As I examine the traces left behind, one thing that strikes me is the rush with which everything happened. Daddy died at Bryce Hospital in Tuscaloosa on Tuesday morning, July 6. It's hard to imagine what my mother was thinking and feeling in the aftermath of her husband's death. Here she was in Alabama, hundreds of miles from the state where she and my father had grown up. He was only forty-five years old, and his death was completely unexpected. Where should the funeral be held? Who would officiate? Where should he be buried? These were things they had never discussed.

But decisions had to be made, and my mother, still in shock, gathered her strength. By the time the *Tuscaloosa News* went to press on Tuesday evening, with Daddy's obituary included, these questions had been answered. The funeral would be held in Greensburg, Indiana, near the place where my father was born and raised, the place where his parents and siblings still lived. Mother, never one to postpone the inevitable, felt the service should be held as quickly as possible. After long-distance phone calls to the funeral home director and minister, the funeral was scheduled for Friday, July 9. On Wednesday morning, the day after her husband's sudden and unexpected death, Mother purchased a single ticket and boarded a train heading north.

I remember her describing the journey:

> That was the worst trip of my life. The conductor told me I had to check the baggage car at every stop because that's where Bert's coffin was carried, and it might get unloaded and sent on to some other destination. I have never felt so alone and frightened in my life.

Throughout my childhood and up to the present moment, I have wondered why Mother didn't take Carol and me with her to our father's funeral. I still feel angry when I think about how alone and abandoned I felt during that long night at the Walkers' house. Not only had I lost my father, but I was deprived of the comfort of my mother's presence during the most traumatic moments of my life.

Trying to imagine things from my mother's point of view, I understand that she firmly believed in listening to the experts, and the common wisdom of the time was that children should be shielded from painful events like funerals. But there was a problem with this decision. Where would Carol and I stay while she traveled north? It would have made sense for us to stay with Tillie and Bubber Nisbet, the parents of my best friends, who lived right across the street. But their house was so small, and besides, they would be leaving on Thursday for their summer vacation in Florida. Although the Nisbets couldn't take us in themselves, Tillie proposed another solution. Why not let the girls stay with her parents, the Walkers? They had a large, comfortable house with plenty of empty bedrooms. Tillie felt it might be good for us to get away from our own neighborhood, which now held so many painful memories.

UNANSWERED QUESTIONS

A handwritten letter I recently found among Mother's papers cleared away some of the fog obscuring what happened in the days after Daddy's death. On July 13, 1954, Tillie wrote to my mother from Shalimar, Florida, where her family was vacationing:

> Your brothers arrived in Tuscaloosa the night you left. I felt so relieved that they were there with your mother and the girls. We left about noon on Thursday for our vacation, and they were planning to leave on Friday morning to drive the girls and your mother up north to Indiana.

What a surprise to learn, more than sixty years later, that Granny had remained in Alabama after Mother left on the train. I have absolutely no memory of her being there. If she stayed there with me and Carol, why didn't we all just sleep at home on Wednesday and Thursday nights instead of moving across town to the Walkers' big house on the lake? And if she was with us in Tuscaloosa, why did I feel so completely alone and abandoned by the adult world? Granny had lived with us for most of my childhood, and I knew I could always count on her for love and protection. However, at this time of terrible loss, no one, not even my grandmother, could compensate for my mother's absence. In my mind, Granny has been erased.

Tillie's letter also solved the mystery of how Carol and I—and Granny—got to Indiana to join Mother after the funeral. Granny's sons (Mother's brothers), Roy and Erwin Stamps, were experienced drivers, and as soon as they learned of the death, they drove to Tuscaloosa from their homes in Pontiac, Illinois, about a hundred miles south of Chicago. They arrived on Thursday, and then on Friday, the day of Daddy's funeral in Greensburg, all five of us left for the drive from Tuscaloosa to Mother's hometown of Evansville, Indiana, where the family was reunited.

I have no memory of that long car trip or of spending the next few weeks with relatives in Evansville.

~

Reading and re-reading Tillie's letter, I'm touched by her genuine love and concern for my mother. "I'm sure you have been under a terrific strain, Ruth, and I do hope you are getting some rest and quiet. I have thought of you each day and wished that I might have been there with you."

Earlier, during Daddy's illness and hospitalization, Mother must have confided her hopes and fears to her friend, who continues in the letter:

> I know what a shock Bert's death was to you, and I know too what you have been through these past few months. You have had such courage to carry on. I can't tell you how concerned we've been through it all. In spite of the heartbreak, if he could never be better, I feel God has been merciful to Bert as well as to you.

The closeness between the two women is a tribute to both of them. Mother was a Northerner who moved to Alabama because of her husband's job. Tillie was a daughter of the South. Not only was her father, Auddis Moore Walker, a prominent physician from an old Southern family, but her husband, James "Bubber" Nisbet, who had been a great football player in his college years, was now assistant coach for the University of Alabama football team, the Crimson Tide. In Tuscaloosa, where football coaches were akin to royalty, Yankee newcomers were not always welcomed with open arms by their Southern neighbors. Somehow, Tillie and Ruth had managed to transcend their differences and form a friendship based on mutual love and respect.

Reading this letter from Tillie so many years after it was written, I realize that I was not the only one with unanswered questions in the

UNANSWERED QUESTIONS

summer of 1954. I empathize with my mother, who found herself in such a difficult situation. Though she never explicitly raised these questions in conversations with me, I know they were weighing on her mind.

> What caused Bert's breakdown?
> Was I somehow to blame?
> Would he still be alive if I hadn't moved him to Bryce?
> If he had lived, what would our future have been like?
> Faced with all this grief and guilt, how can I go on living?

As July turned into August and then September, my mother and I—with our questions still unanswered—made our way into the unknown of a future without Daddy.

13

Crying

IN SEPTEMBER, CAROL AND I went back to Northington Elementary School in Tuscaloosa. She was in first grade, and I was in fourth. Mother went back to school too. After years of being a stay-at-home mom, she accepted a job teaching sixth grade at Northington. Every morning, the three of us would head off to school together while Granny stayed home.

It seemed strange to have Mother driving us to school. This had always been Daddy's job because Mother didn't have a driver's license. Daddy had tried to teach her to drive before we were born, but the lessons didn't go well. I remember her telling me about a time when she was out driving with Daddy, and she panicked and ran the car off the road. Sitting on the side of the road, thinking about what had just happened, she was terrified. What if she had had an accident? What if she had hurt someone? After that, she didn't touch the wheel again for many years.

Shortly before Daddy got sick, she decided to try driving again. In the fall of 1953, she had volunteered to tutor a little boy who had a heart condition and couldn't go to school. His mother was so grateful to have an experienced teacher helping her son. She wanted to do something to show her gratitude but wasn't sure what that might be. Then she had an inspired idea: "Driving! I will teach Ruth to drive." The lessons went much better than they had with Daddy in the passenger seat, and after a few months of practice, Mother passed the driving test and got her license.

CRYING

In later years, she would often say, "What would I have done after your daddy died if I couldn't drive the car?" But she never really felt comfortable driving, and, despite her struggles, she never mastered shifting gears on the Ford's standard transmission. Carol and I sensed her nervousness. The only time when our mother, normally so confident and controlled, seemed unsure of herself was when she was behind the wheel.

And that was where it happened. Mother was driving us to the Methodist church in downtown Tuscaloosa. Carol and I were both in the Christmas pageant, and we had an evening rehearsal. We were singing softly in the back seat: "Oh little town of Bethlehem . . . ." Suddenly, we heard a strange sound. Mother pulled the car over to the side of the road and just sat there sobbing. She rested her head on the steering wheel and cried and cried. Carol and I had never heard our mother cry before. In the months of Daddy's illness, she just kept going, holding everything together, keeping us safe. Even after Dr. Walker came to the door to tell us Daddy had died, she was strong and steadfast. During the weeks after the funeral, she sometimes looked sad, but she never, ever cried.

Listening to our mother's sobs, Carol and I sat like statues in the back seat. We almost stopped breathing. After what seemed to us a very long time, the crying subsided. "Oh, girls, I'm sorry. I don't want you to see me like this." She pulled some Kleenexes out of her purse and blew her nose. "It's just that it's Christmas, my favorite time of year. And I feel so alone without your father here." She went on, "When I heard your sweet voices, I couldn't hold my grief in any longer."

~

After that scene in the car, we didn't see Mother crying again. Christmas came and went. A new year started, 1955. Somehow the months passed by—January, February, and then it was March, a year since Daddy got sick.

Someone, I don't remember who, had given me a wonderful beach ball. We had to blow it up with a bicycle pump. When fully inflated, it was about three feet in diameter, and it was beautiful. Shimmering rainbow colors swirling and running together like a giant marble. Shades of purple, lilac, blue, aqua, moss green.

I was playing with the ball in the living room, tossing it up and catching it; watching it roll along the floor toward the front door or in the other direction toward the screened-in porch on the side of the house. All of a sudden, there was a hissing sound, and in less than a minute, all that was left was a limp, lifeless puddle on the floor.

I looked at what remained of my beautiful ball, and I started to cry. Not a soft leaking of tears but loud, wrenching sobs. I sat on the living room floor and cried and cried. Mother came in from the kitchen and tried to comfort me, but I just kept crying. Finally, after all the sad, quiet months, I could actually cry. And soon I realized that I wasn't really crying about the beach ball. Sure, it was beautiful. Sure, I liked it. But not enough to cry like this. I was crying because my father was dead and never coming back. I was crying because when he got sick, he had changed into a totally different person, so angry and scary, nothing like the gentle father he had been before. I was crying because when we visited him in the hospital in Birmingham, I didn't know which version of my father I would find there. I was crying because then he just died, and I never got to say goodbye. I was crying because my mother left me and my sister with strangers when she went to the funeral in Indiana. And I was crying because we were going to be leaving Tuscaloosa and the only home I had ever known and moving way up north to Indiana.

I don't remember how long I cried. It felt like a long, long time. And it felt good. Finally, all the sadness was coming out, and I didn't have to hold it in and pretend that everything was fine. Nothing was ever really fine again after my father died.

~

Looking back on all of this, I often ask myself why my mother didn't—or couldn't—cry after my father's death. She had lost so much. She was married to a handsome, accomplished husband, a college professor. Finally, after so many years of longing for a child of her own, she had two precious daughters to care for. Since moving to the South with her husband in 1945, she had been quick to make friends, and she was fulfilled by her volunteer work for important social causes. With the pressures of parenthood and her husband's career, the marriage was not as idyllic as it had been in the early days of their love. Bert sometimes seemed distracted and stressed. Still, her life was full, and she was happy.

With the sudden onset of my father's mental illness in 1954, my mother's world was shattered. But she did what she had always done. She just kept going. She had to be strong. People were depending on her, especially her two little girls, and it would be self-indulgent to cry.

So many questions hovered around the edges of her consciousness: How had things gone wrong in her marriage? Why hadn't she seen the breakdown coming? Why had her husband died so suddenly, without any warning?

Pushing these questions aside, she told herself there was no time for such unproductive thoughts. She had to be mother and father to her girls. Crying could come later. For now, she took all the emotions of that year and pasted them into a big black scrapbook. Every get well card and note of sympathy, the cards and pictures that Carol and I crafted for our hospitalized father, condolence letters from Daddy's psychiatrist and the chaplain of Bryce Hospital, where he died, and memorial tributes from the university and his professional organization. Then she shut the book and put it on the top shelf of the closet.

What went through her mind, I wonder, as she made this book to preserve the traces of Daddy's final year? Was she hoping to contain her grief between its covers?

In June of 1955, as she packed up the family's belongings for the move to Indiana, she tucked the scrapbook into a sturdy cardboard box along with hundreds of letters she and Bert had exchanged over the years. As she got everything ready to go into the moving van, she was far too busy to process her complicated emotions. Maybe some day.

14

Summer on Alvord Boulevard

WE ARRIVED IN JUNE 1955 with our summer clothes packed in suitcases plus a few things we couldn't live without. Carol brought her teddy bear, Jimmy, and I had Jean, my favorite doll, named after a friend I left behind in Tuscaloosa. Granny had the patches of the quilt she was working on. Mother brought the books she planned to read that summer. Everything else went into storage until we could find a home of our own.

For me, a ten-year-old girl from Alabama, Aunt Pauline's house on Alvord Boulevard was like something out of a Hollywood movie. Driving by it now on visits to Evansville, I see a rather modest brick bungalow built in the 1930s. But until that summer, I had never been inside a house with more than one bathroom, a whole series of bedrooms running down a long hall, a modern kitchen, and a full basement with its own bathroom. Most fascinating to me was an inconspicuous door at waist height mounted on a wall near the bedrooms. This was the laundry chute. You just tossed your dirty clothes in the chute, and they arrived in a basket near the washing machine in the basement.

Pauline, despite being the youngest of Granny's seven sisters, was the family matriarch. Born with a dominant personality, her status was further elevated when she married Edward Goeke, who had inherited the family business on Main Street. Edward F. Goeke and Son had sold hay, grain, feed, and produce to generations of local farmers.

Uncle and Auntie, as we called them, owned a series of large, beautiful homes. Whenever Aunt Pauline got bored, she started looking for a new house to buy and decorate. Not able to have children of their own, they often shared their home with girls in the extended family. When Granny moved to Chicago in the 1920s to find work, Mother lived with them for several years so she could graduate with her class from Central High School and then attend Evansville College to earn her teaching credentials.

Aunt Pauline ran a tight ship and had clear expectations for the girls she helped to raise. Mother's assignment was to dust every stick of furniture in the elaborately furnished living room each morning. Auntie often bragged to friends and family members: "The room just sparkles by the time Ruth leaves for school." The message was not lost on my mother. Keep everything spotless, and you will be praised and accepted. You might even be loved. And though she didn't always show it, Auntie did love Ruth.

During that summer at Aunt Pauline's house, people were always coming and going. A typical day might begin with Stevie and Butchie (Charles, Jr.) being dropped off for the morning by their mothers, Wilma and Betty, two of Aunt Pauline's many nieces. Wilma and Betty's parents, Uncle John and Aunt Rose, had eight children and very little money. Pauline and Edward had the opposite problem—plenty of money but no children. We never knew the details, but when Wilma and Betty were teenagers, they went to live with Auntie and Uncle. The girls were not formally adopted, and they always regarded John and Rose as their parents. But they were supported in style by their aunt and uncle, who paid for everything, including college educations for both of them. Now, Wilma and Betty were adults living in Evansville with their husbands and rambunctious young sons. Aunt Pauline volunteered to whip those little boys into shape.

Carol and I weren't interested in joining the boys' games, but we liked to follow them around observing their antics. One morning, Stevie, the older of the two, climbed the apple tree in the back yard. Butchie followed suit. About halfway up, he lost his grip and tumbled onto the ground. He let out a loud shriek, which brought Auntie out into the yard. She stood there in her bib apron with her legs apart, looking at Butchie on the ground and Stevie high up in the tree.

"You both know better than to climb that tree," she fumed. "Stevie, you're the older one. You should be setting a good example for your cousin." Speaking in a stern voice, she added, "Come down this minute."

Slowly, he climbed back down and stood in front of her, hanging his head.

"You know what's next," she said as she pulled a big scissors out of her apron pocket and handed it to Stevie. "Go cut a switch."

He went over to the apple tree, snipped off a small branch, and handed it to Auntie. She stripped off the leaves and whipped it through the air to see if it was suitable. Carol and I, watching through the kitchen window, could hear it whistle as she flicked it.

"All right," she said. "You're first, Stevie." He turned around, and she delivered two quick whacks on the bottom. Then it was Butchie's turn. He winced but didn't cry. She never really hit very hard. She just wanted to teach them a lesson. I don't know if they learned a lesson, but Carol and I did. We would make sure this never happened to us.

Lunch was an informal affair. There was plenty of food in the refrigerator, and we helped ourselves and ate in shifts at the dinette set in the kitchen. After lunch, Auntie always retired to her bedroom to take a nap. Mother and Granny rested in their room. Carol and I used this time to explore. Sometimes we would go outside and walk around the neighborhood. Alvord Boulevard was a wide street with a grassy median strip running down the middle. Sometimes we walked as far as Lincoln Avenue—a busy thoroughfare running across town—before turning back. It was fun to imagine the lives of the strangers living in these neat brick houses.

On the way back, we could spot Aunt Pauline's house about a block away because of the brightly colored zinnias growing in her front flower bed. After climbing a few stairs to the porch, we pulled open the heavy front door. The living room was large and well furnished. If the house was still quiet, Carol and I would go straight to the matching swivel chairs near the door. They were armless with high backs and upholstered in a closely woven red and black fabric with a skirt that went down to the floor. We would sit there and propel the chairs around and around with our feet. They went so fast it was almost like being on a Tilt-a-Whirl at an amusement park. We prayed Aunt Pauline wouldn't catch us. If she did, we were pretty sure we would have to go out to the back yard and cut a switch.

Gradually, around two o'clock, the house came back to life. We could hear Aunt Pauline moving around in the bedroom. Some days Mother would get a phone call from the realtor and drive across town to look at another house on the market. Granny would go to the kitchen and start dinner preparations—peeling vegetables or making pie crust.

The rhythm of the house changed around five o'clock when Uncle arrived home from work. He would leave his shiny leather shoes by the door, put on his slippers, and sit down in his comfortable armchair. Auntie would scurry into the kitchen to prepare his nightly highball. Neither of my parents ever touched alcohol, so this drink was a source of fascination to me. It came in a fancy red cocktail glass with ice cubes clinking around. I was sure it must taste delicious. Sitting there in his chair and drinking his highball, Uncle Edward basked in his role as the *pater familias* of this all-female household, so different from the cutthroat world of "bit-ness," as he always pronounced it, where he spent his days.

Most days, he would call Carol and me over and ask us to guess what he had in his vest pocket. We pretended not to know. Then he pulled out a delicious chocolate. Sometimes he would ask me to choose a record from his extensive collection. Carefully removing it from its sleeve, I would put it on the turntable and position the needle. Sound would burst from the machine, perhaps the great tenor Caruso singing an Italian aria or an orchestra performing "Swan Lake."

Everything stopped when Aunt Pauline appeared in the archway between the living room and the dining room and announced, "Dinner is served." We all moved to the table.

Several sets of dishes were stored in Auntie's glassed-in china closet. For family dinners, she usually chose the Franciscan Ware in the popular apple pattern. I loved those dishes with apples and branches twining around the rims of the plates. Aunt Pauline's house was always filled with flowers, and she knew how to arrange them artistically. Every night there would be a flower arrangement in the center of the table, perhaps a white bowl of pink roses, baby's breath, and sweet peas or a crystal vase filled with red, yellow, and orange zinnias. There was always a stick of real butter on the table in a cut-glass butter dish. This was thrilling to me since at home we only had margarine. We knew to sit at the same spot every night because the cloth napkins were refolded and left at our places after dinner. We used the same ones until it was wash day. Auntie did not believe in waste.

There was always talk and laughter around the table, but Uncle Edward, usually so jovial, was almost entirely silent. He had read in the *Reader's Digest*, that for proper digestion, it was important to chew your food—even bananas, he insisted—a hundred times. He would sit there counting and chewing away throughout the meal.

Dinners on Alvord Boulevard were delicious. We might have braised pork chops, mashed potatoes, and steamed cauliflower with cheese sauce.

Dessert was Granny's specialty, perhaps a fresh peach pie served with vanilla ice cream or one of her kuchens, a coffee cake topped with fresh fruit mixed with butter and brown sugar.

After the dishes were washed and stowed away, we would spend the rest of the evening in the living room. Several times a week, other relatives would come over to watch TV or play cards. Aunt Katie and Mother's cousin Caroline were regulars at the card table. They would gather in the living room and play for hours. This was the era of Canasta, a game that required two decks of cards, too many for players to easily shuffle by hand, so they used a mechanical shuffler. I loved it when they let me crank the handle and watch the cards come spewing out into the tray, ready to be cut and dealt. Canastas could be "clean" or "dirty" depending on whether you polluted them with wild cards to make seven of a kind. Sometimes the discard pile would get huge. Then, when someone "picked up the pile," there would be groans or cheers. Canasta was serious business for these raucous competitors.

When it was time for Carol and me to go to bed, Mother would walk us down the hall to our bedroom and tuck us in. I dreaded Thursdays. That was the night when, instead of playing cards, the grownups watched *Dragnet* on TV. The sound was turned up high because Uncle Edward was hard of hearing. When I heard the theme song—*dum da dum dum*—I knew the show was starting. It began with the same words every week: "Ladies and gentlemen, the story you are about to see is true. The names have been changed to protect the innocent." More dramatic music would follow. And then the policeman's voice: "This is the city. Los Angeles, California. I work here. I'm a cop." After that, the volume dropped a bit. I couldn't hear all the words, just the serious voice of Jack Webb, the actor who played Sergeant Friday. Every so often, dire-sounding music would break in again, and I imagined things getting worse. Carol was asleep in the bed beside me so I couldn't talk to her. I would put the pillow over my head to try to block the sound. It always took me a long time to go to sleep on Thursday nights.

When I woke up in the morning, everything seemed fine. The sun would be shining and the house bustling with activity.

One morning in July, Aunt Clara came over with a huge bucket of sour cherries from her farm in Darmstadt. These would be delicious in cherry pies, and we could freeze the rest in Auntie's new chest freezer in the basement. But first we had to remove all the pits. There were quarts and quarts of cherries.

After breakfast, Carol and I went down the basement stairs to help with the cherries. None of the houses in Tuscaloosa, where we used to live, had basements, so this cool open space with its smooth concrete floor had a special mystique for me. Going down these stairs felt like entering a secret underground kingdom.

Aunt Clara, Aunt Pauline, and Granny were already seated on folding chairs with Tupperware containers for the pitted cherries on their laps. Aunt Clara handed Carol and me a few metal hair pins and showed us how to insert the rounded end of the pin into the cherry, using it to gently pull out the pit.

Once I got the hang of the process, I fell into a rhythm. Soon my hands and arms were dripping with cherry juice as a pile of cherries mounded in the container on my lap. Every once in a while, when the aunts weren't looking, I would lick my hands to stop the dripping. I loved the sour, acidic taste.

While Carol and I concentrated on our work, we listened to the talk going on around us—talk about growing up on the family farm in Darmstadt, the neighbor families, the dances, the corn huskings, the marriages, the babies. There were lots of names we hadn't heard before and lots of laughter. At times, the sisters would switch to German, speaking in hushed tones as if they didn't want us to hear, even though we couldn't understand a word. Once in a while, in the middle of a sentence, we would hear our own names. "Carol this" or "Becky that." Speaking in German, they sounded like girls again, sometimes bursting out laughing in a conspiratorial sort of way. Hearing them talking, I thought of a photograph Granny always kept on her dresser. It was an old-fashioned black-and-white portrait of her with three of her sisters. Minnie, who later became my granny, was the little one sitting on top of a pillar. Bertha was the oldest and tallest, then Katie, and then Clara, a baby in a high chair. All of them were wearing beautiful dresses made by their mother, my great-grandmother, Kate Moser Stofft. Every time I saw this picture, I found it astonishing that my Granny had once been a little girl. But during that summer at Aunt Pauline's house, I began to understand that old people had been young once too.

One morning a few weeks later, I woke up and felt a burning sensation on my stomach. Pulling up my nightgown, I saw angry, itchy red blotches running down one side of my abdomen. The week before, Carol had come down with chickenpox, but I had already had chickenpox, and you can only get it once. When I told Mother and showed her the rash, she made a quick call to Dr. Faith. He said he'd come out to the house after his last patient for the day.

It didn't take him long to make a diagnosis. "Shingles. It's caused by the same virus as chickenpox. Becky was exposed when Carol became ill." He continued, "It's unusual for a child so young to get shingles. It's usually old people who get it, and it's often triggered by stress." There wasn't much he could offer in the way of treatment. Soothing baths and cool compresses. They didn't help much.

For the next two weeks, I was miserable and had to stay in bed most of the time. I had a stack of books from the library, but I didn't feel like reading. With all that time alone, I couldn't keep myself from thinking about the future. Mother had been looking for a house for weeks, but none of the houses the realtor showed her were right—too expensive, too small, in the wrong school district. As I lay in the quiet bedroom, questions came to my mind. Would we ever find a home of our own? Where would I go to school in the fall? Would I meet new friends? And why did I get shingles, a disease triggered by stress, a disease that children hardly ever get? The biggest question of all had to do with my father. Where was he now? He had only been gone for a year, but nobody ever seemed to talk about him. It was as if he had never existed. With all the fun and excitement of living at Aunt Pauline's house, I was able to block out the stress and uncertainty and grief from my conscious mind, but I couldn't fool my body.

And where was my mother in the summer of 1955? Looking back, it's hard for me to picture her in the tapestry of life at Auntie's house. For someone who was always so vibrant, so present, she seemed strangely absent.

Mother was an accomplished teacher who had led organizations and won awards for her civic work. But this summer, living in Aunt Pauline's house, she must have felt like she was just Ruth, Minnie's daughter, a middle-aged widow who needed a place to live. She felt the need to do something to demonstrate her competence within the family. Her choice was a surprising one. She decided to tackle a sewing project of all things—a dress for me to wear when school started in the fall. She wanted to prove that she could hold her own at the sewing machine just like her mother and her aunts.

After paging through the Simplicity pattern book at the sewing center, she chose a fitted dress with a dropped waist and selected a beautiful fabric—a bluish-gray cotton with tiny butterflies woven into it in a darker shade. The three-quarter-length sleeves would be highlighted with cuffs of navy blue, and there were tiny buttons down the front. She decided to cover the buttons with the same cloth, positioning a little butterfly in the middle of each.

I can't imagine why she imposed this task on herself. In her younger years, she had been too busy with her books to learn to sew. By contrast, from childhood on, her mother and aunts had been rigorously trained in needle skills. They took special classes focused on basic techniques like basting and hemming, and they created portfolios with samples of their work.

As far as I knew, my mother had never made a dress before. The morning after she bought the pattern and fabric, she laid everything out on the dining room table, pinned the pattern pieces made of tissue paper to the cloth, and cut them out. Then she retreated to Auntie and Uncle's large, sunny bedroom. Enshrined in a place of honor in the bay window was Aunt Pauline's Singer sewing machine, the latest electric model, free-standing in its cherry case.

Day after day, Mother would go in there after breakfast and sit in front of the machine. Sometimes I'd come into the room to see how she was getting along. As I watched her sitting there, mid-project, I thought she might burst into tears at any moment. She was so frustrated. The pieces wouldn't seem to fit together, the bobbin would run out of thread in the middle of a seam, and covering those tiny buttons turned out to be a nightmare. Yet she refused help from Granny or Auntie. She wanted to prove to herself and others that she could do this. Somehow by the end of the summer, the dress was finished. I treasured it all the more because of the struggle that went into making it.

~

As July turned into August, the weather in Evansville was getting muggier, fed by humidity rolling off the Ohio River. Carol's birthday was approaching. She would be turning seven. Back in Tuscaloosa, Mother had always planned the most wonderful birthday parties—lots of kids gathered in our back yard with games and prizes and a beautifully decorated cake. Here in Indiana, we didn't know any other kids except for Stevie and Butchie. And Mother was too exhausted from her summer of house hunting to organize an elaborate party.

August 4 fell on a Thursday that year. Granny made a fresh coconut cake, Carol's favorite, and decorated it with seven candles. We sang "Happy Birthday," and Carol made a wish and blew out the candles. After dinner she opened her presents. It was a low-key affair compared to earlier birthdays.

Then on Saturday afternoon, the relatives began to arrive at Aunt Pauline's house—Aunt Katie and Caroline, Aunt Clara, Aunt Lou, Uncle John and Aunt Rose. They told Carol and me to wait upstairs while they went down in the basement. About half an hour later, Aunt Clara called up in a loud voice, "Surprise!"

When we got down there, we *were* surprised. They had decorated the basement with balloons and crepe-paper streamers. And there was a big handmade sign that read, "Happy Birthday, Carol and Becky!" I was so touched that they included me, sensing that my birthday in May had been overshadowed by the impending move to Indiana. Now I understood what they had been planning when they spoke to each other in German to keep Carol and me from understanding.

They didn't have to say it, but I knew that they knew this had been a hard year for all four of us, Mother and Granny included. They knew we could use some cheering up. When I went to bed that night, I felt happy. This was what it felt like to be part of a family.

15

A Change of Scenery

When Daddy was alive, we almost always visited his parents on their small farm during the summer months. Now that he was gone, Mother wanted these visits to continue as a link with our father.

We had been living at Aunt Pauline's house since June—more than two months. My mother still hadn't found a suitable house to buy, and school would be starting in just a few weeks. She thought a change of scenery would be good for Carol and me. She would have to stay in Evansville to keep looking for a house, but now that I was ten, she figured we were old enough to spend a week with our grandparents without her there. A few days after the surprise birthday party in Evansville, Uncle Edward drove us up to New Pennington, a tiny dot on the map of Indiana.

"That's it," I said to Uncle when I saw the yellow bricks and the shiny gazing globe that sat on a stand in the front yard. He parked the car in the driveway, and we got our suitcases out of the trunk. Grandma and Grandpa came out on the front porch and waved us to come in.

Grandma reached out to hug Carol and then me. She held on so tight. When I pulled away, I could see tears streaming down her face. "Oh, girls," she said, "the last time I saw you, your dear daddy was with you." Grandpa didn't say anything. He just smiled in a gentle way and patted our heads with his big hand.

Walking into the old farmhouse, everything looked so familiar. Compared with Auntie and Uncle's house with its modern conveniences, this place seemed stuck in time, almost like a museum. Just inside the front doors were two parlors separated by French doors. The room on the west side looked out toward the barns. Resting on the big wooden window seat was the vase that had always been there. It was filled with cattails that someone must have cut years ago near the old quarry pond. Some of the dried brown suede-looking pods were bursting open, and white fluff was spilling out. Grandpa's big oak desk was against the back wall. It had cubbyholes where he sorted papers related to his work as a township trustee.

Grandma was strict about proper behavior inside the house, and normally children were not allowed to enter either of the parlors. Today was different because Uncle Edward was there, so she invited all of us into the east parlor to visit. Uncle sat on a stiff upholstered chair, and Carol and I sat on the big sofa under the windows. I was wearing shorts, and the old horsehair fabric scratched my bare legs. While the grownups talked, I looked around, trying to see if anything had changed. The piano was still in its place against the wall. Grandma insisted that each of her daughters take piano lessons. The wind-up Victrola in its wooden case was still there. Next to it was the glassed-in oak cabinet where Grandma displayed her most precious belongings. Daddy's baby cup decorated with blue flowers highlighted in gold was on the top shelf, as always. On the middle shelf was a framed photograph of Daddy's brother, our Uncle Dwight, looking handsome in his army uniform. Grandma had put the photo there when he was overseas during World War II, and she kept it there after his safe return. Now there was a second photo next to it—a picture of Daddy out in the woods on a collecting trip.

Sitting there looking around the room, I wondered how my father, who grew up in this quiet farmhouse, could have ended up becoming a professor and working at a place like Oak Ridge. It must have been hard traveling from the past to the future in just a few years.

Soon it was time for Uncle Edward to head back to Evansville. Before he left, he carried our bags upstairs. As we walked toward the stairs, I saw the old oak telephone with its hand crank and black mouthpiece attached to the dining room wall. I was surprised that they were still using this old thing to make phone calls. Looking into a long narrow room on the left, I saw that it had been turned into a bathroom with a toilet, sink, and tub. I remembered how I used to dread using the old outhouse in back near the barn, sitting on the wooden toilet seat above a big hole in the ground.

Upstairs, the house smelled exactly the same as always—like dust warmed by the sun. Uncle Edward put our suitcases in the front bedroom, where Carol and I had slept on earlier visits. I climbed up on the big double bed and looked around. The wallpaper, with its full-blossomed roses, felt like an old friend, though there were a few more water stains where the roof had leaked. I felt safe and comfortable in this room where nothing ever changed.

The next morning, after Grandma served us breakfast, Grandpa asked if we'd like to come along while he did his chores. He didn't have to ask twice. This was one of our favorite things about visits to the farm. Carol and I put on our shoes and walked with him out through the back porch, where tomatoes sat ripening on the windowsill. On his way out, Grandpa grabbed the half-full slop bucket sitting by the door. He saved all these food scraps to feed to the pigs. Just outside the back door was a huge vegetable garden. Both Grandma and Grandpa loved working in the garden. They grew all the vegetables they needed, and there were Mason jars in the cellar filled with the food Grandma had canned to get them through the winter. Grandma was also proud of her flowers and made sure to keep the beds watered and weeded.

We followed Grandpa over to the big barn. It was kind of rickety, with some boards beginning to rot near the ground, but it smelled so good out there, so farmy. After we walked into the barn, Grandpa shooed the hens off their nests and handed Carol and me a basket to collect the eggs they had laid since yesterday. When we put the eggs in the basket, they were still warm.

Then it was time to milk the two cows that were tethered to a wooden post near the door. Grandpa explained that they were a special breed called Brown Swiss. They gave the sweetest milk, and when they got too old to give milk, they could be used for meat. Grandpa sat down on a wooden chair. I could hear the milk pinging into the metal bucket, but before long, the sound changed to a regular swish. After he finished with the first cow, he asked Carol and me if we'd like to try milking the other cow. We shook our heads. Grandpa smiled and said, "Don't be afraid. Even if you don't want to milk her, you can pet her. She's friendly." We reached out to stroke the cow. Her coat felt like velvet.

A CHANGE OF SCENERY

When Grandpa was finished with the milking, we went over to the pig pen. He glanced into the west window to see if Grandma was looking, and then he pulled a half-smoked cigar out of a pocket in his overalls. Lighting it with a corn husk he picked up off the ground, he puffed on it to get it going. The tobacco smelled wonderful, mixing with the smells of the barnyard. He called for the pigs in a voice that was loud and piercing, nothing like his quiet speaking voice. Then he poured the contents of the slop bucket into the feed trough. A big sow came right over and started gobbling up the scraps. About a month before, she had given birth to eight piglets. They were running around, squealing and trying to nurse from their mother. Covered with soft pink fuzz and twitching their curly tails, I thought they were the cutest things I'd ever seen.

After he finished his chores, Grandpa said, "Excuse me, girls. I need to go out and check on the crops." He had been troubled with rheumatism for the past few years, and it was getting hard for him to climb up on his big orange tractor, but once he was seated there, he looked proud, like a knight riding off to battle on his steed. You could tell Grandpa loved being a farmer.

There really wasn't much to do in the house since Grandma liked things to be quiet and orderly. There were many places we were not allowed to go and things we were not allowed to touch. So instead of going back in the house, Carol and I wandered over to the small field past the vegetable garden. It was really just a vacant lot covered with weeds. I had to look down to keep from tripping, and I saw a few old bricks lying on the ground. I remembered hearing Grandpa say that he had donated this land for a new Methodist church, which later burned down. Maybe that's where these bricks had come from. Then I spotted something else. Half-buried in weeds was an old gravestone. The words etched into the stone were covered with moss and hard to read. Tracing the letters with my fingers, I could make out a name, "Rhoda Pate," and the dates "1835 – 1928" underneath. I wasn't that good at math and had to use my fingers to figure this out, but then I said to Carol, "This woman lived to be very old. When she died, she was ninety-three." Below the dates, it listed the names of her children. One of them was our grandfather, Thomas Jefferson Williams. I liked the saying at the bottom of Rhoda's stone: "Gone but not forgotten."

We were still out in the old graveyard when we heard Grandma ringing the bell she used to call everyone in for meals. Lunch was the biggest meal of the day on a farm. Some of the food was strange to me, not like Mother's or Granny's cooking. But I had two big helpings of Grandma's special Jello salad. It was bright green and tasted delicious. When we were finished eating, Grandma left everything on the table and covered it with a big cloth.

After lunch, she always took a nap. She had been told to take it easy because she had a heart condition. Before she laid down, I asked if it was okay for Carol and me to walk over to the pond. "If you promise to be very careful," she said. "When you hear a car coming, go way off to the side. And when you get to the pond, stay at least three feet away from the edge. That pond is very deep."

As we walked down the road toward the old quarry, the air was hot and still. Not a single car drove by, and the only sounds were the clicking of cicadas and the occasional call of a song bird. I began to wonder if we had gone too far, but finally, I spotted a rickety wooden gate off to the left. I unlatched it, and we followed the rutted path through the overgrown field that led to the pond. Peeking through a row of pine trees, we could see it, surrounded by wildflowers and reeds. It looked like a dark jewel gleaming in the sunlight, untouched by time. As we walked closer, I held Carol's hand just in case she wanted to get too near. Standing there looking out over the still water, I tried to imagine

A CHANGE OF SCENERY

my father as a young boy rowing a small boat across the pond, trailing his hand in the cool water.

On the way back to the road, we passed the remains of the family orchard, full of old apple and pear trees with gnarly trunks. We could see a few small greenish apples on some of the trees, but none were ripe yet. There was a lone persimmon tree on the edge of the orchard near the road. Looking at that tree, I thought of something my mother was fond of saying: "Your daddy was always planting trees." I wondered if this was one of those trees.

When we got back to the house, Grandma was sitting in the small room off the dining room watching TV. It was surprising that in such an old-fashioned house they already had a TV set. Her favorite thing to watch was Billy Graham. Even though he was a Baptist and she was a Methodist, she believed every word he said. When there was nothing good on TV, Grandma and Grandpa would sit in this room and read the Bible out loud to each other. I was glad they never asked me to do this. Even though my parents wanted me to go to Sunday school, we never read the Bible at home.

Supper at our grandparents' house was a simple meal. Grandma just uncovered the leftovers from lunch and added a few freshly sliced tomatoes and cucumbers from the garden. After supper, Carol and I helped her clear the table and wash the dishes. The small galley kitchen had a distinctive smell, a bit like hard boiled eggs. Maybe it was gas escaping from the water heater. I never knew what caused it, but I liked it. To me, it just smelled like Grandma's kitchen.

On this visit, I was happy to see that they finally had hot and cold running water, but the heater could only handle a small amount of water at a time, so we had to be careful not to waste it. Even so, washing dishes was a lot easier than it used to be when we had to pump water from the well with a hand pump mounted next to the sink and heat it in a big pot on the gas stove. We were still in the kitchen helping Grandma with the dishes when the two bells on top of the old wooden phone started to jangle. The sound was so loud and unexpected that I jumped. These bells were so much louder than the ringer on a modern rotary-dial phone. Grandma dried her hands on her apron and picked up the receiver. Then I heard her say, "That sounds nice. Let me ask them." Still holding the receiver, she said, "Girls, this is your Aunt Goldia. She wonders if you would like to stay over at their farm tonight and spend tomorrow with your cousins."

Carol and I looked at each other and smiled. We loved spending time on the Miller farm. There was always so much to do there, and it was great to have other kids to play with. "Sure," I said. "We'd love to."

Once we finished putting away the dishes, Carol and I went upstairs and packed a few things for the overnight visit. Then all four of us went out to the front porch to wait for Uncle Carl to pick us up.

In the light from the setting sun, we could see Grandma's clematis vine climbing up a wooden trellis on the west side of the porch. It was covered with beautiful purple blooms. Carol and I sat on the wooden swing suspended from the ceiling. As we rocked back and forth, I realized that the last time we were swinging next to each other was on the swing set in our back yard in Tuscaloosa. That seemed so long ago.

Grandma sat in a straight chair facing the road, and Grandpa settled into an old rocker next to her. It was so quiet there on the porch. The only sound was from the occasional car or truck passing on the road. This was nothing like evenings on Alvord Boulevard, with all the talking and laughing and card playing. Grandma and Grandpa didn't talk much, and when they did, their voices were soft. Sometimes, if Grandpa said something amusing, Grandma would start to smile and then cover her mouth with her hand. They seemed happy just to be sitting there on the porch with Bert's children at the end of an August day on their farm.

A CHANGE OF SCENERY

I felt happy too, sitting next to my sister, looking across the road at the corn plants swaying in the breeze. Gradually, as it got darker, I saw one, then two, then hundreds of lightning bugs darting in and out between the corn stalks. Their little lights looked like twinkling stars. No wonder Daddy felt at home in the natural world. This was the world he grew up in. After he left the farm in New Pennington, he could always go home again. All he had to do was step out the front door and go for a walk in the woods.

16

Living on Tenterhooks

FOR JUST A FEW SECONDS after I woke up, I felt confused. Was I at Aunt Pauline's house in Evansville? Or at my grandparents' farm in New Pennington? A window across the room was just starting to turn from black to gray. Then I heard noises. Other people moving around in the upstairs bedrooms. And sounds of cooking in the kitchen. "Oh," I remembered, "I'm at the Miller farm with my cousins."

The older boys had to get up and get dressed while it was still dark to help their father in the fields before it got too hot. Aunt Goldia was in the kitchen cooking a big breakfast to give them the strength they would need for this hard work.

I yawned and rolled over. It felt luxurious to lie there in this comfortable bed and imagine the day to come. Carol and I loved visiting our cousins. Arlene was the oldest. She had been like a second mother to her seven siblings, but now she was married and lived in Virginia. Jimmy, Lowell, and Larry were teenagers, but they worked like grown men around the farm. Even Dyar, who was only nine years old—a year younger than me—was learning to drive the tractor and had to help out around the farm. Peggy was seven, the same age as Carol. They were born just a few days apart in August and had the same middle name, June. Doug was four. Sue was the youngest, only two years old. With her sweet smile, bright blue eyes, and yellow curls, she was adorable.

Peggy was sleeping in a twin bed on the other side of the room. I could hear her stirring, and then she got up and tiptoed over to see if Carol and I were awake. "Time to get up," she said. "Mom will have breakfast waiting for us downstairs." I climbed out of bed and grabbed a pair of shorts and a top from my suitcase. Carol rubbed her eyes and got up too.

As we walked down the stairs, wonderful smells wafted up from the kitchen. Aunt Goldia was standing with her back to us tending several skillets on the stove. As she turned around, a beautiful smile spread over her face. When she looked at you, she stopped whatever she was doing and gazed into your eyes. She made you feel like you were the most important person in the world.

"Good morning, Becky," she said. "I hope you woke up with an appetite." Even though the table was quite small, there always seemed to be room for everyone, including any nieces or nephews whose parents thought it would be good for their children to spend a few days on the Miller farm. As soon as I sat down, I felt like I was at home.

Aunt Goldia went back to the stove, where she was flipping pancakes. She kept them coming as long as anyone had room for more. They were delicious topped with her homemade raspberry jam. She was also frying bacon made from their own hogs at butchering time. It was even better than Oscar Mayer's, my favorite brand.

"Who would like some eggs?" she asked after we had eaten all the pancakes we could. "I think I'll scramble a few in the bacon grease." I didn't think I could eat another bite after all those pancakes, but I had to taste the eggs because they came from their own chickens. They were so much better than eggs from the grocery store.

When none of us could eat another bite, we pushed back our chairs and took our dishes over to the sink. "Why don't you kids go outside and find something to do?" she said. "Oh, and remember. Your cousin Jerry is having an operation on his heart today at a big hospital in Chicago. I'm sure everything will go well, but you might want to say a prayer for him."

As we walked out through the back door, we passed a huge vegetable garden. On the side of the garden closest to the house, Aunt Goldia had planted flowers—sunflowers, zinnias, marigolds, and sweet peas. I didn't know how she found time to tend those flowers with everything else she had to do, but like her mother, our Grandma Williams, she didn't consider flowers a luxury for those who had extra time on their hands. They were a necessity, a living reminder of the beauty of God's world.

Peggy held little Sue's hand and led us out to the sheep house next to the big barn. She explained that one of the ewes had had triplets about a month ago, and she didn't have enough milk for all three lambs, so the smallest one had to be fed from a bottle. She let Carol and me take turns feeding the little lamb. She showed us how to kneel down in the straw and hold her gently around the neck. She was so cuddly with her curly white fur, pointy ears, and little black feet.

After the lamb had finished her bottle, we went outside to hunt for eggs. Looking for the small eggs laid by the banty hens was like an Easter egg hunt. We found one nest where a couple of the shells were cracked and empty. If the chicks hatched before anyone found the eggs, the tiny chickens just scrabbled around like the others, eating whatever they could find around the barns.

With all this excitement, the morning flew by. Soon Uncle Carl and the boys were back from the fields and washing up for lunch. Carl loved children, and he knew how to make them happy. "Would anyone like to have a ride on Queenie?" He went out to the big barn and came back leading a horse on a rope. She wasn't saddled up, but she did have a nice soft blanket over her broad back. Our uncle lifted me up first because I was the biggest. Then he put little Doug behind me and Peggy in front so that she could hold the reins. We held onto each other as Uncle Carl led the horse around the yard.

I had to sit up straight and grab onto Queenie with my knees to keep from falling off. When the ride was over, and we were down on the ground, we got to take turns feeding her apples and carrots. I was afraid she might bite me with her big teeth, but my cousins showed me how to hold my hand out flat with the apple on my palm. She just scooped it up and licked my hand with her wet tongue.

Some of us kids tagged along as Uncle Carl took her back to the big barn. As soon as I walked through the door, I felt a change. Light filtered into the barn from a few windows up high. The air smelled grassy and clean from the fresh bales of hay stacked up above in the haymow. There were big wooden posts every few feet. Looking up, I saw rough-cut beams that had been made from huge old trees when the land was cleared for farming more than a hundred years ago. They looked so strong and solid bracing up the barn. In July, at Aunt Pauline's house, I had read a book called *The Hunchback of Notre-Dame* about a huge cathedral in France. Standing here in the big barn, looking up at the rafters overhead, I felt like I was inside another kind of cathedral.

Once Queenie was back in her stall, we followed Uncle Carl outside. Aunt Goldia told him that lunch wasn't ready yet, so he said he thought he'd take a little drive to check on his crops. He asked Carol and me if we'd like to come along. We jumped at the chance. We loved going for rides on the straight country roads that seemed to stretch out into eternity.

"It's going to be a good year for corn," he said as he drove his big Buick out of the driveway. The stalks were taller than I was, and the bright green leaves rippled in the warm summer breeze. In June, he had planted watermelon and pumpkin seeds along the edge of one of his corn fields so that the vines could twine in between the corn. By now, he thought there should be some melons worth harvesting. Just as he was pulling the car off to the side of the road beside the field, a blue pickup truck drove up next to us. Our cousin Jimmy was driving. He leaned toward his father with a worried look on his face. "Mom got a call from someone at the hospital in Chicago. Little Jerry didn't make it through the operation. His heart just stopped beating. There was nothing they could do."

We sat there in complete silence. How could this be? Jerry was only three years old. His fourth birthday would be on Saturday. How could such a young child, with his whole life ahead of him, just die?

Uncle Carl was the first to speak. "Girls, I'm so sorry you have to be here at such a sad time. I think I'd better take you back to be with your grandparents now until we see what the plans are."

When we got back to the house, Grandma's eyes were red from crying, and Grandpa was holding her hand. In their sadness, they looked smaller than I remembered. I felt myself getting smaller too, small and alone, just like I felt when Daddy died and Mother left me and Carol in Tuscaloosa while she went up north to Greensburg for the funeral.

LIVING ON TENTERHOOKS

    This time we were near Greensburg, and Mother was down south in Evansville. I never really understood why she didn't come to Jerry's funeral. She wasn't a confident enough driver to make the trip alone, and maybe none of the relatives were available to bring her. Or maybe the thought of losing a child was just too painful for her to face so soon after losing her husband. I don't think we ever talked about why she didn't come to the funeral. Carol and I were here, and she was there. It was as simple—and as complicated—as that.

~

Two days later, we got dressed in formal clothes to go to Greensburg for something called visitation. I had never seen Grandpa in a suit before. He looked so different in his black suit, white shirt, and dress shoes. Grandma had on a plain black dress with her long hair coiled into a bun at the back of her neck. Carol and I didn't have any black clothes, but we wore the dresses we had packed in case we went to church while we were in New Pennington.

    The drive to Greensburg took about half an hour. Grandpa parked the car on Franklin Street, just a short walk to the Oliger-Pearson Funeral Home. Walking up the front steps behind my grandparents, I suddenly felt afraid. "You go in first," I said to Carol. I often counted on her to go first in scary situations. She was my little sister, but she was braver than I was.

    Once inside, things didn't seem so frightening. It was just a big old house with lots of rooms with comfortable chairs where people could sit and talk, holding cardboard fans to stir the still August air. One of the rooms held a tiny white coffin surrounded by flowers. I stood for a long time near the doorway, afraid of what I might see inside. Finally, my curiosity got the better of my fear. I walked over and peered into the open casket. Jerry's face, framed by his wispy blond hair, looked almost transparent. It was hard for me to believe he was dead. He looked so perfect, like a beautiful doll.

What I remember most clearly though from that day at the funeral home wasn't my little cousin but the inconsolable grief of his mother, my Aunt Agatha. She sobbed and wailed for what seemed like hours. Her husband, Denzil, was standing beside her with his arm around her waist. He looked so sad, but he wasn't crying. Denzil was Daddy's youngest brother, and he looked a lot like my father, over six feet tall with hazel eyes and curly black hair.

No matter which room I went into, I could still hear my aunt's high-pitched cries, almost like a police siren, punctuated with shuddering breaths as she filled her lungs to go on crying. Her grief was so public, so uncontrolled, so different from my mother's stoicism and restraint. I had never seen anyone cry like this. For some reason, instead of feeling frightened, I was fascinated. Knowing that a person could feel this much pain and still go on living was strangely comforting.

Finally, though, when I couldn't stand the crying any more, I went out on the old-fashioned front porch. After a few minutes, Aunt Ercil came out for a breath of air. She was the wife of Uncle Dwight, Daddy's other brother, the one who had fought in World War II. A breeze was riffling the leaves on the stately elms that lined the sidewalk. It was pretty and peaceful out there.

"It's hard to believe, Becky," she said, "but it's already been a year since we came to pay our last respects to your father. Right here in this same funeral home."

I didn't want to say it, but it seemed like much longer than a year to me.

When I went back inside, I kept thinking about Daddy. He had been in the hospital for three months, and then he was just . . . gone. After his death, Mother disappeared too—on a train to Greensburg, where friends and family gathered at the funeral home to say goodbye. But I wasn't there. I was four hundred miles away, staying with strangers, wondering, worrying, left alone to imagine what would come next for our family.

Hearing Aunt Agatha's agonized cries as she grieved for her little son, I kept trying to imagine my father's funeral. His coffin would have been so much bigger than Jerry's. Was he finally at peace as he lay there with his big hands linked together over his waist? I could picture my mother, standing straight and tall beside the open casket, welcoming friends and relatives, easing their awkwardness and discomfort. Never shedding a tear.

Many years later, I discovered a letter that my father's Aunt Lydia wrote just five days after the funeral, a letter Mother preserved in the scrapbook she made after his death. Growing up, I often heard family members speak of Lydia with affection and respect. She was Grandmother Williams's older sister, and she was married to Reverend Thomas J. Hart, a Methodist minister, who had baptized my father as an infant in 1909 and married him to my mother in 1936. Reverend Hart, Lydia's husband of many years, had died in 1937, when she was only fifty-seven years old. She was no stranger to grief.

I treasure Lydia's note for its snapshot of my grieving mother. "You certainly seemed to be a very brave person in your sorrow, Ruth." Then she added, "But I know, too, something about your heart-ache." She knew that, deep inside, the gracious, self-possessed woman standing beside her husband's coffin was suffering from a broken heart.

~

Thinking about the different ways my mother and my aunt grieved their terrible losses got me wondering why, even now, in my late seventies, I have so much trouble experiencing and expressing grief in an honest way. The sadder I am, the harder it is for me to cry. Tears only come later, when I'm watching a sentimental movie or reading a poem that taps into my grief. When something sad happens, my first instinct is to start moving, to tidy up the kitchen or fold the laundry, anything to distract me from the fear and pain in my heart.

By a quirk of fate, Carol and I were staying with Grandma and Grandpa Williams when Jerry died in 1955. My grandparents didn't read psychology books about child rearing. They didn't wonder about whether children would be traumatized by seeing a dead body. They just did things the way they had always been done. When they were young, people died at home, and the funeral ceremonies were held there as well. Friends and relatives gathered to view the body and mourn—talking and eating and laughing and crying together. Children were not excluded. So, when our little cousin died, they didn't agonize about whether Carol and I should go with them to the funeral home. Saying goodbye to the dead was something that families did together.

Perhaps if I had been able to share in the rituals of mourning for my father, I could have expressed some of my grief instead of holding it all inside. If my mother had talked or cried more often and more openly about my father in the years that followed, I might have gradually found my own way to acknowledge my grief. But we hardly ever talked about him and never mentioned his mental illness. I sensed that this was a taboo subject, so I never discussed it, not even with my sister.

Instead, I built up a lot of fear inside. If illness and death were too scary for children to see, too scary to even talk about, they must be more frightening than anything I could imagine. This fear—the fear of not knowing, of not seeing—grew into a haunting anxiety, a fear that something terrible might happen unexpectedly, something that would overtake me and destroy those I loved if I wasn't constantly on guard, ready to do whatever was necessary to prevent it.

LIVING ON TENTERHOOKS

You could be lying in bed on a summer morning, listening to the birds and smelling the honeysuckle, and then you might hear a knock at the front door. Or you could wake up at your cousins' farm ready for a day of fun and adventure, but around noon, riding down a peaceful country road with your uncle, a truck might drive up next to the car. Everything could change in an instant without any warning. You never knew what might happen when you least suspected. It was like living on tenterhooks, nerves stretched tight, always waiting for the worst.

17

2719 Short Marion

It was the middle of August. School would be starting in a couple of weeks, and we still didn't have a home of our own. Aunt Pauline's house was on the East Side of town, which now felt a little bit like home, but the school where Mother would be teaching was way over on the West Side.

Mother's house-hunting efforts during the summer had been unsuccessful. With little money for a down payment, her options were limited, and none of the houses she looked at were suitable. Then, a few days after Carol and I returned from visiting our relatives in Greensburg, Mother got back from another real estate appointment with a look of relief, even excitement, on her face.

"I think you girls are going to like the house I saw today." It was on the West Side, just a stone's throw from Reitz High School, and less than a mile from Centennial Elementary School, and it was big enough for Granny to live there with us. "I made an appointment for all four of us to go out and take a look tomorrow afternoon."

~

The woman who owned the house greeted us on the front porch and invited us in. She gave us a complete tour of the house and basement. Afterwards, as we stood in the living room, she became emotional. "This house saved my husband's life," she explained. "Building it with his own hands gave him a reason to keep going after his heart attack in

1950." She seemed about to cry and then changed the subject. "The S. stands for Short, not South," she said. This street was indeed short. 2719 S. Marion was one of only three houses on a dead-end street connected to two narrow, unpaved alleyways. But to the four of us, this small house built into the side of a hill felt like a promise. Light poured into the pine-paneled den at the front of the house, and the oak floors gleamed in the sun. The kitchen, tiny by today's standards, looked ultra-modern with its linoleum floor, pink appliances, and blue Formica counters. The builder must have had some Formica left over, because he made a kitchen table out of plywood and covered the top with the same indestructible material. A year or so after completing the house, he died of heart disease.

The house had two bedrooms—one for Carol and me and one for Granny. Mother said she could sleep on a daybed in the den, which would also serve as her study. There was a full basement that was partly above ground, with large windows to let in the sun. It could easily be finished and turned into additional living space later on. Mother didn't have to think twice before she signed the contract.

In a way, that little house saved our lives too. Slowly, we began to put the trauma of the past year and a half behind us. Before Daddy got sick, our life in Alabama had seemed ideal, a real-life version of *Father Knows Best*. But then our father, who had always been so calm and kind, turned into a different person, and just three months later, he died of a sudden heart attack.

Living in a new house in a new town, we tried to pretend that none of this had happened. Mother started her new job, teaching U.S. history classes at Reitz High School. She walked to school every day through the alley at the bottom of our driveway. Carol and I also walked to our school, Centennial Elementary, about a mile away. Granny helped with the cooking and cleaning and talked to her sisters on the phone—no longer an expensive long-distance call—while we were at school.

Spending the summer at Aunt Pauline's house had been exciting. There was always something happening, with relatives coming and going. But it was also unsettling. I felt uprooted, like a plant pulled out of its native soil. Now on Short Marion, I was beginning to put down a few roots again.

It helped to have so much love and support from the extended family. Granny's sisters, in keeping with their German upbringing, showed their love through deeds rather than hugs and kisses. They decided that Ruth needed help decorating the house. There were all those big windows in the living/dining room. It was the era of floor-length drapes with pinch pleats hung on traverse rods. The drapes would have to be lined for privacy and light control. Custom-made drapes would cost a fortune. But three of Granny's sisters—Pauline, Clara, and Katie—came to the rescue. Mother picked out an elegant fabric, a floral design in shades of rose and green highlighted in metallic gold. Once the fabric had arrived—yards and yards of it—Granny's sisters came with their portable sewing machines and turned the dining room table into a workspace. It took many days of intense work, but the finished drapes were beautiful. I still remember that heavy fabric and the feeling I had whenever I went over to pull the cord to open or close them. A warmth seemed to radiate from them, reminding me of the love that went into making them.

Mother was so proud of her new house. Granny had never owned a home. She and Mother had lived in a series of rentals in run-down neighborhoods. In 1945, when my parents moved to Tuscaloosa, they rented the house on Cedar Crest from the Carlson family. Dr. Carlson was on a one-year sabbatical to do research at the University of Tennessee. At the end of the year, he accepted a permanent position there, and my parents bought the house they had been renting. During the ten years they lived in that house, Mother never felt a sense of true ownership. To her, it still felt like the Carlsons' house.

2719 was different. Finally, she had a home of her own. Once the new drapes were hung, the furniture she had brought from Alabama looked kind of shabby. She decided to keep Daddy's big armchair, but she bought a new couch. The living room rug had seen better days, but she decided to keep it until she could afford to install wall-to-wall carpeting. That dark mahogany dining room set was out of style and carried too many painful memories. One Saturday, she went to Finke's furniture store in downtown Evansville. She ordered a dining room suite made of limed oak—very 1950s. It included a large table, eight chairs, and a buffet to hold the good china.

In Evansville, the school year started in early September. I anticipated my first day of fifth grade with a mixture of excitement and trepidation. Early that morning, I got up and put on the dress Mother had made for me during the summer. It was a typical Evansville day for that time of year—hot and humid. Wearing that dress with its fitted bodice and long sleeves, I was sweating by the time we got to school. But there was no way I would wear anything else after her struggle to finish it during our summer at Aunt Pauline's house.

Mother drove Carol and me to Centennial that day, even though it made her late for her own class at Reitz. As we walked into the old brick building, I was struck by a distinctive odor—a fusty smell as if the windows had been closed all summer with no air circulation in the sweltering heat. On either side of the central hall, oak staircases led to the upper floors. Hall monitors, boys and girls wearing special sashes, were stationed beside the stairs to direct traffic and make sure none of the kids pushed or shoved. As I climbed the steps to my homeroom on the second floor, I looked down. The old oak treads were worn and cupped in the middle from the thousands of children's feet that had climbed these stairs since the school opened in 1876—just in time for the nation's centennial.

After the first few days, Carol and I walked to and from school together. She was still just my kid sister—but I loved spending time with her on these walks. Though I wasn't conscious of it then, we had been forever bonded to each other by all we had lived through in Tuscaloosa after Daddy got sick. Walking her home from school made me feel responsible for her in a way I hadn't before.

At the end of the school day, I would wait outside her second-grade classroom until the teacher dismissed the class. Then we would begin the eleven-block walk back to Short Marion. If I had a few coins in my pocket, we would stop at the little corner store and put the coins into the gumball machine. I always hoped I'd get grape. I would suck on the hard outside, enjoying the grapey sweetness, and when I couldn't stand it any longer, I'd chomp down and start to chew. Sometimes I would show off by seeing how big a bubble I could blow before it burst all over my face.

2719 SHORT MARION

We had to be very careful crossing the Division Street Expressway, with cars whizzing every which way, but it was easy going after that. We knew to turn left on Lemcke Avenue. The house on the corner had a concrete retaining wall topped with beautiful geodes. Some were round like small bowling balls, but others had been cracked open to show the crystals inside. We liked to count them as we started walking up the long hill toward our house.

~

Living in southern Indiana, things began to feel almost normal. Nobody knew what had happened to Daddy in Alabama, and we tried our best not to think about it. But by the time the three of us got home after a long day of school, it was hard to keep pretending.

Mother and Granny were both good cooks, and our meals in Alabama had been delicious. Even on a weeknight, we might have fried chicken with fresh green beans and a homemade fruit pie for dessert. Suppers at 2719 were not like that. We often made do with Campbell's tomato soup and tuna noodle casserole. Dessert might be canned pineapple or chocolate pudding from a mix. The four of us would squeeze in to fit around the small kitchen table. It just didn't seem right to sit at the dining room table without Daddy there. The thing that made us a real family was missing.

In late September, it was getting dark earlier and earlier, and we all felt a bit lost after the dishes were washed and put away. Then one evening, while Mother was sitting in Daddy's big chair reading the Evansville Press, an ad for Bob Schaad's Appliance Store caught her attention. You could have a television set delivered to your home on trial to watch the World Series. After the Series was over, you could return it. No charge.

FROM SEED TO TREE TO FRUIT

We hadn't had a TV in Alabama, even though most of our friends did. I suspect part of the decision was financial. Money was always tight in our family. But there was another reason as well. Watching television would take us away from the things my parents valued—reading, thoughtful conversations, and spending time outdoors.

But by the fall of 1955, after all we had been through, we needed a distraction. Granny was a rabid baseball fan. As someone who had experienced so many losses in her life, she identified with losers. Her favorite team was the Brooklyn Dodgers. She listened to all their games on the radio, sometimes yelling out loud in excitement or exasperation. This year, the Dodgers had made it to the Series—the fifth time in nine years that they had achieved this feat. Once again, they would compete against their archrivals, the New York Yankees. In their earlier matchups, the Yankees won every time. But the Dodgers never gave up. Their motto was "Wait till next year." Wouldn't it be wonderful if the Dodgers finally won in 1955? Wouldn't it be wonderful if Granny could actually see what was happening on the field instead of just listening to the radio announcer? It didn't take Mother long to make a decision. When she told us, she was careful to add a postscript: "We'll just keep the set for the World Series and then return it to the store."

The next day, after school, we drove over to Bob Schaad's on Franklin Street. We selected a Philco. It had a limed oak case, like the new dining room suite, and stood on splayed-out legs, making it look very modern.

A few days later, a big truck pulled up in our driveway, and two burly men carried the set up the front steps and installed it in the living room. By the time the Series started, we were familiar with the dials and knobs on the front panel. Often the black-and-white image would get all snowy, and we would have to fiddle with the rabbit ears on top. Then the picture would start to roll, and we'd play with the controls to try to get it to stop. But these were minor problems. The new set gave us a window on a wider world.

To make things even better, in 1955, the Dodgers finally won the World Series, defeating the Yankees in game seven—the first and only time the team won the championship while they were still in Brooklyn. When the Series was over, no one mentioned returning the television set. Mother got out her checkbook and started making payments on the installment plan.

Having access to television changed my grandmother's life. She stayed home all day while we were in school, and she hardly ever left the house, but TV allowed her to experience worlds very different from her own. She would sit on the couch for hours with her sewing in her lap, watching her favorite shows. She especially enjoyed pro wrestling. Something about the wigs, the costumes, the violence, the fakery. It was almost like opera without the singing, and she had always loved opera. She was also a fan of the subtle humor of Groucho Marx and the urbane patter of Jack Paar, the host of NBC's *Tonight Show*. When the late-night show came on, she would turn the sound down low and watch until the program ended around midnight. At that point, a recording of the national anthem was played with the American flag waving on the screen, and then a test pattern appeared until programming resumed in the morning.

For Carol and me, TV helped to fill the void of Daddy's absence. On Saturday mornings, we watched *Howdy Doody*, a show that featured a marionette and his human friend, a man in a cowboy suit named Buffalo Bob. I knew it was corny, but I watched it anyway. Even cornier was a program on WEHT, a local station, starring Peppo the Clown. I watched that too. My favorite show was *Fury*, a drama about an orphan boy who was adopted by a rancher in California and the boy's heroic horse, Fury. In the evenings, we sometimes watched more sophisticated shows such as *Playhouse 90* and *Alfred Hitchcock Presents*. I didn't completely understand them, but I could tell they were good.

Since Granny was home all day, she watched the soaps in the afternoon. Her favorite was *The Edge of Night*, which started at 3:30. As Carol and I walked home from school, I would check my watch. If we were running late, we would race up the huge staircase by the Reitz football stadium and jog the last few blocks to be home in time to hear the dramatic piano music announcing the latest episode of this soap opera. We didn't want to miss any of the exciting adventures of Mike Karr, a policeman who was training to be a lawyer. With his dark, glossy hair, dimpled chin, and penetrating eyes, I thought he was the handsomest man I'd ever seen. The subject matter of this show was definitely not suitable for children, but the writers and actors found a way to keep viewers of all ages tuning in to find out what would happen next.

Mother was happy to see all three of us enjoying the new television, but she hardly ever watched it herself. She was too busy trying to keep her grief at bay. From childhood on, her way of coping with pain had been to lose herself in work. "No use crying over spilled milk" was one of her favorite maxims. She had never taught high school before, so she needed to spend a lot of time preparing her lessons in U.S. history. She would get up at five o'clock every morning, do any last-minute planning for her classes, and leave for school around 7:30. She'd arrive back home between 3:30 and 4 o'clock. The only downtime she allowed herself was the twenty or thirty minutes she spent each day after school sitting in Daddy's big chair to read the newspaper. We knew not to bother her while she was reading the paper. She needed these few minutes to recover from her busy day. When she was done, she would fold the paper and put it on the little table next to the chair before going into the kitchen to prepare the evening meal. After supper, when the rest of the family was settling down in front of the TV, she would go into the study she had set up in the den and start preparing her classes for the next day.

In Tuscaloosa, she had been such an involved parent. She had served as the leader of my Brownie troop and president of the school's PTA. Now she had no time for volunteer activities. But she still wanted her girls to be active in the life of the community, so she enrolled me in a Girl Scout troop and Carol in the Brownies. Both groups met at Simpson Methodist Church, and she signed us up for Sunday school there as well. For the first few Sundays, she met us as our classes were dismissed and walked with us into the sanctuary to attend church. Sitting there in the quiet church, she couldn't contain her grief any longer. During the hymns, which she had known by heart since childhood, her tears would begin to flow. The music brought out all the sadness she was trying to push away. After two or three Sundays, she stopped attending.

Always so positive and optimistic, my mother had never learned how to grieve. As a result, Carol and I couldn't either. All three of us just kept going from one day to the next, trying to make the best of things. There was something missing from our lives, but we didn't know what might help to fill the void.

Surprisingly, it was Mother's cousin Caroline (pronounced Kar-leen) who came to our aid. Caroline had never married. Her last name was Stofft—like Granny's before she married Bill Stamps. Caroline lived with Aunt Katie, Granny's older sister, and worked for years as the office assistant for Dr. Weiss, a respected physician in town. For me, a ten-year-old girl, she was an important role model of a successful professional woman. Like all the Evansville relatives, she wore sensible shoes and dark-colored dresses. She was twelve years younger than Granny, but to me she seemed old. She was also very kind.

In November of 1955, Caroline had a talk with Mother. She thought the girls needed something to cheer them up. Not a small thing easily broken like a new doll. These little girls needed something to love and care for. They needed a dog.

Mother had never had a pet dog. In her opinion, dogs were dirty and smelly. She cringed to think of a dog shedding all over her beautiful new house.

"You have that whole big basement with windows to let in lots of light," Caroline countered. "It's the perfect place for a dog."

Mother began to understand what Caroline was saying. "I'll have to have a serious talk with Becky and Carol. They need to understand that if we get a dog, it will be their responsibility. They will have to feed it and keep the water bowl filled. They will have to walk it several times a day." When she brought up the idea of adopting a dog, we were thrilled. Of course, we'd take care of it.

A few weeks later, Caroline called to say she had heard of a dog that might be available. It barked so much while its owners were at work that they finally let it run loose. Then it started going to the neighbors' houses begging for food and tagged along with the mailman on his daily route. The mailman liked the dog, but he and his wife already had a dog. The owners said they'd be glad to have their pet go to a good home. They added, "She loves children."

The next day, Caroline arrived in our driveway. Cowering in the back seat of her car was a dirty, bedraggled mutt, a long-haired dog with fur that needed to be brushed. The dog's owners said she was a cocker spaniel, but it was hard to see any resemblance to the popular breed. Her ears were much shorter and her tail much longer. It had never been docked, the standard practice for pure-bred cockers.

Caroline wrapped her in a blanket and carried her in through the basement door. Once Carol and I peered into those liquid brown eyes, we were in love with this poor scared dog. For the first few weeks she trembled in silence, creeping around the basement with her tail between her legs. She never barked or whined. We put a little bell on her collar so we'd know where she was when we came downstairs to feed or pet her, and that inspired her new name—Tinkerbell. Like the fairy in Peter Pan, this little dog lit up our lives in an almost magical way.

Gradually over the next few weeks, she became less frightened. One day when I went down to feed her, the tail came out from between her legs and she waved it in a tentative way. A few days later, when I was petting her, she licked my hand. She was beginning to feel at home at 2719—just like us.

Every day, after school, I would attach the leash to her collar and take her outside to walk around the neighborhood. One day I walked up the street to Marion Avenue—past the Holders' and the Foxes' and the Lashleys'. Then, as we walked back down the hill, I saw another girl walking her dog in the alley at the foot of the hill. She was tall like me with medium-length hair and glasses. She was wearing a pretty dress and saddle shoes. Waving, she said, "Hi! I didn't know you lived near me." I recognized this girl, though I didn't know her name. We were both in Mrs. Hitch's homeroom at Centennial. Her dog began straining at the leash and pulled her up to where I was standing. The dogs sniffed each other warily, and then they both wagged their tails.

"I'm surprised," she said. "Poochie usually hates other dogs." He was a distinguished-looking black-and-white terrier. "I usually have to keep him on a tight leash when there are other dogs around, but he seems to like your dog." We talked for a few minutes, and I learned that her name was Patty, and she lived just a few houses away from me on Hartmetz Avenue.

A couple of weeks later, I was at my first slumber party ever, hosted by a classmate named Barbara Springer. Being so new in town, I didn't know most of these girls. What a relief it was when I saw that Patty was there too. When Barbara's mother said it was time to settle down for the night, we spread out our sleeping bags next to each other and started to talk. We talked for hours before we finally went to sleep. It turned out we had so much in common—including little sisters who were both seven years old and in the second grade at Centennial.

Patty and I never ran out of things to talk about. In the months and years ahead, I told her everything. Everything except the story of my father's mental illness. All she knew was that he died young of a sudden heart attack. That's what we told everyone.

Years later, after we had graduated from Reitz High School and gone off to different colleges, she called long distance to tell me that her mother had tried to commit suicide. Sitting on the wooden seat in the phone booth in my dorm, I remember my hands shaking as I held the receiver. "I never told you this," I said in a quiet voice, "but my father died in a mental hospital." Sharing the pain of our parents' lives brought us even closer.

~

As 1955 came to an end, I was happier than I had been in a long time. I had a dog I adored, a best friend, a dear little sister, and a grandmother who was always there for me. Most important of all, I had a brave and loving mother, the pillar of my childhood. Every night before bedtime, she would come into the room Carol and I shared and sit down to read us a story. By that time, we could both read for ourselves, but there was something special about hearing these stories in our mother's voice. She often chose a comedy—the fantastic adventures of the English nanny Mary Poppins by P. L. Travers or the hilarious antics of a group of animals chronicled in *The Hollow Tree and Deep Woods Book* by Albert Bigelow Paine or the exotic doings of Dr. Dolittle, a physician who could talk to animals. Carol and I would smile or giggle as we heard about these wacky adventures. But our favorite book from this time was not a comedy. *The Swiss Family Robinson* was the story of a hard-working and resourceful family—father, mother, four young sons, and two pet dogs. They had survived a shipwreck and ended up on a deserted island, where they created a new home for themselves after losing everything—everything, that is, except each other.

Mother would read us a chapter or two each night. We always begged for "just one more," and usually she relented. Finally, she would kiss us both, turn out the light, and say good night.

After she closed the door, I would lie in bed listening to the night sounds of our neighborhood on the hill. I loved to hear the trains whistling in the distance, the same sounds that had soothed me to sleep in Tuscaloosa. Hearing them now reminded me that the two places were connected, that I hadn't just slipped off the edge of the earth, the way I felt during that long summer at Aunt Pauline's house. The sound of the trains lulled me to sleep, almost like being rocked in my mother's arms. Maybe, I thought, as I drifted off, things are going to be okay.

PART III

"Ask and it will be given to you; seek and you will find; knock and the door will be opened to you."

—Matthew 7:7, New International Version

18

Opening the Book of the Past

I AM NO LONGER that fifth grader adjusting to a new home and a new life. It is the middle of August 2020, and I am seventy-five years old. A few months into the global COVID-19 pandemic, my husband and I are isolating at our country house in Plainfield, Massachusetts. I sit at the kitchen table staring at a heavy scrapbook bound together with a black faux-leather cover. My sister had left it on the table when she came for a brief visit a few days earlier. "This is one of the things I took when Mother died," she explained. "I think it might help you with your memoir."

Mother was always making scrapbooks. For her, this was a way of tidying up the past as she selected bits and pieces of our family life—newspaper clippings, photos, personal notes and letters—and organized them on blank pages. This scrapbook was different. This was the book in which she carefully preserved traces of our life in 1954, the year that changed our lives forever. For days, I sat at the table in the quiet house, turning the thick, yellowed pages, trying not to tear the brittle paper.

Paging through the scrapbook, I found clues related to some of the questions I had about my father's mental illness and death, questions that had gone unanswered for sixty-five years. Sitting quietly with a cup of herbal tea, I wondered what motivated my mother to preserve these artifacts. And where did she find the time and energy when she was working so hard just to hold the family together and figure out a way for us to keep going after Daddy died?

As I read through the pages, it occurred to me that perhaps making this book was Mother's way of compensating for not being able to talk about our father's illness with me and Carol when we were children. Maybe it was her way of saying, "Here it is, the story of his last year. I couldn't tell you this when you were younger. But I knew you would want to know someday. I saved this for you."

~

Looking back, I remember that Mother wasn't always so secretive about Daddy's illness. During his hospitalization, she treated me almost like an adult confidante, telling me about her conversations with his psychiatrist and explaining her need to rescue the family from financial disaster by having him transferred to the state hospital. During the years that followed, however, she relied on a defense mechanism she had used during her childhood. Don't talk about sad things. Just pretend they never happened. My mother, with her indomitable energy and optimism, had an uncanny ability to sweep painful realities under the rug. In her German-American family, cleanliness was a virtue, and from childhood on she had earned praise for her strenuous efforts to keep things clean and tidy.

During the year after Daddy died, she decided to move the family to Evansville, Indiana, her hometown. "Teachers' salaries are so low in Alabama," she explained to me at the time. "I will double my salary by teaching in Indiana. And I want to protect you girls. People in the South still don't understand that mental illness is a disease. They won't forget that your daddy was in the state hospital, and they might say mean things to you."

After the move, she worked hard to create a new life for us. She was busy with her teaching, and there was no room in this life for the tragedy that had derailed our life in Alabama. Whenever she talked about Daddy with Carol and me, she never mentioned his illness or his hospitalization. Instead, she held him up as the perfect husband and father, the archetype of what we should look for when we were ready to marry. But then a few years after Daddy's death, I was shocked to learn that she was looking around for a new husband. She signed up for ballroom dancing lessons at the Arthur Murray studio and started going to dinner dances at the Hadi Shrine Temple in downtown Evansville. In my opinion, none of the men she met could begin to compare with my father, and the new teenaged me was explicit in letting her know what I thought. I destroyed at least one budding relationship with my anger and resentment. But I relaxed when she started dating a man named Freeman, a skilled iron worker active in the union. I was sure she would never marry him since he wasn't anything like my father. He made grammar mistakes when he talked, and he never read books.

Then in May 1960, six years after Daddy had died, she made a stark announcement to Carol and me. She and Freeman were going to get married. I started crying hysterically and tried to change her mind, explaining that this went against everything she had ever told us about the foundation of a good marriage. But she could not be swayed. She said she was tired of being alone. She needed a man to go out with on Saturday nights and fix things that broke around the house, and Freeman needed a wife. He was a widower with two daughters to raise, and he wanted them to have a woman's influence as they were growing up. This would be a marriage based on practicality rather than shared intellectual interests and dreams of eternal love. They were married in a private ceremony at Howell Methodist Church on Evansville's West Side on June 18, 1960. I did not attend.

FROM SEED TO TREE TO FRUIT

Our house was bigger than Freeman's, so after the marriage he and his daughters moved into 2719 Short Marion. Granny moved to a nice apartment a few blocks away, and Anne and Glenna shared the bedroom across the hall from Carol and me where Granny had slept. Freeman renovated one side of the basement into a nice living space, complete with its own kitchen and bathroom. Mother and Freeman slept down there.

Once they moved in with us, it was like 1954 had never happened. But it had happened. Some of the events of that year were indelibly engraved on my memory. They could not be erased.

~

For years, I tried to avoid thinking about what had happened to my father. Even in fiction, mental hospitals terrified me. In 1964, during my sophomore year in college, everyone was reading and talking about *One Flew Over the Cuckoo's Nest*, Ken Kesey's novel about the horrors of life in a psychiatric institution. I bought a copy of the book but only got a few pages into it. Skimming to the end of the first chapter, I read these words spoken by a patient known as Chief Bromden:

> I been silent so long now it's gonna roar out of me like floodwaters and you think the guy telling this is ranting and raving my *God*; you think this is too horrible to have really happened, this is too awful to be the truth!

Feeling shaken by this stark portrait of life on the wards, I got up from the desk, walked over to my crowded bookshelf, and wedged that paperback between two others on the bottom shelf. I never touched it again.

In 1966, when I met Frank, the man who would become my husband, I told him about my father on our second or third date. I sensed he would understand and empathize. He did. It seems strange, but I never considered talking about this with my mother, the only one who could have answered some of my questions. The unspoken rule of silence was too strong.

After I graduated from college, married Frank, and moved to New York City in 1969, my questions became too insistent to ignore. In the spring of 1971, with a referral from a trusted physician, I made an appointment with a psychiatrist. I was twenty-six years old when I finally confronted all the fears and doubts I had been harboring. After several sessions, he said, "Nothing is as frightening as not knowing. You need to talk with your mother about this." I knew he was right. I decided to call her.

Long-distance calls were a big deal in those days. I remember sitting with the telephone receiver in my hand, my finger poised over the dial, trying to get up the courage to call and ask her the questions that were clamoring for answers. I heard the distinctive rings, two shorts and a long, and then she picked up. As usual, she was thrilled to hear from me, and after a few minutes of casual talk, I said, "Mother, there's something I need to ask you."

"What is it?" I could hear the concern in her voice.

"I have some questions about Daddy, about his nervous breakdown and the time he spent in mental hospitals."

There was silence on the other end of the phone, and finally she said, with genuine shock in her voice, "I had no idea you knew about that!" Her defense mechanisms were so effective that, at least in her mind, they could not only repress her own painful memories but mine as well.

Staying calm, my own default mode when scared or upset, I said, "Mother, I was nine years old. I could see him falling apart. I was there when those men came to the house and took him away in an ambulance. You brought me and Carol to visit him in the hospital in Birmingham. How could I not remember?"

She didn't deny what I was saying. My mother was not devious or intentionally false. She just was not conscious of the psychological forces that shielded her from painful truths. Thinking back on those silent years, she recalled, "I agonized about whether I should tell you girls about your father's mental illness."

She told me that one summer a few years after Daddy died, she was living in a dormitory at Indiana University in Bloomington, taking courses toward a master's degree to enhance her teaching credentials. While she was away at the university, my sister and I stayed home in Evansville, cared for by our grandmother. During her weeks at the university, Mother became friendly with a Catholic nun who was living down the hall from her in the dorm. One day she confided in her new friend. "There's something that has really been bothering me," she said. "A few months before my husband died, he had a nervous breakdown and was committed to an institution. My daughters were very young at the time, and lately I've been wondering if I should tell them about their father's mental illness."

The nun was quiet for a long time and then said, "You should pray about this. God will help you decide what is best."

I don't know if she ever received an answer to this prayer. I only know that once she was back home and busy with all the tasks of daily life, she never got around to talking with me or Carol about our father's illness.

After that phone call, Mother and I agreed that we should continue to talk, and the opportunity for these conversations soon arose. On June 22, 1971, our third wedding anniversary, Frank and I moved into our new home—a beautiful but dirty and run-down brownstone in the Park Slope section of Brooklyn.

We both had full-time jobs, and even though we worked on the house in the evenings and on weekends, we soon realized that we needed help. Mother was sixty years old at the time, still a strong and eager worker. We decided to invite her to visit for a couple of weeks to see our new neighborhood and wage war against the layers of dirt that had accumulated over many years of neglect.

The days were long at that time of year. I remember one evening when Mother and I were sitting in the dining room after dinner, looking out at the oak tree in front of the house. It was a young tree then, its crown barely reaching up to the third-floor window. Taking a deep breath, I turned to Mother and said, "I need to ask some more questions about Daddy's illness."

Both of us stared out the window at the tree, our eyes seldom making contact. We had been putting off this conversation for so long. The details of what we said are lost in the mists of memory. I do remember that I asked her if she ever sought professional help to sort out her own feelings about Daddy's illness and death. "Oh, yes," she said. "I talked with a psychiatrist." She paused. "It didn't help."

"How many times did you go?" I asked. "Once." I smiled and shook my head. "You know, if you want to make any progress, you have to go more than once." This was so typical of my mother. Trying to make complicated things simple, expecting to deal with her grief and confusion in one tidy session. No wonder she never talked with me about Daddy's illness after we left Alabama. In her mind, that was all in the past, neatly filed away in a drawer labeled "Do not open."

There was another question that had been hovering around the edges of my consciousness since that phone call a few weeks ago. My father died only a few days after being admitted to Bryce Hospital. What if he didn't really die of a heart attack? What if he took his own life? Taking a deep breath, I asked whether he had committed suicide. Mother's reply came quickly and with certitude. "Oh, no. He died of a massive heart attack." She had a knack for repressing unpleasant or frightening things, but she wasn't a liar. I knew she was telling me the truth.

By the time Mother flew back to Indiana about a week later, I had answers to some of my questions. But so many things were still unexplained. Gradually, working with several therapists over many years, it became easier for me to think and talk about my father. My stomach didn't feel quite so tight. My voice didn't sound quite so remote when I got up the courage to talk about what had happened.

When I was in my forties, I began to focus more often on the positive memories, the kind of father he had been before he got sick. I talked with Mother about this, and a few weeks later, a large envelope arrived in the mail. "I thought you might be interested in reading some of Daddy's letters," she said the next time we talked. "They can tell you a lot about who your father was."

These letters were a revelation. I had always thought of my father as so quiet compared with my talkative mother. He never told us much about what he was thinking. In the letters he was like a different person, so open in expressing his thoughts and feelings.

But after reading all the letters in the package, I still had questions. What had my father's life been like during the three months he spent in mental institutions before he died? Who were his doctors and caregivers? What kind of treatments did he receive, and how did he respond? Behind those locked doors, what thoughts went through his mind?

~

Reading through the memorabilia in the scrapbook nearly fifty years later, I was actively searching for answers to these questions. Two typed letters captured my attention. The first was on letterhead stationery of the Frank Kay Clinic in Birmingham and signed by Dr. John Elmore, the psychiatrist who treated my father when he was a patient at Jefferson-Hillman Hospital. The second was also typed, this one on a piece of stationery with a small picture of Jesus in the upper left corner, and signed by Rev. Otis Daniel Thomas, a Methodist minister and the chaplain of Bryce Hospital in Tuscaloosa.

The letter from Dr. Elmore was addressed to my mother and dated July 8, 1954, only two days after my father died. It began:

> A Mr. McKee telephoned today to inform me of your husband's unexpected death. We were all quite unprepared for such saddening news of your bereavement and wish that we could adequately express to you and your family our feelings of regret and sympathy.

He thanked my mother for her "unusual helpfulness in planning together for your husband" and went on to say, "I regret that our plans have had such an untimely interruption, but we can take comfort in knowing that everything possible had been done for him."

Well, there it is. Confirmation of my childhood recollection that my father's psychiatrist had been instrumental in having him transferred to the state hospital. In his professional judgment, my father would never again be well enough to return home and resume a normal life.

Who was this Dr. Elmore, the man who could predict my father's future? A quick internet search revealed the basics. He was born and educated in Alabama, attended Tulane Medical School in New Orleans, graduating in 1945, and completed residencies in psychiatry at the New York State Psychiatric Institute and the Bellevue Psychiatric Hospital, both in New York City. In 1951, he accepted a position at the Kay Clinic and worked there until his retirement in 1989. He was well respected in his profession, serving as professor of psychiatry at several colleges and as a member and officer of many professional organizations. He died on February 21, 2014, at the age of ninety-one. In 2016, a large gift to the University of Alabama from the estate of Dr. Elmore and his first wife created three endowed professorships. One of these went to Dr. Kim

Caldwell, an outstanding young female professor of cell and molecular biology. Daddy would have liked that, I thought. Dr. Elmore's generous legacy went to support the department he had served, the place where his career as a professor of botany had begun—and ended.

Reading Dr. Elmore's obituary, I felt consoled by these details of his life and career. Though the doctor was a native of the South, he had done his specialty training in New York City. As a New York snob about all things medical, I found that reassuring. I was impressed to read about his long and distinguished career. And I found it touching that, through his estate, he was supporting outstanding young professors at the university where my father had worked.

But one thing really shocked me. He was so young! Fourteen years younger than my father, who himself was only forty-five. When this man made an iron-clad pronouncement that my father would never recover and recommended the transfer to the state hospital, he was only thirty-one years old. He had been practicing psychiatry for only three years. How can a person that young and inexperienced be so sure of what the future will hold?

The other typed letter, the one from the chaplain of Bryce Hospital, was also dated July 8 and addressed to my mother. The letter began:

> We here at the hospital realize the great sorrow which you and other members of your family are experiencing due to the death of your husband, Dr. Bertice Clarence Williams, who passed away here July 6, 1954. This letter will let you know those of us who have known and tried to minister to your husband during his hospital illness are thinking of you at this time.

In closing, the chaplain wrote the kind of words you expect to read in a condolence letter from a minister: "We know God has never failed us in trying times, and we commend His love to you, and extend a loving hand of sympathy and understanding." He enclosed a small printed pamphlet entitled "The God of All Comfort" by Keith L. Brooks, D.D.

My initial reaction to this letter was anger. I assumed this was a form letter sent out on a fairly regular basis to the families of patients who died at Bryce. If there was a God, it certainly seemed to me that He had failed my father and the rest of our family. How could this man claim to understand what we were going through? Who did he think he was?

A quick internet search helped me to answer that question, and my anger began to soften. His obituary revealed that Otis Daniel Thomas had lived a long and fruitful life. Born in Alabama, he received his master of theology degree from Southern Methodist University in Dallas and, later, a master's degree in sociology from the University of Alabama. He died in June 2003, at the age of 104, less than two months before my mother passed away. When he died, he was the oldest person in the Alabama retirement system and one of the four oldest Methodist ministers in the entire country.

I was intrigued to learn that he had been the first chaplain of Bryce Hospital, serving there from 1951 to 1965. The obituary mentioned that, late in his life, he had published a book about his experiences at Bryce, *Through These Eyes: My Ministry to the Mentally Ill*. Knowing that he would have been working there when my father was a patient, I ordered a copy of this book through a used-book seller.

While waiting for the book to arrive, I scoured the internet to learn what I could about Bryce Hospital. When it opened in 1861, the Alabama State Hospital for the Insane was the most progressive and humane institution of its kind in the United States. Inspired by the social reformers Dorothea Dix and Thomas Kirkbride, the hospital's philosophy was to treat patients with kindness and respect at all times, allowing most of them to move freely on the beautiful two-thousand-acre campus that included a billiards room, tennis court, library, and chapel. The original Italianate building included three wings and featured a front entrance with impressive columns and a circular courtyard complete with fountain. The building was not only beautiful but also functional—the first large structure in Alabama to have central heat and gas lighting. In 1865, during the Civil War, the university, located nearby, was burned to the ground by Union troops, but the hospital was not touched.

Dr. Peter Bryce served for twenty-seven years as the first superintendent of this state-of-the-art mental hospital. Trained in Europe in the latest, most humane methods, he had been recommended to the board by Dix herself. Under his leadership, the institution was like a small city, with patients growing much of their own food and publishing a newspaper entitled *The Meteor*. The institution was renamed in his honor around the turn of the twentieth century.

By the time Reverend Thomas came to work there in 1951, things had deteriorated badly. Dorothea Dix would have been horrified to see this distortion of her dream. The place was terribly overcrowded. In a facility built to house 250, nearly five thousand patients were served by a meager staff—seven doctors, one dentist, and eight registered nurses. During the 1950s, the amount of funding for each patient's care was only two dollars a day, increasing to three dollars in the 1960s. The conditions at Bryce were often compared to those at a concentration camp.

As Thomas describes it in his memoir, his first day as chaplain was a fitting introduction to these horrific conditions. It began at 8 a.m., when he attended the daily staff meeting in the office of the hospital's superintendent, Dr. James Sidney Tarwater. One of the doctors reported the death of a seventy-four-year-old patient after a shock treatment. The doctor surmised, "It must have been caused by a weak heart." Another doctor reported an attempted suicide by a woman who had cut her neck with a broken razor blade. Yet another said that one of his patients, an elderly man, was found dead in his bed that morning, apparently of natural causes. He had been a patient at Bryce for sixty years. No relatives could be located, so he would be buried in one of the four cemeteries on the hospital grounds. Clearly, death was not an unusual occurrence at Bryce Hospital.

I was especially struck by the details of the first case of the day, the death following a shock treatment of a patient with a "weak heart." My father also had a weak heart as a result of having had rheumatic fever as a child.

In the 1950s, before psychotropic drugs like Thorazine became widespread, electroconvulsive therapy (ECT) was the primary method for treating psychosis. Chaplain Thomas was appalled by the severity of these treatments, which he described in minute detail in the second chapter of his book.

At Bryce, ECT was usually given three times a week for a total of ten treatments. The shock was so severe that it could cause convulsions, sometimes even resulting in broken bones. To prevent that, the patient was given medication beforehand to reduce the spasms, but this sometimes resulted in a short period when he or she could not breathe, a terrifying sensation. During the treatment, the patient lay on a padded table, held down by three nurse's aides. A registered nurse would place the electrodes on the patient's head, and a physician would open a circuit to send an electrical charge through the patient's brain; the usual protocol was 120 volts for 3/8 of a second. The patient would then be put on a stretcher and carried to a nearby ward to be monitored for the rest of the day. Some patients did experience temporary relief of symptoms as a result of these treatments, but the side effects were severe—memory loss, confusion, and a blank facial expression that lasted for hours after the treatment.

Writing years later, in the mid-1990s, Thomas explains that ECT was no longer used at Bryce, but in extreme cases, milder versions of these treatments would be administered as a last resort—and only after approval by a committee of experts—at a regional medical center. The side effects of these treatments were less extreme, and patients were able to walk soon after the treatment.

From my earliest memories of my father's illness, I knew that he received shock treatments both at the private hospital and at Bryce. I remember my mother telling me that during his time in the hospital he would sometimes become almost catatonic, and the shock treatments seemed to bring him back to reality. But now I wonder how strong these treatments had been. What precautions would have been taken if a patient was known to have a weak heart? When Dr. Elmore tried to console my mother by saying "everything possible had been done for him," I wonder what this really meant. Maybe, instead, "everything possible had been done *to* him."

Reading Thomas's book, I felt sick to learn about the institution where my father spent his last days. There were almost a hundred wards at Bryce, and during his orientation period, Thomas had visited all of them. The conditions he observed were abysmal:

> I remembered the ugly walls, dark gray throughout most of the hospital, except where the plaster had fallen off and been replaced with a rough patch of lighter gray. There were no pictures on the walls and no curtains at the windows. Dark brown benches lined the walls. All the wards looked much alike, bleak and barren. A peculiar stench like none I had ever known had penetrated my nostrils on several of the wards.

With no training in ministering to the mentally ill, Thomas accepted this job only because he had not been reappointed as the minister of his church in Tuscaloosa. In his memoir, he explains that in one of his sermons he made the mistake of referring to Adolf Hitler in connection with Jesus's command "to love our enemies and pray for those who despitefully use us." That evening, the church board met to discuss the situation, and at the next annual Methodist conference, he learned that he was to be transferred to a church 150 miles away. He decided not to accept that appointment, and after a period of financial insecurity, he reluctantly accepted the position of chaplain at Bryce Hospital. Still, once there, he came to see this as his life's work and left the hospital after fourteen years only because he had reached the mandatory retirement age. Looking back on his career, he writes:

> The patients there—my charges, sometimes my friends—rewarded my ministry to them with such responses as they were able to give: occasionally scornful, frequently loving, usually candid, but always giving me a sense that I was exactly where God wanted me to be.

Thomas describes his interactions with many of the patients and details the conditions on the wards, areas in varying stages of filth and neglect. In one chapter, he describes a foray into the locked area known as the bull pen, where some of the men were allowed to go for outdoor exercise. Enclosed by a nine-foot-high concrete wall, this huge yard was barren of vegetation except for several tall trees. Men were milling about or engaged in a variety of bizarre activities—throwing an invisible baseball; claiming to be Prince Edward, the king of the world; endlessly circling one of the trees; lying spread-eagled on the ground; standing in a far corner masturbating. As he looked out over the masses of men in the bull pen, Thomas was reminded of cattle in a stockyard or lions in a zoo, "the desperate pacing of creatures wanting to be free—free from what? Who could say? Was it to be free from locked doors and barred windows? Or free from haunting fears and guilt feelings?"

It is difficult to picture my gentle, dignified father in a place like this. Perhaps his death was a blessing.

~

After writing these words, I sat at my computer staring at the tree outside my window. It was only September, but already a few leaves were beginning to turn. Looking back at the computer screen, I realized that, finally, I had faced the horror of my father's last days. But I didn't feel relieved or enlightened or even emotional. I felt detached, dissociated. I simply could not allow myself to feel that much pain.

Hoping for an answer, for some kind of resolution, I opened the scrapbook again. My eyes fell on a page unlike any of the others. Nothing was pasted on this page. Instead, my mother, in her beautiful schoolteacher handwriting, had copied three quotations "from Bert's notebooks."

The first was a line from "The Old Astronomer," a poem by Sarah Williams, published in the 1860s:

> I have loved the stars too truly to be fearful of the night.

The second was from Etienne Gilson, a French philosopher. In March 1940, he delivered a series of lectures at Indiana University in Bloomington. Audiences of around a thousand people attended these lectures, and my father must have been among them since he was a student there at the time, finishing coursework for his master's degree in botany. He was struck by Gilson's words and copied them into his notebook:

> We are alone in death—we often find God in death.

The third quotation was the most meaningful for me because these are my father's own words. In a letter to his Aunt Lydia, also from March 1940, he wrote:

> The anticipation of my own inevitable death is not unpleasant when I reflect that I will then be with God and at peace spiritually and alive physically in the beautiful plants which I love. In some very real senses life is harder than death. Yet life can be very beautiful.

Sitting at my kitchen table in Plainfield, I realize that, like me, my mother must have been searching for answers. Unable to express her grief, her anger, her confusion, she looked to my father's writings for some resolution, some hint of an explanation, some words of comfort. I suppose that's what I am doing as well. Examining the evidence, trying to make things add up, hoping at last to move beyond grief and guilt and fear.

19

Letters from the Psych Ward

It was Thanksgiving Day, 2020, but it didn't feel like a holiday. Since March 15, Frank, and I had been living at our country home in Plainfield, Massachusetts, trying to avoid the deadly new coronavirus. In November, we drove to Brooklyn to spend a few days in our brownstone but were planning to head back to Plainfield later in the day.

Before we left the house, I hoped to find some family documents I needed for my memoir in progress, including the baby book my mother kept during my first year of life. Opening the doors of the linen closet in our bedroom, I spotted a shoebox on the top shelf labeled "Important Family Papers." Wondering what might be inside, I opened the box and saw a pile of old letters, some in their original envelopes, a few black-and-white photos, and some scraps of yellowed paper. As I sifted through the contents, a small envelope caught my eye. It bore a three-cent stamp with the image of Thomas Jefferson and was addressed to my mother, "Mrs. Bert C. Williams." The handwriting was one I knew well—my father's neat, legible script. Scanning the date on the postmark, my heart stopped. "May 18, 1954." My father had written this letter from Jefferson-Hillman Hospital in Birmingham.

Quickly, I scanned the other papers. There was another letter to my mother from the hospital, this one postmarked June 3, 1954, just a month before he died. These were letters my mother had saved but hadn't included in the scrapbook she compiled to document her husband's final year. These were letters he had written from the psych ward. I stood there in shock.

By this time, I was steeped in the details of that year, having processed everything in the big scrapbook. Finally, in my mid-seventies, I had forced myself to think and write about my father's breakdown. But I was still not ready to face what frightened me most—an accounting of what he was thinking and feeling during the months he spent alone at Jefferson-Hillman and then at Bryce Hospital before his sudden death in July. Here, in a random pile of old papers, were possible clues to the man my father had become after he fell apart so suddenly in March of 1954, a month before my ninth birthday.

Scanning the rest of the items in the box, I pulled out a few other things—a yellowed clipping from the New York Times dated November 25, 1951, entitled "Using Shock Therapy: Present Methods of Applying Treatments Questioned," an old postcard with a picture of Jefferson-Hillman Hospital in Birmingham, some notes my father himself had written about the committee meeting where he became violent and had to be removed, several other letters he wrote to my mother during his hospitalization, an undated letter to his psychiatrist in Birmingham, and finally a large sheet of paper with the corner ripped off containing penciled notes in my mother's handwriting.

Part of me didn't even want to touch these papers, fearing they might burn my fingers. But I also couldn't pretend that I hadn't found them. Without thinking, I grabbed a used manila folder from another pile, put the papers inside, and stuck it in my black shoulder bag. I can't face this now, I told myself. Reading these things will have to wait.

My mind was a blur as I finished packing for the trip north. About an hour into the drive, I said to Frank, "I can't believe what I found in the bedroom closet. Some letters my father wrote to my mother during his time in the mental hospital. They were postmarked in May and June

1954, just weeks before he died." My voice sounded flat, uninflected with any emotion. That period had always been a blank space in my mind, something I trained myself not to think about. Frank didn't say a word. He just kept driving. But I could tell he understood how frightened I was by these new discoveries.

About two hours north of the city, we stopped off in Connecticut to share Thanksgiving dinner with my sister and her husband, Bob. Fearing that one of us might be harboring the virus, we were afraid to hug or even touch one another. We had been duly warned about the dangers of gathering inside, so we ate on TV tables on the front porch. The weather was unexpectedly warm, the turkey and dressing were delicious, and it felt almost normal to talk with Carol and Bob and to greet a few neighbors passing by on the sidewalk. As we were leaving, I motioned my sister aside and told her what I had found in the closet. Her eyes widened in surprise. I could see she was as scared as I was. "This is going to take a while for me to face," I told her.

~

Once Frank and I were back in Plainfield, weeks passed before I forced myself to open the folder holding my father's letters and the other papers related to his breakdown. Finally, one Saturday afternoon in January, I took the folder from my bag, grabbed my reading glasses, and settled down on the couch in the living room. Reading the first letter, I recognized the voice I remembered from my childhood: calm, rational, polite, ever the scientist. Feeling relieved—he sounds so sane, I thought—I began to read aloud to Frank, who was sitting across the room in the recliner. Frank never met my father, but over the years he has come to know and admire him from what others have said. When I finished reading everything in the folder, Frank didn't say anything. I don't think he knew what to say, and I was actually grateful for his silence. I didn't need commentary or analysis, just acceptance of my quest to understand. "That was hard," I said, putting everything back in the folder and setting it aside.

Months went by, and the folder, now stored in a bluish-green plastic envelope, sat untouched on top of the filing cabinet in the bedroom. Some days, I checked to make sure it was still there. Reflecting on my reluctance to open this envelope, I decided I must be experiencing what psychologists call an approach/avoidance conflict. Part of me was driven to keep following every lead, to trace every clue, to document everything related to my father's illness and death. Another part was terrified of what I might discover about a time that was never discussed, a time I never expected to learn about, a time that still terrified me nearly seventy years later.

~

The weeks came and went. The snow melted on the hills outside my window, and the barren trees began to turn green. We were still isolating in the country, but in early March, Frank drove to Brooklyn for a few days to take care of some business matters. Sitting alone in the Plainfield house, drinking my morning coffee, I decided it was time to take a closer look at those letters. I removed the folder from the plastic envelope and put it on the table beside the wood stove. After getting another cup of coffee, I sat down and began to read, looking for clues.

This time, as I opened the folder, I felt a little calmer, a little more detached, like a scholar trying to answer a research question. That's it, I told myself, I will approach the contents of this folder like one of my oral history projects, reading through the transcripts again and again, looking for recurring themes, searching for meaning. I started by arranging the papers in chronological order.

The first item was a three-by-five-inch piece of paper with a typed message written before the committee meeting on March 26.

> Bert, in connection with the "no-comment" directive you carry with you this afternoon:
>
> There will doubtless be submitted to your committee some suggested "COMMITTEE REPORTS" for ~~voting~~ approval by all members. Will it not be appropriate for you to make sure that any controversial "committee report" carry this statement that of the Biology Dept's action (if you <u>abstain</u> in our behalf, that will be an important part of the record for our purposes).

The note is initialed in pencil "EGP" in a script that does not appear to be my father's. The reverse side of the note has a comment written in ink in my father's hand:

> He had been sickened by the rumor he had heard of the tactics the Dean was using to gain control of his faculty.

Reading this cryptic note, I noticed that my hands were trembling. I was beginning to lose any scholarly detachment I had summoned up. I knew my father's breakdown had happened at an important meeting. He had been asked to represent the biology department on the University Committee on Nuclear Studies, a logical choice because of the summers he had spent doing research at Oak Ridge. Mother told me that serving on this committee had been very stressful for him, a man who could not tolerate open expressions of anger or conflict—from himself or anyone else. He had been dreading this meeting, which took place on March 26, 1954, a Friday.

Re-reading this little scrap of paper, I was puzzled. My father often typed his notes. I don't know if this one was typed by someone else, someone whose initials were EGP, or if he typed it himself and then initialed it as EGP in a different-looking handwriting. The handwritten note on the back was definitely my father's because the capital D in "Dean" is unmistakably his. The rest of the handwriting does not resemble his, perhaps a sign of his impending breakdown. In any case, I wonder why he referred to himself in the third person. And what, in his view, the dean had done that was so sickening.

I found the next document even more puzzling—a numbered list written in pencil in my father's neat, legible script on lined notebook paper. The heading reads: "1:30 AM 3-27-54." I'm shocked. My father must have written this just a few hours after he became violent and had to be forcibly removed from the meeting. Like a scientist noting the sequence of an experiment in his lab notebook, he recorded his version of the events at the meeting, even including the meeting's time ("4 PM, March 26, 1954") and location ("101C Morgan Hall"). Reading my father's report, I am mystified.

1. We were reminded that news reporters were not present.
2. Later the Chairman mentioned that some of us might not be free to talk.
3. I mentioned said that all I could say was "no comment," and asked if I should stay as an observer or not.
4. I was asked to stay.
5. The committee was about to vote on something (no record was kept while I was there) when it was mentioned that Mr. Williams was not a member of the committee since he could not participate.
6. This was about 5 PM, and I felt that if I was not a member of that committee any longer perhaps I should leave.

7. I asked again if I should stay—especially since it had been stated that I was not a member of the committee any longer.

8. Mr. P said that "perhaps Mr. Williams would be more comfortable elsewhere."

9. Naturally I left [note: some words have been erased here; the original sentence, with some words still faintly visible, ending with "walked out."]

10. The meeting broke up soon after this, apparently.

11. About 9 PM the chair called to report to me that the action of his committee would allow the Dean to proceed as he wished in the faculty meeting today.

12. Two other members of his comm. called to apologize to me—though I'm not sure why.

For me, these notes raise more questions than they answer. What really happened in 101C Morgan Hall? What mental gymnastics were going on in my father's mind as he recorded his version of events? And the biggest question of all: Why had such a calm and rational man had a violent outburst in the middle of a university meeting?

~

As I placed these papers back in the folder, I took a few deep breaths to try to regain my composure. Part of me felt like that eight-year-old child who saw her father falling apart in front of her eyes. Part of me still felt helpless and afraid when faced with this horror. Suddenly, I realized that my hands and feet were freezing. I opened the lid of the wood stove and saw that the fire was almost out. Grabbing a poker and stirring the coals around, I watched as a few embers began to glow. As soon as I saw that beautiful orangey-red, I began to feel warmer. I added a few sticks of kindling and went to the kitchen to get another cup of coffee. Once I was back in the living room, I sat down to examine the next item.

It was a postcard mailed from Birmingham on March 31, 1954. On the front was a picture of an impressive sixteen-story building, the Jefferson-Hillman Hospital where my father had been taken by ambulance on March 27. A notation on the back explained that it was affiliated with the University of Alabama in Tuscaloosa and was regarded as a "monument to medical advancement." The card contains a message from Daddy's brother Dwight, who had flown from Indianapolis to Birmingham on March 30 to support my mother and assess the situation.

He wrote this card from his brother's hospital room to his parents in Indiana.

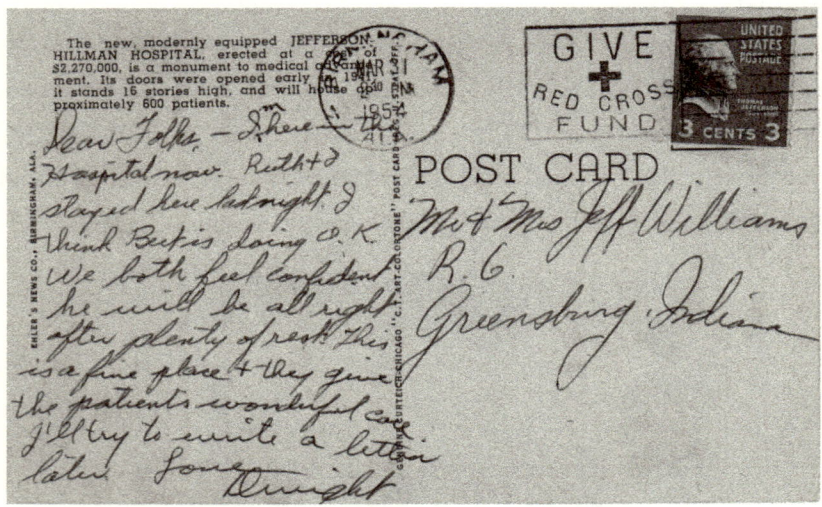

With Daddy in the hospital in Birmingham, the rest of us tried to resume life as usual. Granny was there to help with the housework and cooking, and Mother had her driver's license now, so she was able to drive Carol and me to school. I continued with my ballet classes and got to dance in the spring recital. Wearing the beautiful costume Granny had sewn for me, I danced on my toes in my pink satin pointe shoes as my long paisley skirt swirled around my legs. I remember feeling strangely elated during the performance, but once I left the stage, I didn't feel anything. I was numb with grief and anxiety.

Despite all the stress and uncertainty Mother was experiencing, she made plans to celebrate my ninth birthday in her usual style with a party in our back yard. All of my friends were there, but it just didn't feel the same without Daddy there to take pictures and eat a big slice of cake.

~

The period between the birthday party and the morning in July when Dr. Walker came to tell us that Daddy had died had always been a blank space in my mind. And now, almost seventy years later, here were these letters he had written during that time. Part of me was eager to fill in some of the blanks, but another part dreaded what I might learn about his state of mind.

Adding a few more logs to the fire, I picked up the next item in the stack of papers—a letter my father had written on May 8, 1954. Opening the envelope, I was impressed by the heavy stationery with its bold sans-serif heading announcing "Jefferson-Hillman Hospital, Department of the University of Alabama."

The letter is addressed to "Dearest Ruth & Family" and is written in the voice I remember from my childhood. "Many thanks for the letters and for the announcement of the DePauw Comm. Sounds like Becky had a wonderful party. I will get her something when I get home. Like that picture also, very much!"

These don't sound like the words of a mad man. Mother must have sent him a clipping about the commencement ceremony at his alma mater, DePauw University, and mentioned my birthday party on May 3. The picture probably refers to a drawing that Carol or I made for him, which Mother included with her letter.

Although my father had been in the hospital for more than a month, he was clearly aware of events in the outside world. "I haven't forgotten that tomorrow is Mother's Day. Let's do something nice for your Mother." How to reconcile this wish to celebrate my grandmother with the violent scene that happened a few weeks earlier in the dining room? Looking back on all of this, I realize that my father must have been compartmentalizing any negative or angry emotions—walling them off from his conscious awareness. Something about the controversies surfacing on the Committee on Nuclear Studies caused a system failure, allowing these dangerous emotions to escape.

Later in the letter, he mentions the shock treatments he had been receiving, which he refers to as "shots." "One of the things the 'shots' do for me is cause me to forget just about everything. Will have you explain a lot of things too me when I get home." Thank heavens the treatments didn't cause him to forget how to write, the way he had used since boyhood to make meaning of his world and communicate with others (the only slip I see in this letter is writing "too me" instead of "to me"). For my father—and for me in my later life—getting thoughts down on paper has always had a calming effect. In the letters he wrote from the secure environment of his hospital room, he could exercise a measure of control that had eluded him in the heated atmosphere of Morgan Hall.

The main thing on his mind was coming home. "Sure will be happy to see all of you again. I love all of you so much!" Later, he elaborates, "I'm going to talk to Dr. Elmore this PM and find out when I can be home—the earliest possible time. So I may be home and see you before you get this letter—tomorrow afternoon."

I realize this was wishful thinking. But given the calm, reasonable tone of his letter, it doesn't seem unrealistic to believe that he could return to live with us at 89 Cedar Crest before too many more weeks. As if to reinforce this thought, he ends with a postscript: "P.S. Don't worry about me. I'm sure I will be all right! And will be home soon. Thanks for the lovely letters! And pictures, etc."

My first response on reading this letter was relief. He sounds so much like the Daddy I remember from my childhood, always so polite, always thinking of others. But on later reflection, I wonder if his extreme politeness, his constant concern for others might have been factors in his breakdown. What a strain it must have been to keep up this polite façade even when things were going badly in his life, even when he was trapped in a hospital room.

Searching my memory for clues to his illness, I remember a few things that didn't quite fit the image he tried so hard to project to the world—and to himself. One of these clues, seemingly a small thing, looms large in my memory. Whenever we were in the car with Daddy, even for daily errands like picking up a prescription at the drug store or shopping for groceries, he always drove into the parking lot through the exit and then, after the errand was completed, drove out through the entrance. Even as a young child, I noticed this and sensed it was a subtle sign of rebellion against conformity, a silent protest against the strictures of society, spoken and unspoken, that circumscribed every aspect of his life.

~

Glancing at my watch, I was surprised to see that almost two hours had passed since I first opened the folder. Now that it was open, I didn't want to close it. There was an immediacy in these pieces from the past, as if my father were speaking to me directly.

The next letter was written in pencil on two small lined sheets and dated "May 14, 1954," a Friday. Addressed to "Dearest Folks," it begins in a style that is typical of the father I remember—upbeat, trying to make the best of every situation, even the serious side effects of the shock treatments he has been receiving. "This is a most interesting experience (amnesia). I hope to be home soon and I hope never (!) to have a recurrence. I hope it does not inconvenience us too much!" In this letter, as in daily life, my father puts the needs of others before his own needs, careful to present a calm and reasonable face to the world. He continues, "Do not think I will need to take too many shots." And then he clarifies and emphasizes, "too many more shots."

He continues in a positive vein, talking about the "beautiful letters & cards" he has been receiving from friends and family and the interesting people he is meeting on the ward, "all kinds," "old & young," including "Emmett, who plans to come to the university this fall." Reading the letter now, I wonder if Emmett was a fellow patient or perhaps a young volunteer on a summer internship. Either way, it must have been painful for a man who was used to being respected as a professor, not seen as just another mental patient.

In these letters, my father's mind is never far from the university. He mentions that he recently told the chair of the biology department, Dr. Walker, that he would be ready to teach in the upcoming summer or fall term. He even explained to his boss that "this experience at Jeff-Hill Hosp. would be of some value in teaching biology, especially to pre-meds." In this letter, he seems almost desperate to appear normal to those in the outside world, as if his experiences in the psych ward were just another experiment he chose to conduct.

Later in the letter, he gives more details about the "shot," the shock treatment, he had that very day. It intrigues me that he consistently refers to the shock treatments as "shots." As a young man growing up on a farm, he used a rifle for hunting, and as a college student, he won a medal for "shooting from a prone position." Now, he has become the target; he is the one getting shot.

> The shot that I had this AM was different than any I have had before and I woke up from it with a more detached feeling, but have had breakfast & have just now finished lunch and am feeling almost normal. I sure hope to get home before too long and to make myself useful and worthwhile.

Folding the letter to place it back in the folder, I wipe away the tears. My poor, dear father. He is trying so hard to be brave. My heart aches to think of him locked in this hospital against his will, struggling to regain his familiar persona and get his life back. Everything he had done in his life up to this point had been an attempt to make himself "useful and worthwhile." The diligent boy who worked like a man around the farm, the high school student who studied so hard that he earned a merit scholarship to DePauw University, and the high school teacher who went on to get a PhD so he could become a college professor.

I turn my attention to the next letter in the sequence. This one is in its original envelope. Holding it in my hands, I feel strangely comforted, knowing that my father and my mother also held it so many years ago. As I run my fingers over the paper, it feels slightly rippled, like the ocean on a calm day. It is addressed to "Mrs. Bert C. Williams" with the return address partly torn off; my mother must have ripped open the left side of the envelope to retrieve the letter inside. Enough is left for me to fill in the gaps:

> Bert C. Williams
> Jeff. Hill. Hosp.
> Room # 1156
> Birmingham, Ala.

The postmark is clearly legible and dated "May 18, 1954, 6 PM." I touch the purple three-cent stamp with the image of Thomas Jefferson, pictured in profile. I wonder if this caught my father's eye as he licked the stamp and glued it neatly in the upper right corner of the envelope. His own father, my paternal grandfather, Thomas Jefferson Williams, was named after the famous president, something I only learned recently, since he was always known as Jeff. The stamp has been cancelled by the post office and bears a printed message in all caps: "FIGHT YOUR INSECT ENEMIES." I have to smile at this public service announcement. How well I remember the war against mosquitoes that was being waged when I was a child in Alabama. Often walking home from school on a small side street, I would smell it before I could see it—a huge, white tank-like vehicle releasing an enveloping fog of DDT. Years later, thanks to the pioneering work of Rachel Carson, we learned that DDT, a toxic carcinogen, was far more dangerous than the insect enemies it was targeting along with everything else in its path.

Removing the letter, I see that it is written on the same small lined sheets as the previous one. Dated "May 18, 1954," with a parenthetical note at the top, "(Pardon pencil)," it begins, "Dearest Ruth, You will never know how beautiful you looked stepping into the room Sunday. You certainly are wonderful."

He continues by reporting how well he has been feeling. "I have had no special care or treatment of any kind for about a week. I am just resting, eating all their food, writing letters, observing the doctors, patients, practices, etc. around here. And thinking of you girls at 89 Cedar Crest."

The letter is filled with hopes and strategies for coming home for a visit. "I am feeling better, more normal all the time." He muses about how he will spend his time once he's home. "I am looking forward to having fun, mowing lawn, trimming hedge, but especially to playing with the girls."

Reading this, I can see my father in our small back yard pushing the old-fashioned lawn mower with sweat streaming down his face or standing alongside the boxwood hedge that divided one side of the yard from the other, hacking away with a heavy pair of hedge clippers. Yard work was arduous in this time before power equipment, but as a country boy, he loved to be out in nature even when it was as domesticated as our little yard. I am touched by the end of the sentence, where he says he is especially looking forward to "playing with the girls." How different our lives would have been if this dream had come true.

He is eager to return to the job he loved, teaching biology at the university, but realizes that will have to wait until the fall. "I guess I will not begin teaching again until this Sept. I am being urged to take a good rest this summer (Dr. Elmore, my mother, etc.) But I really do feel fine right now." It's intriguing that he's getting the same advice from two authority figures—his psychiatrist and his mother.

Since he won't be teaching, he is already making plans for a family trip to Indiana and Illinois to visit friends and relatives, "mentioning it tentatively in the little letters I write" to the folks at home. "We really can have a lot of fun, I am sure."

He is most excited, though, about the upcoming visit to his wife and daughters in Tuscaloosa. Figuring out how to make the 120-mile round trip is challenging. "Let us go on the bus? If you will come up we will go together on the bus and you won't need to worry about getting the Ford up here. OK? I can hardly wait."

In closing this letter of May 18, he refers to a recent news event. "How do you feel about the Supreme Court outlawing Segregation? I am in favor as you probably guessed." For my father, who was so sensitive and attuned to the suffering of others, living for ten years in the segregated South must have been terribly painful. His reference to this momentous Supreme Court decision, which had been announced the previous day, is one of many unexpected finds in this trove of letters—sparks of light in the darkness.

He ends on a note of longing. "Sweetheart, I plan on going with you on the bus Saturday. I am so happy to report that I feel so good—and without any treatment at all. See you soon with all my love—to all of you. Bert."

Reading this letter, filled with love and longing, I feel comforted, as if my father were speaking to me and telling me that everything would soon be okay.

Picking up another one of the miscellaneous papers I found on Thanksgiving Day, my feeling of comfort turns to dismay. Gone is the gracious tone I recognized in the letter of May 18. Written in pencil on a piece of lined notebook paper ripped out of a ringed binder, the kind of notebook my father always kept handy to record his musings, it begins simply: "Dr. Elmore."

This undated letter to his psychiatrist may have been a draft he wrote in his notebook intending to recopy it later. Or he may just have been thinking on paper, a practice he used throughout his life in his journals and notebooks. In the first paragraph, he mentions receiving a visit from "Ruth and Becky" the previous morning along with "Henry," Dr. Walker, the chair of the biology department. This aligns with my own memories of visiting the hospital in Birmingham—the walk down that long corridor to my father's room, the sickening hospital smell, the sinking feeling I had when I saw my strong, handsome father looking so helpless and trapped.

In this letter, he seems to be trying hard to ingratiate himself with his doctor, hoping to be allowed more privileges. "Henry (& I) think that you and the staff are doing a fine job—an excellent job!"

He mentions that he slept well the night before and feels "better than ever today." He says that his eyes are "extremely good," with "no double vision at all this morning." All of this is building up to asking for a favor—permission to drive the family car when he is cleared for a home visit. "I think I could handle the Ford now as well as I ever could. You're the Dr. so may I?"

He ends with another request, this one regarding someone named Bobby. "I would like to spend some of the time at home playing C. C.

with Bobby if you think it would do him any good and if you think he could stay away from your special equipment for a few days. OK! Then we'll pick him up Saturday—if it is ok." The letter ends there, abruptly, with no closing or signature.

I sigh and shake my head as I refold the page. Unlike the letters he mailed home to my mother, this one doesn't sound like the father I remember. Even the handwriting looks different—bolder, less controlled than his usual careful script. And the tone, trying so hard to put a good face on things, does not sound like the modest self-effacing man I knew. What does he mean when he says "no double vision this morning"? Was double vision a symptom of his illness? A side effect from the shock treatments? Or was it the way he was now experiencing the world? A double vision of reality?

Most puzzling of all is the part about Bobby. My parents often talked together about their many friends, but I never once heard them mention a person named Bobby. Who was this man? My father seems to be asking the doctor for permission to bring Bobby home with him on the upcoming visit if "he could stay away from your special equipment for a few days." Was Bobby a fellow patient? Are psych patients ever allowed to bring other patients along when they go home for a few days? What is this special equipment he mentions? I can only surmise that he's referring to the machines used for the shock treatments. And what is C. C.? Could it refer to Chinese Checkers, a game our parents often played at home and one likely to be available in the common area of a psychiatric hospital, a simple game with orderly rules, a pastime that might help to calm the nerves of anxious patients?

These notes addressed to my father's psychiatrist are strange and unsettling, scary for me to read even now. And yet, having started on this quest to understand, I can't stop myself. Removing the next piece from the folder—a yellowed sheet folded into a square with one corner ripped off—I see that the penciled notes on this page are in my mother's handwriting. Unlike my father's letters with their neat, controlled script and coherent sentences and paragraphs, this sheet contains cryptic notes jotted down in list form with disjointed words and phrases. It is not dated, and the handwriting is hurried and lacking in control. The left-hand column reads:

> Parting shot – any different
> trailing us – Jeff Hillman
> ~~Dale's~~ Restaurant – shouldn't I have known a lot of those people
> Sedation ?

The notes continue in a second column:

> Sleeplessness
>   Tues.   angry – dawn
>   Wed.   caught in a trap
> ~~Concern~~   Extreme talkativeness
> Concern for Bobby – hates women – dream – world end in 7 days
>   Candy – practicing psychology on him –
>   I wanted you to bring it in.
>   Heard Bobby other night
> Don't need any more treatments
> Bent on driving the car
> No concern for the children – more concerned about Bobby
> Hostility – mixed up biologists – psychologists
> Not nearly as well as he seemed Sunday

With trembling hands, I fold the paper back into the neat square that has held these secrets for almost seventy years. Although I have now read this page several times, with every repeated reading, I am stunned and shaken. These are clearly the notes my mother took when my father returned home for a trial visit in the middle of May. What an ordeal this must have been for her as she recorded the transformation of her kind and gentle husband into some strange and unrecognizable version of himself, so different from the familiar self he always presented to the outside world—and even now in his letters from the hospital.

To control my own anxiety, I try shifting into my comfort zone, the role of a detached researcher studying a transcript. In these hastily scribbled notes, I see certain themes and patterns. There are signs of paranoia in my father's thoughts that someone from Jeff Hillman (the hospital in Birmingham) is "trailing us." Anxiety is reflected in his "sleeplessness," his dream about the world ending in seven days, and his feeling of being "caught in a trap." I wonder about the phrase "parting shot," the first item on the list. Since he consistently refers to the shock treatments he has been receiving as "shots," maybe he mentioned receiving a "parting shot" before leaving the hospital.

Especially disturbing is his preoccupation with the mysterious Bobby, a man who "hates women" and appears, uninvited, in my father's thoughts and dreams. Mother notes that he "heard Bobby the other night" and that he seems "more concerned about Bobby," showing "no concern for the children." This was not the husband she had been married to for almost twenty years. In his place was a sleepless and talkative man, a hostile man who was "bent on driving the car" and insisting he "didn't need any more treatments." My mother assessed the situation differently. This man was "not nearly as well" as he had seemed on Sunday.

My only memory from the home visit is the scene at a rest stop, described earlier, when Daddy got into the car and started to drive away, but only as far as the nearest gas pump. I now wonder if this happened at Dale's Restaurant, a place mentioned in Mother's notes.

Once we got home to Tuscaloosa, the rest of the visit is a complete blank for me. Perhaps this was my mind's way of protecting me from memories too painful to recall.

My mother didn't have the option of forgetting. At least not yet. She had to report back to my father's young psychiatrist, Dr. John Elmore. Ever the good student, she took notes to aid her memory as she and the doctor would need to refer to them when they discussed the options for further treatment. There is no record of that conversation save for the words in the doctor's letter of condolence after my father's death thanking her for her "courtesy and unusual helpfulness in planning together for your husband."

~

By now it was after noon, but I didn't feel hungry. The fire had burned down again, and the room was getting cold. After putting a few more logs in the stove, I turned back to the folder with a feeling of resignation. I had come to the last piece in the collection that emerged so unexpectedly on Thanksgiving Day of 2020. My father's handwriting on the envelope is unmistakable. Like the other letters, it is addressed to "Mrs. Bert C. Williams," with the return address, "Jeff. Hill. Hospital, Birmingham, Ala." The first time I saw the postmark, I was stunned: "June 3, 1954, 6 PM." This letter was mailed just a month before he died, and he was still in the private hospital. I had always believed that he spent months at Bryce Hospital, the wretched state institution in Tuscaloosa where he died on July 6. The postmark on this envelope tells me his stay there was brief. I am consoled by that fact.

The letter itself is dated "June 2, 1954," and addressed to "Dearest Ruth." Although the handwriting is familiar, this letter looks different from the others. The only one written in ink, it is on unlined yellow paper, the color of a daffodil. I conclude from the date that it was written after the disturbing home visit and probably also after the decision had been made to transfer him to Bryce. However, this letter shows no traces of the angry, restless man described in Mother's notes from the visit. Instead, it speaks to me with a feeling of hope and love. "I sure am missing you & Mom and the girls and sorry that I am not with you now. I don't think it will be long, however, and please tell your Mother we will go to Indiana pretty soon—especially if she would like."

He says he would love to help out at the university in the summer and definitely plans to be in the classroom in the fall. Then he turns to events in the outside world. "Did you vote? How does the election suit you?"

As if it's an afterthought, he mentions, "I got another shot yesterday afternoon. Maybe that will be the last one. Everyone around here speaks of how well I look and act. I feel fine now. Sure will be happy to see you all—the sooner the better!" And then he continues, "Everyone who saw you when you were here tells me how sweet, young, and beautiful you are. It sure makes me happy. See you all soon. Kiss the girls for me often." He signs this letter, the last he would ever write to my mother, "All my love, Bert." This was a love letter to his wife and family—and a goodbye.

Like my mother, I scarcely ever cry, but as I refolded this letter and placed it gently back in its envelope, I could hardly see through my tears.

~

Once the letters were back in the plastic envelope, I felt sad but also relieved. I was sure this would be the last message my father wrote before his death. But a few weeks later, as I was revising what I had written so far, I opened the large plastic bin where I've been storing materials related to this project and found a page torn out of the Autumn 1953 issue of the Bulletin of the American Association of University Professors. My father had written notes in the margins. This must have been another one of the things my mother saved but didn't include in the scrapbook.

It contained a list, dated June 4, 1954, of "adjectives for hospital experience." Optimistically, he numbered the list from 1 to 10 but only filled in the first two slots: "interesting" and "profitable!" At the bottom of the page he wrote, "I feel fine now. Very, very well psychologically! & physiologically!"

He was still in the private hospital in Birmingham at this time since he wrote that Dr. MacQueen, one of the psychiatrists from the Kay Clinic in Birmingham, "came in this AM, in his wheelchair. He said he was in hospital for 600 days from 1944 to 1946." He noted that he told Dr. MacQueen he was getting homesick, and the doctor said that was a "good sign."

I learned later, from an internet search that this man, Dr. James William MacQueen, died just two months after my father. He suffered a fatal heart attack at his home in Birmingham on September 8, 1954. He was fifty-four years old. His obituary states that he had formerly been the director of Jefferson-Hillman Hospital and that he had recently "engaged in the practice of psychiatry." While working as a physician, he had also published eight mystery novels under the pen name James Edwards, including *Murder in the Surgery* (1935), which was made into a movie. He lost the use of both legs in 1946, the result of a crippling disease, and decided, against the advice of other physicians, to have both legs amputated. After the surgery, he spent twenty months in hospital, just as he had told my father.

I feel such tenderness for this doctor as I picture the scene in the hospital—the last glimpse I will ever have of my father. It comforts me to imagine these two damaged men, both of them doctors, sharing their humanity and their hopes for the future—a future that would be much shorter than either of them realized at the time.

LETTERS FROM THE PSYCH WARD

A few days after this chat with Dr. MacQueen, my father left Jefferson-Hillman for Bryce Hospital in Tuscaloosa. I am relieved that his stay there was brief. No letters from Bryce survive.

20

Double Vision

Thought while stapling a Biology-1 examination:
One's impression of reality is determined by his situation in time and space—one's impression or feeling about anything depends upon his point of view—perspective is one of the objective factors in Einstein's Relativity—it goes into his calculations to give a more authentic picture of reality—

—Quotation from a notebook my father kept in 1949

WHY DO I KEEP GETTING these messages from my father? Just when I think I've found every surviving piece of evidence, something new and unexpected emerges from the trove he left behind. The latest discovery came in January 2022, when I opened a box of memorabilia and lifted out one of my father's tiny notebooks with *1949* embossed in gold on its leather cover.

The entry that riveted my attention was the one quoted above. Sitting at his lab bench, stapling together the mimeographed pages of an upcoming exam for his Biology 1 students at the University of Alabama, he speculates about the way one's perspective can influence his perception of reality.

Maybe that was what happened in the spring of 1954. His long-held view of reality fractured, and a side of himself that he had held in check for so long burst out. After his breakdown in March, my father was indeed experiencing a kind of double vision, a symptom he mentioned in a note he wrote to his psychiatrist. I imagine he was speaking of double vision in the accepted sense of seeing two images of the same thing. But I'm wondering if he might have been suffering from another kind of double vision. Sometimes he saw the world through the eyes of Bert, the quiet, modest Daddy I remember from my childhood, the man who wrote those letters home from Jefferson-Hillman Hospital. At other times, and particularly during his catastrophic home visit in May, he seemed to be seeing through the eyes of Bobby—an angry, unpredictable man who hated women, another side of his personality that emerged in 1954. Looking back on all of this, I realize that Bobby may have been part of his persona for many years, but a side he managed to suppress until his "situation in time and space" shifted so drastically in the days before the committee meeting where everything changed.

~

Paranoid schizophrenia. This was the label affixed to my father by the medical establishment in 1954. Over the years, I have described his condition to several therapists. Most of them have questioned this diagnosis. "Sounds more like depression to me," one of them said. "I think he was bipolar," another opined. Or maybe it was just situational: "This was all brought on by stress. That committee assignment just pushed him over the edge." The experts disagree.

I wish there could be a definitive diagnosis. For me, there is comfort in calling things by their proper names. How can we hope to understand something if we don't even have the words to describe it? In my struggle to comprehend, however, there is no one correct phrase, no clear-cut category, no neat description in the Diagnostic and Statistical Manual of

Mental Disorders that can explain what happened to him. There were just too many complex forces at work inside my father.

One force was heredity. He was the oldest of six children. Three of the six showed signs of mental illness at some point in their lives. His youngest sibling, a brother, developed psychotic symptoms in mid-life. There was talk of institutionalization, but his wife insisted there must be a physical cause for his altered behavior. It turned out she was right. This man was a professional truck driver, and carbon monoxide had been leaking into the cab of his truck. When the leak was fixed, the psychotic symptoms disappeared and never recurred. Another sibling, one of my father's sisters, was treated in her later life with psychotropic medications, drugs that had not existed during my father's lifetime. She was never institutionalized and lived into her nineties, though she did suffer side effects from the powerful drugs. Given this family history, it seems likely that my father had a biological predisposition for mental illness.

Certain physical conditions may have played a role as well. Having had rheumatic fever as a child before the ready availability of antibiotics, he was left with a heart murmur. Years later, on the morning of September 14, 1953, the day he left Oak Ridge following his summer research, he had a physical exam in Knoxville. This didn't surprise me. The authorities were careful to monitor the health of everyone working at Oak Ridge, especially those working with dangerous substances like radioactive phosphorus as my father was.

What did surprise me were the detailed notes on heart disease he included in the Memoranda section of his pocket diary for 1953. Probably quoting from some source he had consulted, he writes about "fibrillation," a medical condition:

> In auricular fibrillation, which is seen esp. in the late stages of mitral stenosis, the condition occurs when the auricles and the ventricles fail to receive the normal impulses therefrom, and in turn beat irregularly.

Mitral stenosis, or narrowing, is most commonly caused by rheumatic fever. His notes about heart damage continue with this sentence:

> Ventricular fibrillation, more serious and usually fatal, follows such severe injuries as electric shock and occlusion of the main arteries of the heart.

That was the diagnosis we received on July 6. Daddy had died of "coronary occlusion" after having had multiple, powerful ECT treatments—the shots he referred to in the letters he wrote from the hospital.

These notes caused me to wonder if the doctor in Knoxville had warned my father about some heart anomalies detected during the exam. Had he learned during this physical that his heart condition was growing worse? If so, he never mentioned it to my mother. What she did know was that the university politics that surfaced in 1954 during the deliberations of the Committee on Nuclear Studies were making him extremely anxious.

I've always wondered what it was about this committee that he found so distressing. It seems likely that he had mixed feelings about the work he and others had been doing at the Oak Ridge National Laboratory in Tennessee. Although he was proud to be conducting research at such a prestigious institution, he must have been disturbed by knowing that Oak Ridge was the primary site for uranium enrichment necessary to produce the atomic bombs that killed and injured so many innocent Japanese civilians. By the spring of 1954, the country was racked with a controversy over whether or not to develop an even more powerful bomb, the hydrogen bomb. Less than a month after my father's breakdown, Robert Oppenheimer, sometimes referred to as the Father of the Atomic bomb, was being grilled in Washington about his association with members of the Communist Party as well as his opposition to developing ever more powerful atomic weapons. Ultimately, he was publicly humiliated by being deprived of his security clearance. This was the atmosphere in which the Committee on Nuclear Studies convened at the University of Alabama at the end of March.

As a scientist, my father had been thinking about atomic weapons for a long time. On February 24, 1950, he wrote in his little notebook:

> Science is international but love is even more so. Love is the medium of God's will and more powerful than the atom (or proposed H) bomb. Love does not explode like the H-bomb but is more subtle and more powerful. It is a high destiny to walk upon the earth with the love of God in one's heart, but it has been achieved by the great and good men of the ages (by Jesus Christ—by M. Gandhi) and the influence of those men and of others is still with us and lighting the way to a higher destiny for every man today and for the entire world of our time. The Hope of the World is the Love of God in the Heart of Man.

A man with these beliefs was bound to feel conflicted about working at Oak Ridge and serving on the University Committee for Nuclear Studies. But discussing these views with those who disagreed would have been painful for him. He had always been uncomfortable with any sign of anger or conflict.

Years later, my mother recounted a frightening episode from my childhood—another event that has been erased from my conscious memory. It happened in our garage in Tuscaloosa when I was about four years old. It was late afternoon, and my mother was rushing to finish the laundry before supper. With sweat dripping down her face, she was bending over our old-fashioned washing machine, taking the clean clothes out of the soapy water and running them through the wringer before dumping them into a big galvanized tub full of clean water to rinse them.

Normally I loved being part of this operation. What child doesn't like splashing around in warm soapy water? But on this day, I was not happy. I kept tugging on my mother's apron, begging her for one of the candies she kept in a jar in a kitchen cabinet. "No, Becky," she calmly explained. "That will ruin your appetite. It's almost time for supper."

I would not be satisfied. Whining became crying and then morphed into a full-fledged tantrum. I was screaming and kicking the tub of the washing machine with the sole of my sandal when my father arrived home from the university. "I had never seen Bert lose his temper," Mother told me, "but he was absolutely furious to see you so out of control. He grabbed you by the shoulders and started spanking your bottom. The more you cried, the harder he spanked. I was terrified." He simply could not tolerate seeing his own child kicking and screaming in the midst of a temper tantrum. And that caused him to lose control of his own temper.

Although I don't remember this episode, I learned my lesson well. I still have a temper. But no matter how justifiable my anger may be, I struggle to suppress it. I'm afraid of losing control, of lashing out in public—or even in private. As a child, I learned that anger is dangerous. Better to bottle it up inside than risk the punishment, even self-imposed punishment, that comes from expressing it.

Bert must have learned a similar lesson when he was a boy. "Hold your horses!" That was one of his most common expressions. Now I realize he must have been following his own advice, always holding his horses, restraining them from breaking away and running wild.

Somehow, in the runup to the fateful committee meeting, his horses were threatening to break loose. As he expressed it in the note he wrote just before the meeting, "He had been sickened by the rumor he had heard of the tactics the Dean was using to gain control of his faculty." Perhaps referring to himself in the third person was a way of distancing himself even further from the intense anger he was feeling. It was becoming almost impossible for him to hold his horses.

~

There had been some precursors to my father's psychotic break in 1954, especially when he was feeling pressure related to his academic work. The first happened during his sophomore year of college. He was taking two courses in zoology and learned, for the very first time, about Darwin's theory of evolution. These scientifically proven ideas upended his mental and religious framework so severely that he had to drop out of college for more than a year, though he eventually returned to the campus and earned his bachelor's degree in 1933.

He experienced a different response to stress in 1946 as he was preparing to defend his doctoral dissertation at Indiana University. A few days before the exam, he took my mother for a drive on the country roads around Bloomington. Suddenly the car veered out of control. Mother, who had never driven, grabbed the wheel and steered them safely onto the shoulder as the car slowly glided to a stop. Seconds later, he regained consciousness. There were no further fainting episodes, and he successfully defended his dissertation as planned. The doctor they consulted at the time labeled the attack as epilepsy though he was never treated for this condition, and it never recurred. At least in my mother's mind, this episode was a sign of Bert's vulnerability under pressure, especially pressure related to his career in academia.

As far as I know, there were no blackouts at the time of his psychotic break in 1954. Those would come later as a result of the shock treatments in the hospital. But there could be no doubt. This time, the rupture with reality was severe. This time, my father had failed to hold his horses and Bobby had escaped. He was suffering from double vision.

~

As I look out the window of my Brooklyn study, I'm surprised to see snow sifting down onto the garden. The whole world feels quieter under this blanket of white, and I too feel a sense of calm, of quietude. Despite all my searching, I haven't found answers to my questions about my father's illness—its causes or a definitive diagnosis—and I now understand that rather than finding answers, the important thing has been to face what happened, to learn as much as possible and then accept it. My understanding, still incomplete, has deepened. In this way, I continue to make meaning of my father's life. And my own.

PART IV

Efficiency says that grief should follow a road map and things should be gotten over and that then there should be that word that applies to wounds and minds both: closure. But time and pain are a more fluid, unpredictable business, expanding and contracting, closing and opening and changing. . . . [S]ometimes you revisit the past . . . to map the distance covered. There is closure and reopening and sometimes something reopens because you can bring something new to it, repair it in a new way, by understanding it in a new way. Sometimes the meaning of the beginning of the story has changed as new chapters are added.

—Rebecca Solnit, *Recollections of My Nonexistence*

21

Holding the Gate Ajar

Two years have passed since I sat in my study in Brooklyn, watching the snow falling outside the window and wondering what it all meant. Now, in the early days of 2024, I am looking out another window, this one in our living room in Massachusetts. In the distance, I see barren hills punctuated by the wintry outlines of trees closer up. Then, as dawn lights up the morning sky, the emerging blue is streaked with a tinge of pink filtering through the bare branches near the window.

My quest to get to know my father has not been quick or straightforward. However, after these intense years of searching, I have come to a different place. I wouldn't call it closure. I still grieve for what I lost by not having my father in my life as I grew older. But now I look back at the past from a new perspective.

At the beginning of a new year, I am called to go back further in time, to get to know the man who fell in love with a young woman named Ruth in the summer of 1935, a man who became my father in 1945, a man who touched the lives of many and whose memory was cherished by all who knew him. Having faced the tragedy of the past, I no longer feel bound to it as I did before. From this perspective, his illness and death are a part of his life but not the whole thing.

Clues to his identity are not hard to find. Stored in a drawer in a large filing cabinet are hundreds of letters my parents wrote when they were young. Some have had parts scissored off—the intimate sections, perhaps. Others have inevitably gotten lost or misplaced. A few of them were rescued by a good Samaritan. When my sister and I were clearing out 2719 Short Marion as Mother prepared to move to an assisted living facility in 1996, we hired a man with a truck to take some unwanted items to the dump. The next day the truck pulled up in the driveway, and the man got out. "When I tossed one of the bags into the landfill, these fell out. They look like old letters. I thought you might want to keep them."

We were so grateful to this man. These were letters that had been treasured by both of our parents, each one saved, most in their original postmarked envelopes. They had survived so many moves and life changes. Carol and I certainly didn't want to be the ones who consigned them to the landfill. Reading them now, freed from the torment I suffered in the past, I savor these glimpses into my parents' thoughts and feelings when they were young and so much in love.

The Great Depression of the 1930s runs like a river through their letters. When our parents met, both of them held teaching jobs in their hometowns in Indiana. During the Depression, when steady incomes were rare, their salaries helped to sustain everyone in their families. Because these jobs were scarce, two teachers who were married were not permitted to teach in the same school district, so even after they married in 1936, they had to live many miles apart during the school year. They didn't actually manage to live together in the same house until 1941—six years after they met and fell in love. Through all these years, letters, written almost daily, sailed back and forth between Greensburg and Evansville, sustaining and strengthening their love.

~

It all began in July 1935 in Professor John Anderssohn's Modern European History class at Indiana University in Bloomington. A tall young man with black curly hair sitting toward the back of the classroom was irresistibly drawn to a straightforward young woman sitting a few rows in front of him. In an era when female students were supposed to be seen and not heard, she was not afraid to ask a question in class or even voice an opinion.

At the next class, the young man made a point of arriving a bit later than usual and took a seat next to the woman who had attracted his attention. At the end of the class, he asked if he might walk her back to her dorm, and she said yes. Their first official date occurred two days later, on July 13. Within a week, they were deeply in love. He was twenty-six years old, and she would turn twenty-four in September.

Writing to his beloved a few months later, Bert reflects on the earliest days of their romance:

> For some unknown reason my memory takes me back to those happy days and dates we had in the summer of 1935. I think of the times we used to sit on the terrace and thrill to each other's presence. Of the nights when we sat on the bridge together and talked of "God and man and the universe." Of the beautiful moments we spent in the sunken gardens. Of the times that we sat on the steps of the field house. Always dreaming and thinking and believing. Always happy and thrilled and knowing that life together for us would be continual love and beauty.

By the time the summer school session ended in mid-August, they were unofficially engaged to be married.

Bert had been back at his family's farm in New Pennington only hours when he wrote the first of so many letters to Ruth, dated August 14, 1935. Before he met her, he was convinced he would never fall in love. All the girls he met in his rural community or even in college seemed shallow and superficial. Just weeks before meeting Ruth, he was convinced that he would need to find all his "inspiration, and contentment, and happiness" within himself. Marriage was not in the cards. Now things had shifted dramatically, and he wished he could move the clock ahead to the summer of 1936, when they would again be together at the university for summer school.

The next day, Ruth, still in Bloomington for a few more days, wrote a long letter to Bert. I recognize my mother's voice in this letter. She was never at a loss for words either in speech or writing. She begins with a litany of what she's been doing since he left the campus, not a very auspicious beginning for a love letter. Finally, on page five, she becomes more personal:

> It's that matter of "private worlds" we were talking about the first night we were up on the terrace. I liked what you said about there being no such thing between people who loved each other deeply. There shouldn't be and yet I've felt this summer that there were so many things I should have liked to discuss with you and didn't. We have so much in common and I love you so dearly that I hope you won't hesitate to hold the gate ajar. Your every thought is sacred to me. More than anything else in the world I want to know the real "you."

When she wrote this letter, she had known Bert for only a month. Over the next year, their letters would enable them to hold the gate ajar, getting to know each other deeply as they discussed so many things—especially the marvel of their having found each other, "the supreme miracle of my life," as Ruth describes it. She misses him terribly but reflects on "how much more terrible it would have been to have gone through life searching hopelessly for you with that unutterable feeling of longing stabbing at my heart."

The next day, she writes again, eight pages of flowing script overflowing with the love she felt after receiving a letter from him. "There were tears in my eyes when I finished reading it. You said so much in such little space. I keep reading it over again and again, and lines from it keep running through my mind."

In her reply, she mentions that they're both considered "serious minded" by others, and the letters show that their love is intellectual as well as emotional. Both Bert and Ruth constantly write about the books they're reading. In this, only the second letter Ruth has written to Bert, she mentions *The Fountain* by Charles Morgan, a novel he had loaned her; *Nature and Human Nature*, another of his recommendations; the novels of George Eliot and the poems of George Meredith; and a new book she just checked out from the library, *Mary Peters* by Mary Ellen Chase. In passing, she refers to conversations they had had during the summer about the ideas of Plato and Aristotle. They were awash in ideas, in literature, in love.

Ruth realizes that, because of their shared reverence for the written word, the letters they will write in the next few months will be "a means of deepening our understanding of each other so that when we meet again we shall feel much closer and love one another more than ever before." Then, Ruth, who was always so direct, mentions something that had come up during the summer. "You remember your asking me about being disillusioned in love and I remarked that it wasn't my heart but another's that was broken."

She explains that she had been engaged briefly to a man who was now a Christian minister. She never truly loved him, she writes. It was "one of those hopeless one-sided affairs," but she finally convinced herself that she could learn to love him and gave in to his entreaties. Fortunately, she eventually "came to her senses" and broke off the engagement.

She reassures Bert that "there never was any question about you. I just loved you almost from the first day I saw you. Your love has made of me a new creature, all life has taken on new meaning and I shout for joy."

Bert replies on August 16 after receiving her letter. The envelope is addressed, as so many will be, to "Miss Ruth Stamps, 112 East Iowa Street, Evansville, Indiana." Ruth has returned home and is living with her mother in a rented house in a rundown neighborhood. Soon her two brothers, Roy and Erwin (known as Erv), will also arrive to live with them, filling the small house to overflowing. Bert is thrilled with the letter he has just received. "Judging from the sample I have, your letters are going to be wonderful." He responds to her apology for writing at such length: "Don't deplore the length of your letters. The more I get the more I want—and that goes for all of you."

Like Ruth, his life has been transformed.

> I have worshiped the beautiful things of nature. I have marveled at the great minds of all times. I have wondered at the glorious spirit of youth. That I should find all these things blended into the personality and form of a beautiful woman is more than the fulfillment of my most sublime dream.

Referring to her confession of the brief engagement, he says:

> I had wondered about the broken heart. You may tell the story if you care to. It doesn't matter to me. I have infinite respect for him. He loved you. I have infinite sympathy for him. He could not win you. I am impressed more deeply with my own infinite good fortune.

What matters now, Bert writes, is their own love, which promises only to increase as they get to know each other better "through the mutual and inarticulate interplay of our spirits."

In Ruth's next letter, written on August 22, she tells the complicated story of her friendship and then her engagement to Carl. Once she starts to tell the tale, she can't seem to stop, going on for twenty-two pages. It's no surprise to me that many of her letters from fall 1935 are stamped "Postage Due 3 Cents." She explains that although she never really loved Carl, he adored her, and she had deluded herself into believing she could enjoy an adventurous life with him if they traveled to Africa to serve as Christian missionaries. At this point, she interjects, "Would you believe that the cynical, irreligious, realistic Ruth you know was ever such a silly, sentimental, misguided little girl?"

As the story winds down, she reassures Bert—and perhaps herself as well. "I think I understand all men better for having known Carl. It was a kind of fire through which I had to go, and now my soul is tempered as steel is."

Reading these old letters, I'm captivated by the story of my parents' young love. Frankly, I had been dreading this part of the project because of the sheer number of pages that had been lying undisturbed in my filing cabinet for decades—and maybe also fearing what new and unexpected revelations they might contain. For months, I had packed up the folders full of letters as I traveled from Brooklyn to Plainfield and then let them sit unread for weeks before it was time to pack them up again for the trip back to Brooklyn. Now that I've started reading, I find it hard to stop. Having faced the pain and grief of 1954, I feel myself opening to a new appreciation of the time when my parents were young and in love. Reading these old letters, I feel that I am there too, an unborn presence, standing right behind them, listening in on their conversations.

In Bert's next letter, he mentions Carl only once in passing. Instead, he focuses on the miracle of their having found each other:

> I am sure there is a powerful and irresistible force drawing us together. I simply could not help asking you to be my wife. My proposal (such as it was) was absolutely unpremeditated, although I had a feeling that I could not be with you long without doing something of the kind.

At the end of August, Ruth was in Darmstadt, a village on the outskirts of Evansville, to visit her Aunt Clara and Uncle Henry for a few days. As a girl, she had spent many summer months living on their farm, and Aunt Clara had become a kind of second mother to her. As she explained in a letter to Bert, "I love it out here in the country. So many happy childhood memories come back, and there's still a halo of glamor about the old place despite its simplicity and lack of modern conveniences."

When her mother—my granny—arrived to join the group, she brought not one but two letters from Bert that had arrived in Evansville.

Ruth was so excited that she immediately grabbed a pen and started to write back. Delayed gratification was not in her nature. If you gave her a wrapped gift, she had to open it immediately. If she received a much-anticipated letter, she would rip it open, read it quickly, and sit right down and write a reply.

She continued her letter the next day when she was back in the city. She is fascinated by Bert's ideas about God, which he had shared in his letter, but confesses that she has lost most of the Christian beliefs that sustained her in her teenage years. She tells him that she had attended Sunday school and church the previous week and was asked to give the opening prayer. "The irony of it! I hadn't prayed for so long that I found it rather difficult. If I had had courage enough, I suppose I would have refused."

While her belief in religion is waning, her dedication to political causes is increasing. She describes a labor struggle currently taking place in Indiana and adds, "Before I met you, Bert, I secretly cherished the hope of someday being a labor organizer or at least an instrument in educating the workers. Can't you just see me standing on a soapbox talking to a crowd of miners?"

I imagine that Bert could see her on that soapbox, and so can I. She wasn't shy about expressing her opinions, and she had a gift for public speaking.

In another letter to Bert, she enclosed a newspaper clipping with the headline "Legion Assails Communism in SCHOOLS OF U.S. Attacks Directed at Dr. Oxnam, President of DePauw." She thought he would be interested to learn that the president of his alma mater was being accused of inviting "radical, pacifist and communist speakers" to the university. Bert's family members, like most farmers in Indiana in the 1930s, were conservative Republicans, and Bert had obtained his teaching position partly through his father's influence as a Republican official in the township. But that didn't prevent him from falling in love with Ruth, who declares in this letter: "I'm not a communist or a 'red' but my whole being cries out against this flood of propaganda which is being directed against everyone who dares to be liberal or to do any thinking about conditions as they exist today."

She goes a step further in her next letter, where she writes, "As you know, I am an ardent socialist and therefore interested in a new social order under the democratic form of government." Reading this, I'm surprised by the strength of my mother's political convictions. I knew that FDR was her hero and that she always voted Democratic, but I didn't realize how committed she had been to socialism in her younger years. Actually, I shouldn't have been surprised. My mother never did anything halfway.

While she was preoccupied with defining her political beliefs, Bert was more concerned with articulating his thoughts on religion. Writing to Ruth in early September, he tries to express what God means to him. Unfortunately, this letter has been lost, but a sense of his ideas comes through in Ruth's reply:

> I deeply appreciate your trying to explain "God" to me,
> but your theory is beyond me I'm afraid. Your explanation
> seems simple enough but I'm not used to thinking in terms
> of physical dimensions and divine calculus. I can just
> see you tearing your hair. I've been so used to thinking
> of a "human" God that it may take some time for me to
> conceive of him as a shifting motivating center in space. I
> suppose you would say God is the controlling force back
> of the universe. Have patience with me, Dearest. I am
> eager to learn and while some of this is a bit too profound,

maybe some day you'll be able to make it clear to me. It will be a test of your ability as a teacher.

Toward the end of the letter, she teases him. "So my Darling is worried because he is less of an angel than he'd like to be." She's been reading a lot of modern books, which have helped her to understand men's emotions better. She too has been having thoughts of sex, but "of course until we are husband and wife, we must be masters of our emotions." She reassures Bert that he needn't worry that she will like his letters better than his physical presence: "I'd rather spend one hour with you than read a hundred letters. Letters have a tendency to make one seem shadowy."

Switching moods, she ends abruptly: "I'm going to a bridge party tonight so it's Adios, Sweetheart. See you in my dreams!"

I see so much of my mother in these letters—her ebullience, her sense of humor, her tendency to switch back and forth abruptly from the ridiculous to the sublime. But I'm surprised to hear her taking such a firm stand against premarital sex. In the 1960s, when I was a student at Reitz High School, where she taught history and psychology, friends would often approach me in the hall between classes and announce, "You won't believe what your mother said in class today." She often shocked her teenaged students with her progressive views on sex.

This was not the case in 1935. In her next letter to my father, she refers to Alfred Adler, the Viennese psychologist, whom she's been reading: "Dr. Adler advises against intimate relations before marriage no matter how deeply people love." This leads her to thoughts of their own marriage. Bert feels they won't be able to marry for two or three years because of their financial obligations to their families. Ruth dreads waiting so long but adds, philosophically, "Time and circumstances will probably dictate our course." Never one to stay on a negative note for long, she changes tone as she closes: "Isn't the moon beautiful these nights? Yours forever and ever. Ruth."

In her next letter, she again waxes romantic.

> The past few months I feel as though I had entered a paradise or pushed my way into some enchanted garden. And you, my dear, are the fairy prince whose kiss has transformed my mundane existence into a dream of happiness. I just hope that our romance ends as all good fairy stories do: "and the prince and princess were married and lived happily ever after."

On the back of the envelope, I see that Bert has copied a quotation from Edward Payson Roe's novel *His Sombre Rivals*: "I have a religion at last and I worship the divine nature of that complete woman."

Placing the letter back in its envelope, I breathe a sigh, knowing that their love affair will not have the fairytale ending they both dreamed of. I wish I could travel back through time to warn them. Handsome and devoted as he was, Bert was not a prince with magic powers. And Ruth was not a goddess who could become Bert's new religion but a real, flesh-and-blood woman, young and beautiful and flawed as all human beings are. Their dreams are so romantic and so unrealistic.

~

As I sit on my couch reading my parents' letters from the mid-1930s, many of the scenes play out in my mind in grainy black and white featuring Gregory Peck as Bert and Katharine Hepburn as Ruth. When I first saw the movie *To Kill a Mockingbird* in 1962, I was mesmerized. Watching Gregory Peck playing Atticus Finch was like seeing my father come back to life. And the little girl who played Scout, Atticus's daughter, looked and dressed and acted just like me when I was eight years old and growing up in Alabama. No wonder I decided to cast Gregory Peck in the role of Bert in the movie playing in my head.

His co-star in this romantic film is Katharine Hepburn. Ruth and Katharine shared the same prodigious energy, mischievous sense of humor, and exuberant enjoyment of life. I remember my mother saying with obvious pride that people often said she reminded them of Katharine Hepburn. In the mid-1950s, when she received an important civic award from the Tuscaloosa Business and Professional Women's Club, she always referred to it mistakenly as "Woman of the Year," the title of the 1942 film starring Hepburn.

I can imagine a scene from a letter Bert wrote after Ruth's twenty-fourth birthday on September 21, with Gregory Peck speaking the lines of the leading man:

> Do you feel a year older now that your birthday is past?
> Ah, yes, you said you feel younger than you did at twenty.
> I feel younger also. I feel as if I shall never grow old. Your kiss has done it.

In another scene, Hepburn, playing Ruth, stands at the front of her classroom of sixth graders. One of the little boys who sits up close to the teacher's desk announces to the rest of the class, "Miss Stamps must have gotten a letter from that boyfriend of hers yesterday." I can just see Katharine/Ruth standing at the teacher's desk, unable to suppress the joy and excitement she feels after receiving a letter from her fiancé. Writing to him the next day, she confesses, "Most of the children suspect that something has come over me. I don't think I've been cross a single time yet this semester, and for the most part the kids have been quite angelic."

Ruth, like Katharine Hepburn, had a more serious side as well. Writing a few weeks later, she comments on how her understanding of Bert increases with every letter: "We must have had much the same struggle; our efforts to build an integrated personality—to find ourselves—seem so much alike." When I was a teenager, I knew my mother was interested in psychology. I had a habit of checking out the books on her shelf, and I remember seeing authors such as Carl Rogers and Karen Horney. But I never would have guessed that as early as 1935 she was thinking about such deep psychological questions. Driven by her insatiable curiosity, she was developing an unusually sophisticated worldview for a young Midwestern schoolteacher in the mid-1930s.

She agrees with a comment Bert had made earlier about their shared commitment to the life of the mind and the need to work for the good of the larger community. "The greater mutuality, the more people have in common, the greater their chances for married happiness." It almost seems like a miracle, she writes, that they found each other.

> We have so much to be thankful for, and together we shall pay our debt of gratitude—make our contribution to the betterment and enrichment of humanity. If we did no more than prove to the world that husband and wife can

remain sweethearts to the end—that there is such a thing as fidelity, loyalty, understanding, and love—we should not have lived in vain.

My mother wrote these words nearly ninety years ago. Despite the shock and pain of Bert's last year, their love was strong and enduring as they found their own unique ways to contribute to the future.

~

In early November, Bert and Ruth managed to have a brief meeting, their first since they parted in August. Bert borrowed the family car and drove south to Versailles, Indiana (always pronounced "Ver-sales"), where he was able to visit with Ruth for an hour or so at a restaurant. She was going with friends to Cincinnati for a teachers' conference, and he arranged to have lunch with the group during their rest stop in Versailles. Frustrating as this short visit must have been, they were consoled, knowing that they would have a real visit over the Thanksgiving holiday.

Ruth wrote practically every day in November—long letters filled with news of her life and her ever-increasing love for Bert. I imagine he wrote almost as often, but not as many of his letters survive. Those that do reveal a serious and reflective man who is very much in love. In mid-November, he writes about the physical aspects of love.

> Our family at home, like yours, is not demonstrative; however, it never embarrasses me to kiss you. I have always taken life and love rather seriously. More seriously than most people. I shall never regret that fact for it has been partly responsible for my waiting for a girl whom I can love for what she really is.

Because of their financial situation, specifically the $1,000 he needs to repay to his father, he feels they cannot marry in June, although they both plan to attend summer school at the university.

> It will be hard to reconcile ourselves to the fact that we can go only so far and no farther in our physical contacts. We will have to lose ourselves in our work I suppose. Your embrace with its glory and promise should be enough to satisfy any man. Spiritually we are <u>one</u>.

Reading this, I wonder how they will manage to contain their natural desires while spending the whole summer together on the beautiful IU campus. It sounds like torture to me.

The Thanksgiving visit gave them a chance to practice being together but "going only so far and no farther." On November 27, Ruth took a bus to Greensburg, where Bert picked her up and drove her to the farm in New Pennington, about ten miles away. She met his parents and siblings for the first time and spent four blissful days with Bert.

In letters written after they returned home, both of them rhapsodized about how wonderful their visit had been. Ruth didn't even wait till she was back in Evansville to write. She grabbed a pencil and scribbled a few pages at the bus terminal in Indianapolis, a place that was "hardly conducive to love letters." During these four days, Ruth says her love and admiration for Bert have increased dramatically.

> I can say with all sincerity that I think you are the kindest, gentlest, most considerate man in the world. If nobility of character is the true measure of success in this life, you have achieved what few have. I wouldn't take anything for the delightful intimacy of last night's conversation. I feel that there is nothing I couldn't tell you about. We are truly one in spirit because of that experience.

In early December, she writes that the pain of separation isn't quite so bad since they will be together again in only three weeks, when he comes to Evansville to spend Christmas with her. She has fallen in love with his whole family and has already written a letter of thanks to his mother and father. Then she asks about Bert's youngest brother: "Has Denzil seen anything of Santa Claus yet?" This makes me smile. I knew my Uncle Denzil only as a tall, handsome man. It's hard for me to imagine him as a little boy hoping for a glimpse of Santa.

Writing a few days later, Ruth mentions that Bert's mother has answered her letter. "You don't know how much I hoped that your family would like me. I am rich now with a new mother and father and all those brothers and sisters to love."

One of the most poignant pieces in the thick folder labeled "1935" is a single sheet written on stationery headed "Greensburg, Ind.," and dated "Dec. 16, 1935." This is the reply that Bert's mother wrote to his bride-to-be. She begins with an apology: "Well I have been a long time answering your nice letter." I can understand why she took a while to write. Her letter in a penciled scrawl is so different from the letters of Bert and Ruth, written with a fountain pen in flowing script. Writing must have been a struggle for this farm wife. She tells of daily events—Bert and Dwight have gone to a ball game, Lois and Denzil are over at the church practicing "for Xmas," and she is planning to visit a hospitalized friend, who "is growing much worse." In closing, she says, "Ruth, we will sure be glad to welcome you into our family we all love you so much." She signs off, "Lovingly Bert's mother," and then adds a postscript: "Excuse the pencil and mistakes."

Reading this simple letter, I feel sorry for my Grandma Williams. She must have been intimidated by Ruth, this well-educated woman who lived in a world of ideas. I remember reading the letter her sister, Aunt Lydia, wrote to my mother after Bert's death. It was so literate, coming from a minister's wife, clearly a well-educated and articulate woman. I can imagine how inadequate my grandmother felt with a sister and a son and now a future daughter-in-law who could dash off a long, eloquent letter on a moment's notice.

While Grandma Williams professed her love for Ruth, I'm not sure the feeling was mutual. My mother adored Bert's father, but she regarded his mother as rather cold and disparaged her for the dust bunnies under the beds in the upstairs bedrooms. Her own mother or her aunts would never have tolerated such signs of sloppy housekeeping.

Now that Ruth was getting to know Bert's family, certain differences in their backgrounds were starting to emerge. The Williams family had owned land for generations and produced all their own food. Bert's father's role as township trustee gave the family an elevated status in their small community. But with the Depression reducing the value of their crops, actual cash was hard to come by. Ruth's mother and father had never owned anything, and she had grown up in poverty, but her years of living with Aunt Pauline and Uncle Edward sparked her desire for the finer things of life.

In the letters they exchanged in December, there was lots of talk about rings. Bert planned to give Ruth an engagement ring for Christmas. She went to the jewelry store to have her finger measured—a size 6. And she also expressed her preference for the gold to be all of one color. Other than that, she left the choice up to him. "I'd rather you'd choose what you think I'd like—something dainty with a pretty mounting." This is exactly how I would describe the ring he gave her, which now sits in a small onyx box on the dresser in my bedroom. But I clearly remember my mother's verdict on the ring as she gave it to me when I graduated from college: "I was so embarrassed when I saw it for the first time! I had never seen a diamond that small, really just a chip!" I feel sad to think of all the thought and love Bert put into selecting that ring—and the hard-earned money that went toward paying for it.

Writing just days before he would travel to Evansville to meet Ruth's family, Bert made an important confession: "You know, Ruth, I sometimes almost get tired of living. If it were not for the prospect and privilege of loving you, life would sometimes become tiresome for me."

This was the first hint I have found in the letters of Bert's struggle against depression. He explains that in the past he worked hard to counteract this tendency.

> I used to be able to philosophize myself out of an attitude like that. Now all I need to do is think of you. My life is no longer "an incompletion" for you have made it whole. The infinite passion and yearning of my heart and soul can be entirely satisfied in you.

In her next letter, Ruth responds to Bert's confession.

> I'd never know from the tone of your letters that you were ever depressed. I hope, dearest, that after we're married you won't be troubled with such moods. At any rate you'll have me to confide in, and it helps so much just to be able to tell someone who understands. I shall love you all the more and do everything in my power to make you happy.

Reading these letters so many years later, I ache for both of them, knowing how their youthful hopes and dreams will end. Even Ruth, with all her courage and determination, will not have the power to grant Bert the kind of wholeness he so desires.

Unlike Bert, Ruth was not subject to depression, and she can hardly contain her joy knowing that in just a few days he will be with her in Evansville. This will be only the third time they've met in person since mid-August, but they know each other so much better now thanks to the letters they've been exchanging over the past four months, letters that Ruth promises to cherish forever.

> I've kept them, every one. To destroy them would be sacrilegious. Someday if ever I have a daughter I'd like to let her read them. That's my chief reason for keeping a lot of stuff that most people would consider trash. My mother's old souvenirs meant so much to me when I was a kid, and I rather think my daughter will be the kind of girl who'd appreciate some of the things I'm saving for her.

When Mother mailed this letter to me in the 1980s, she wrote a message on the outside of the envelope in red ballpoint pen: "Take time to read this letter!" In a sense, my parents were holding the gate ajar for me as well as for each other. And as usual, Mother's instinct was right. I did turn out to be the kind of girl who appreciated all the stuff she saved for me. Reading the letters now, almost a hundred years after they were written, I'm able to understand so much about what my parents were thinking and feeling, about who they were and what their lives were like when they were young and idealistic and so much in love.

22

This Force We Call Love

JANUARY 1936 WAS the coldest month Indiana had experienced in many years. But there was nothing cold about the letters that flew back and forth between Bert and Ruth. They had spent nearly two weeks together over the Christmas vacation, and their love had become more physical. The theme of every letter in the weeks that followed is the same—their ever-growing love, devotion, and sexual attraction. As I read through their correspondence, Ravel's *Boléro* plays persistently in the back of my mind. Their love is so intense. And the questions they face are urgent. When will they finally pay off their debts to their parents and be free to marry? Will they be able to control their passion until they are husband and wife? Will they ever find jobs in the same town so they can actually live together? There is repetition here and suspense.

Both of them endorse the goal of waiting until after they marry to consummate their love, but this is becoming more difficult. As Bert writes, "We are both idealistic and highly sensitive. Fortunately, we have all our lives suppressed our strong physical passions, so that now we can give ourselves entirely to each other." In his next letter, he writes of his unending love and commitment:

> I simply <u>cannot</u> think of sex and that relationship in terms of any other woman. And I <u>never</u> will. Somehow with you I can be free and natural, and the intimate physical relationships become highly glorified and spiritual because

you have the mind and intelligence to see them in their
true significance and beauty.

Two days later, he writes again. It's twenty degrees below zero, and he wishes he and Ruth were together to keep each other warm. Thinking about his desire, he feels the need to explain about a young female teacher at the school where he teaches who has a crush on him and had "insisted on kissing" him when they went together to the Junior-Senior reception. "Never you fear," he reassures her. "Seeing other women only makes me love you more."

Writing the next day, Bert is struggling. He describes a time when he was in great pain:

> Although I have suffered a great deal mentally and
> spiritually, it does seem that a kind fate has been watching
> over me. I can say that especially now that fate (or God)
> has given me <u>you</u>. Surely our fates won't desert us now.
> The only way they could really hurt me now would be to
> take <u>you</u> away.

As I put this letter back in its envelope, I feel a sense of trepidation. He seems so fragile in this letter written in the cold days of January, so dependent on Ruth for his stability.

A few days later, he is desperate to be with his beloved. "I am unsettled. I am restless. I need <u>you</u>! I need <u>you</u>!" Resuming this letter the next morning, he announces that "the turbulent mood of last night has passed." He adds, "My ability to control that mood is the thing that has saved me. And now that I have met you, I thank all the Gods there be that I have always controlled myself." He recalls a night in 1933 when he nearly lost control. He was a senior at DePauw, and it was a beautiful warm spring evening. "I was with a girl (not by choice but by accident). She evidently was willing and eager. And so I had more than just myself to control." He did manage to restrain himself—and the girl. In fact, he never even kissed a girl until the summer of 1935. And, he tells Ruth, "You know who that girl was."

Ruth too has been struggling and hoping for self-control.

> I love you in every way that it's possible to love, so naturally I love you very passionately at times, but I pray that I may always be able to exercise complete self-control. I don't want to make it hard for you, and it's as much my responsibility as it is yours.

Ruth was no stranger to responsibility. As the oldest child in her family, she had needed to assume responsibility at a young age. As a seven-year-old, she had to do most of the housework and care for her two younger brothers while her mother was at work, struggling to support the family without a husband to help her. Responsibility came naturally to Ruth, so I'm not surprised that she volunteered to help Bert in restraining their passion until they were married.

In a letter written on a beautiful snowy Sunday, Bert mentions how much he appreciates Ruth's frankness and her "freedom from complexes and affectations with your beautiful body in my presence. If I want to kiss you from head to foot, you yield so gracefully. You will never know how easy it is to kiss you. How hard to keep from it sometimes."

Both Bert and Ruth had felt isolated in their own families, so it's understandable that they were thrilled to find someone who shared the same values and loved them for what others saw as eccentricities. Both were the oldest of several siblings. From childhood on, they were drawn to books and learning in a way that none of their relatives were. Ruth explains in one of her letters:

> Even as a child, if I'd be cleaning out a pantry and saw an interesting article in the old newspaper that was on the

shelf, I'd have to stop and read it. I've received more than one scolding for that.

In another letter, she talks about how misunderstood she felt during the six years she lived with Aunt Pauline and Uncle Edward. Her mother had moved to Chicago to get work and took her two young sons with her. Ruth desperately wanted to stay in Evansville to finish high school with her classmates, and her aunt and uncle offered to take her in. I had always envisioned this as an idyllic period in my mother's life, so it came as a shock to read, "All my life I've been tortured and made fun of by my relatives because they couldn't understand me." She remembers Aunt Pauline and Uncle Edward mocking her religious beliefs and ridiculing her "for going into raptures over a tree or a sunset." Uncle Edward, who had attended college for a few years though he never graduated, was fond of saying, "Ruth has plenty of book sense, but when it comes to common horse sense, she just isn't there."

Sharing all of this with Bert, she knows he will understand. "I think you've experienced enough of the same thing to appreciate my position." People in his hometown considered him odd because of his interest in nature and book learning. Though he was never ridiculed, as Ruth was, he too was seen as an outsider. When he was living at home again after college, he was aware of how distant he felt from his mother and sisters. "In spite of the fact that I have lived with these folks all my life, there is not one to whom I feel as close to as I felt to you that first Saturday night we were together." His sophisticated, philosophical views on religion set him apart from others in the community—especially from his mother, who took the Bible literally. She, like so many others, he writes, "is religious in the orthodox rather than in the true sense." He sees her as "a fine woman" but knows there will always be an unbridgeable gulf between them.

This distance from family members, which Ruth also experiences, helps to explain her need to cling to Bert as a source of strength and refuge. "I need you so much more than ever before. Just to have someone who really understands, and who loves you in spite of your so-called idiosyncrasies. No wonder I was so utterly lonely at times before I met you."

One thing that earned Bert the reputation of being odd was how he chose to spend his spare time. In May 1935, after his teaching responsibilities for the year had ended, he had some free time before summer school began. Instead of going hunting or fishing as other young men in his community would have done, he decided to spend part of every day writing in a special notebook. His goal was to articulate his philosophy of life.

In early 1936, he began to include excerpts from this writing in his letters to Ruth as she had requested. The section below is typical of the questions he was pondering just weeks before he met her.

> In nature, everywhere we see evidence of never changing faithfulness and consistency in the steadfast pursuit of certain ends. Has the sun ever been known to cease its regular rising? Or has it ever risen in the west? Did you ever find oranges on an apple tree, or oak leaves on a maple?
>
> In some ways it seems diabolical that vacillating, irregular, weak, and perplexed <u>man</u> should be made responsible for the direction of such sublime and seemingly self-sufficient powers as we see at work all around us. Then a genius with the intelligence, and the will, and the spirit springs up in our midst. And Luther Burbank justifies God for

> having made man to rule over the wonderful natural judgment here on earth.
>
> Still man is subordinate and the mighty power of the universe prevails.

Where did he come from, I wonder, this twenty-six-year-old from rural Indiana who spent his leisure time reflecting on such existential questions?

Reading this excerpt from his philosophical writings, I'm reminded of the time in 1953 when I went with him to visit his lab in Oak Ridge. Even as an eight-year-old child, I sensed that something about this work was disturbing to him. He must have felt terribly conflicted working at a place where geniuses even more brilliant than Burbank had manipulated the powers of nature to create weapons capable of such horrific destruction. For Bert, there would have been something very wrong about the way these men tampered with "the mighty power of the universe."

Although Ruth and Bert shared a love of reading and scholarship, they differed in ways that seemed to complete them as a couple. Bert was an introvert, a dreamy philosopher who lived mostly in his head. He spent much of his time alone, writing in his notebook or going on long walks on the farm. He looked to Ruth as a stabilizer, and she willingly accepted this role, having essentially held her family together since she was a young girl.

Ruth, an extrovert, was the practical one who got things to happen. She loved being with others and often went straight from teaching her classes at the elementary school to hear invited speakers at the YWCA or attend meetings of the Business Girls Club, where she served as president. Other after-school activities included bowling, bridge games, an art appreciation class, and tap dancing lessons. There seemed no end to her interests—or her energy.

I was intrigued to learn about one meeting that took place at the Y early in 1936. Five "Negro" girls from different occupations met with fourteen White girls to discuss what were then called "race relations." Ruth says the Black girls were "lovely persons to know" and "the discussion was sincere and frank and did a great deal to promote that sympathy and understanding which is basic if race prejudice is ever to be eliminated." She explains that she has been reading Will Durant's *Story of Philosophy*, and she asks Bert how the famous philosophers of the past felt about relations between people of different races. Speaking personally, she can't imagine that "a true philosopher could feel racial prejudice toward any group." These are the kinds of questions no one else in her family would understand, but she knew that Bert would welcome them.

~

In a letter postmarked on March 9, Bert declares that the bitter cold has finally broken:

> There is a strong south wind, the nights are warm and spring-like, and everything combines to make me love and need you more. It seems that I write of love—love—love—all the time <u>love</u>. I can't seem to help it. You are about all that I can think of these days.

All he could think about and write about was love, but still he spoke of delaying the marriage until 1937. It's true that he wanted to repay his debt to his parents before marrying. But I wonder if his reluctance was also related to something deeper. Did he fear that he was not stable enough, not flexible enough, not lovable enough? Did he prefer to remain in a fantasy land, dreaming of eternal love and fulfillment rather than face the realities of married life with a living, breathing woman?

Whatever Bert's doubts may have been, Ruth did not share them. And in March, she began to martial the arguments for marrying sooner rather than later. "I'm in the mood for love," she reports in one of her letters. Perhaps this is because she's been attending talks by Mrs. Morgan, a Columbia-educated psychologist and counselor. She spoke privately with this woman after one of the talks. "I went in to ask her about our school's club program and ended up telling her how terribly in love I was." Mrs. Morgan felt it would be a mistake to postpone their marriage until 1937, that by doing so they would be "wasting just that much happiness." She encouraged them to keep trying to get jobs in the same school system but to go ahead and marry at the beginning of the summer even if they still had to live apart during the school year.

A few weeks later, it's clear that Ruth has won the day. Bert writes, "Now that you have convinced me that a postponement of marriage is, to some extent, a postponement of our happiness, I am equally anxious to be married as soon as possible." He acknowledges that spending the summer together in Bloomington "without the privileges that a license will give us" might be "worse than nothing. We might destroy the uniqueness and beauty of the whole thing by failing to take advantage of this psychological moment."

He is getting support for the marriage from an unexpected source. Earlier in the evening, his mother surprised him by saying it was "all right as far as she was concerned" for them to get married in June. He credits Ruth for his mother's generosity: "She likes you exceptionally well."

Reading these letters from the 1930s, I have learned so much that I didn't know about my parents' early lives as I piece together the chronology of events in those years. Ruth's letter postmarked March 17 has a new return address: 17 East Tennessee Street. She and her mother and brothers have moved to another rented house in Evansville, and they don't like it. "There's no hot water and without an attic or cellar we don't know where to store things." They're looking for a better house and hope to move soon. But as it turned out, they were stuck in this small house for more than two years. They just couldn't afford anything better.

Ruth's letter of mid-March reveals that they have chosen a date for the wedding—June 9, 1936. Despite (or perhaps because of) the fact that they have a specific date, tensions are running high for both of them. Ruth recently had a fight with her younger brother. Jack Benny was on the radio, and Erv insisted on listening to the program even though she needed peace and quiet to finish her lesson plans for the next day. She was so angry that she slapped him and then broke down in tears. Bert reports that he too "has been so highly strung lately." He got into an argument with his mother about something that really wasn't important, and for the first time ever, he broke down in tears in front of her. "My convictions are absolutely unchanged, but I have sworn off trying to explain myself and my motives to her." Fortunately, spring vacation was only days away.

~

Easter fell on April 12 in 1936, and the letters paused for a few days as the lovers spent time together. Ruth had a friend who lived in Bloomington, and they were able to stay with her and enjoy some much-needed privacy. Once Bert was back on the farm, he writes to Ruth:

> I was a little disappointed not to get a letter today. My life is in your hands! Just by not writing you can kill me.
> I honestly believe that nothing but death could stop me from marrying you this year if you will have me. If you wouldn't have me, that would probably be death.

Ruth is effusive in her apologies. "Will you ever forgive me for not writing Sunday night? If I had known you'd be expecting a letter, I'd have written no matter how tired I was." From her point of view, the Easter vacation was perfect. "You are such a wonderful lover, Bert. You leave nothing to be desired and I count myself the most fortunate of women. You are deeply fervent and yet possessed of a self-control that is remarkable."

After receiving Ruth's letter, Bert is still unsettled.

> I am afraid I must confess that I am almost unhappy at times when I must be away from you. I can hardly control my desire for you. If I could just be near you—just see you or touch you.

It distresses me that Bert feels so utterly dependent on Ruth. He seems to be counting on her for his very survival.

Fortunately, Ruth likes being needed, a role she has always embraced. She is sorry that he finds the separation so hard and wishes there were something she could do to make it easier for him. She herself has "never been as happy or as mentally healthy" as in the past few months.

> When I'm with you, all earthly cares and troubles actually fade into thin air. I seem to forget everything but you and our love. No wonder a visit with you serves as a tonic to buoy up my spirits and give additional beauty and zest to this business of living.

She looks forward to the summer when "we can be completely free" and "won't have to worry about what other people might think."

School ends early in New Point since the kids are needed to help with spring planting. As Bert's teaching responsibilities wind down toward the end of April, he has time to focus on the wedding. He has written to Aunt Lydia's husband, Reverend Thomas (Jeff) Hart, to ask if he could officiate at their wedding, and he has asked his dear friend from DePauw, Ebert Whipple, to serve as best man. Thinking ahead to the summer, he writes, "For me it will be the easiest, most natural, and most beautiful thing in the world—to start living with you. Nothing seems worthwhile any more unless I can share it with you."

In Evansville, Ruth is busier than ever with teaching and her many outside activities. But as the wedding approaches, she is overflowing with energy, love for life, and love of Bert. She recently gave a talk entitled "Why We Are as We Are" at the YWCA. "Rather a presumptuous title, don't you think? But it was handed to me." In planning the talk, she identified "heredity and environment" as the basic determinants of one's personality as well as "childhood scars which prevent people from attaining psychological maturity." She plans to end with "some suggestions for achieving a wholesome, well-integrated personality."

I have to wonder who invited a twenty-four-year-old elementary school teacher to hold forth on such a complex subject. But as she describes the content of her talk, I'm impressed. She seems wise beyond her years and unusually forward-thinking for a woman of her time and place. In fact, her views still seem relevant today, more than a hundred years after her birth.

In May, Ruth wrote to Bert almost every single night no matter how busy her day might have been. In one letter, she describes a problem involving three girls at the school where she teaches: "They have been using terribly vulgar language and to boys as well as among themselves. They are so boy-crazy they'd resort to almost anything to get a little attention." One of these girls has the highest grades of any student in the school, and Ruth has taken it on herself to visit her mother to discuss the problem. Afterwards, she concludes that the woman is a "religious fanatic" who has probably never told her daughter anything about sex. As a result, the girl "has developed a morbid interest in the subject."

As if dealing with this tricky disciplinary problem wasn't enough for one day, Ruth had a terrible time trying to get back home. The streetcar she would normally have taken was blocked by a train engine that had jumped the track and ended up in the roadway. She had to walk about two miles to catch another streetcar and didn't get home until after 7:30.

In her typical stream-of-consciousness letter-writing style, she transitions from the frustrations of her day to a testament of her love for Bert: "I only wish I could find words to tell you how much I appreciate you. I marvel at your self-control, your tenderness, your unselfishness, your sympathy and understanding, and above all your desire to make me supremely happy."

Shifting abruptly from the sublimity of their love to practical concerns connected with marriage, she mentions a book she has been reading, *The Sex Factor in Marriage: A Book for Those Who Are or Are About to Be Married* by Helena Wright. She tells Bert that the book "had quite a bit on the various positions suitable for intercourse, but I didn't think it very suitable to write in a letter. Some were a bit surprising to me." Never one to be intimidated, Ruth concludes, "I'm sure that with practice we'll have no difficulty at all."

Bert replies that he has been reading as well. The May 1936 issue of the *Readers Digest* has just arrived at the farmhouse, and he has read an article entitled "How to Live Happily Even After." The author of this article recognizes that, among other things, "sexual technique" is important for happiness in marriage and refers readers to Helena Wright's book "as one of the best." Bert is impressed. "Leave it to you to find the best!"

Reading Bert's letters, I'm touched by his sweetness and sincerity. Ruth's letters have these qualities as well, but I often find myself laughing aloud at things she says. For example, her letter of April 25 begins, "My dearest, how does it feel to be a farmer, or didn't you work today? If you could see my face and arms, you'd think I'd been plowing all day." She had just returned from an adventure with the Girls Athletic Club. She had hiked six or seven miles to Evansville's Burdette Park, a "W.P.A. project and a grand place for an outing," and then played baseball for a while before walking back home. When I knew Ruth as my mother, she rarely ventured outside and would never have played baseball. But in these years, she seemed to be up for anything, on fire with love and the energy of youth.

Much of the rest of this letter is a recitation of Aunt Pauline's plans for their wedding. I always felt it was generous of Auntie to volunteer to host their wedding in the garden of her lovely home on Stringtown Hill. And it was. But it came with strings attached. Ruth had gone out there the night before to talk about plans for the wedding.

> As I feared, she had everything planned out. She is a woman who is used to having her way. Despite my protests, I'm afraid this wedding is going to be much more elaborate than I wanted, but after all I'm "merely" the bride.

Her aunts have decided that she must have two of her girl cousins as attendants. Bert's uncle, Reverend Hart, has agreed to conduct the ceremony, and Ebert Whipple will be the best man. Ruth's childhood friend Maggie will serve as maid of honor, and she will walk in with Ruth's brother Roy. There will be two little flower girls to strew petals over the garden path. And Uncle Edward will give her away. As an aside to Bert, she writes, "That's a silly custom, isn't it? As if I hadn't already given you my very soul!" Aunt Pauline has even decided what the men will be wearing: "dark coats, white flannels, and white shoes." What was this Midwestern *Hausfrau* thinking as she planned Ruth's wedding? She seemed to envision it as something out of *The Great Gatsby*.

Ruth appreciates all her aunt is doing but confesses to Bert, "If I had my way about it, I'd follow Mom's suggestion and run away and get married." She was serious. When I was starting to plan my wedding to Frank in 1968, she offered to pay us $500 if we would just elope. We opted for a simple church wedding instead, and she was a good sport about it, but I know she meant it when she offered to pay me rather than host a wedding.

Realizing that Bert has simple tastes and a limited budget, she apologizes:

> I hope you won't mind too much, darling. When you think of all the hours we'll have alone together this summer, perhaps we can reconcile ourselves to a little fuss for this one great occasion. As far as I'm concerned, I don't care about anything but making you happy. What difference does it make whether I'm married in a satin wedding gown or a house dress?

The next day she writes again. She is missing Bert and feeling terribly lonely. "Lovers just weren't meant to be apart in springtime." She fantasizes that if they were together, they could take a walk in the woods where the wildflowers are blooming and "stretch out in the sunshine and bask like two lazy seals." I laugh as I try to imagine my mother and father sunning themselves like seals amid a sea of wildflowers. Where did she get the colorful language she uses in these letters? Perhaps it was her wide reading combined with her innate love of the sound of words. She often told me that it was her father, the much-maligned Bill Stamps, who taught her to love poetry. Sometimes, reading these letters, I feel like a little girl again, listening to my mother telling me a bedtime story.

In his reply, written a few days later, Bert says that he is planning to come to Evansville for a few days to visit Ruth and see if there are any teaching opportunities there for the fall. He closes this short letter with a pet name for Ruth: "You Old Sweet Thing! I love you more and more."

THIS FORCE WE CALL LOVE

Hearing this phrase brings back memories. During my childhood in Tuscaloosa, my father would sometimes come up behind my mother as she was standing at the stove or washing dishes at the sink and put his arms around her, kiss her on the top of her head, and whisper, "You Old Sweet Thing." Both of my parents had grown up in families where open displays of emotion were rare, and they did not do much hugging or kissing in front of my sister or me. But the warmth and affection were always there. Whenever Daddy called Mother "You Old Sweet Thing," I knew how much he loved her.

As the wedding date neared, the letters began to focus more on practicalities, but the dominant theme was the same—their ever-growing love and devotion. In a letter written early in May, Ruth tries to imagine what the summer will be like for them living in Bloomington as man and wife. "To be near you all summer would be sublime but to be yours completely, to be your wife, will be better than just being sweethearts as we were last summer." Reminiscing about the early days of their courtship, she writes:

> How mysterious is this force we call love. Little did I dream the first day you sat beside me in history class that some day our relationship would be the closest that can exist between two human beings. How wonderful that within so short a time, you have grown dearer to me than anyone else in the world. Oh, how I love you!

In another letter written in May, she mentions that her mother had commented on how appreciative Bert was for all Aunt Pauline was doing in connection with the wedding. "He's just like that all the time, Mom," she explained to her mother. "You can't help wanting to be good when you're around him. There is a certain gentleness, a certain humility of spirit about him which only 'God's noblemen' possess."

She admits that at first she was attracted to Bert because of his good looks. Then she was impressed by his intelligence. But now, she explains:

> The thing that strikes me and keeps growing is an appreciation of the real you, 'the soul of you.' I know that come what may, you will never fail me, that you would never do anything that would make me unhappy or ashamed of you.

As the wedding approaches, Bert seems to be feeling more sure of himself and of Ruth's love. The letters he writes in May have a grace and assurance—a peace and contentment—that even show up in the fluidity of his handwriting. He tells Ruth how much he appreciates "the frankness and openness of your mind on all questions, including sex."

Ruth's letter of May 21 starts with some "good news." She has received her teaching contract for the next school year and is thrilled to learn that she will be making $166 a month, "a rather magnificent salary." She plans to save enough to pay her mother $700 in the next year. She suggests that she and Bert pool their resources for living expenses over the summer and imagines that they will both choose to live simply. Ruth is glad Bert wants to have children but adds, "If only we can delay their advent into the world until we are in a position to provide for them."

Responding to her comment about the need to delay having children, Bert mentions that just the other day he did something he had never done before. He went into a drug store and bought some condoms. I can't keep from laughing as he describes the items he had just purchased. "I had seen them before (in their unused state), but never before appreciated their unusual strength and delicacy. I didn't suppose rubber could be made so delicate and yet so strong. If one gets a good quality, they should be neither unsafe nor inconvenient." Nothing seems to escape the observation and descriptive powers of this dedicated scientist.

Ruth too has been thinking about contraception. She has been to see a gynecologist, Dr. Ehrich, who shared his opinion that the sex instinct is even stronger than that of self-preservation. He assured her that there was no need to have children until they wanted them and advised that for the first two or three months, Bert should take responsibility for controlling conception, and after that initial period of adjustment, Ruth should make an appointment to be fitted for a diaphragm. She adds, "I imagine that's the device I was telling you about."

Ruth and Bert are so earnest! They approach every decision like a school research project. Still, I have to admire their success. They were married for nine years before they decided to start a family. As my mother told me on more than one occasion, "You were conceived the first time we made love without using the diaphragm."

In her next letter, Ruth says she is proud of Bert for purchasing the "cundrums," one of the few words she misspelled in all these letters. "We talk like old married folks instead of prospective bride and groom. What would our children think if they read this letter? Maybe by that time a much better contraceptive will have been discovered and this letter will seem horribly old-fashioned." I marvel at her foresight. Yes, indeed, getting a prescription for birth control pills was so much easier and more effective than what she and Bert had to go through.

In a letter written near the end of May, he describes "a most disturbing dream" he recently had. He and Ruth were happily married and attending a party with friends. She went outside, and when he went out to find her, he sees that she had fallen and struck her head on a rock. It was clear she was dying. "The shock to me was so terrible that I awoke immediately. The dream was so clear and vivid, and my anguish was so real that I can't forget it."

Ruth had also been feeling anxious. "You must be careful, darling, working on the farm. If anything should happen to you, I couldn't go on living. You're all on earth I care for."

At the beginning of June, Bert seems calmer. Soon, after all the waiting, they will be free to consummate their love. "Just one week from tonight," he writes, "will be our first night together with the license to do as we please. Far from being embarrassing, it will be the most natural thing we ever did—to sleep (?) together. If we see that intercourse is going to prove inconvenient on Tuesday night, do you suppose we can wait if we use our self-control and will power?" In an earlier letter, Ruth had discussed the details of her menstrual cycle with him, and she feels they should be in the clear on June 9. He thanks her for being so frank with him about this natural function "in the midst of a society that has built up so many complexes around the vital sexual life."

Bert has calculated the number of hours before they will be "united in holy matrimony," 141 to be exact. Now he feels it would have been "impossible" to delay the marriage for another year. In the past year, his love just kept "growing and growing" and "has carried over into all phases of life and living." He signs this letter with a sacred vow: "I am yours forever with all my body & mind & soul. I love you so, Ruth dearest!"

On June 4, Ruth replies in a letter filled with news of parties and showers and gifts in celebration of the impending marriage. "I do believe I'm the most fortunate girl in the world. I'm sure I'm the happiest. I just feel like I'm going to pop inside—I'm so excited and thrilled about everything."

Toward the end she writes, "I suppose this will be the last letter I shall write to you, dearest, for a long time, and I'm glad of it. I love your letters, but nothing can compare with actually being with you." Perhaps in response to his concern about whether having sex on June 9 might prove "inconvenient," she goes on without even starting a new paragraph. "Is there any reason, dear, why we shouldn't be able to have intercourse Tuesday night?" Ever practical, she suggests that rather than setting out on their honeymoon after the ceremony, they might want to book a hotel room in Evansville.

That same day, Bert writes his last letter—just 117 hours until the wedding, according to his calculations. Like Ruth, he reports that he is happier than he has ever been in his life "and it is all because I am thinking of you and writing to you." He too is glad there will be no need for letters for the rest of the summer. "And so I must finish my last reply to the most heavenly correspondent I have ever known. When I address you in a letter again, it will be from a fuller experience and to you as my wife." It seems hard for me to believe after reading all these letters in which they spoke from the depths of their souls that they had known each other less than a year.

Now, only hours before their marriage, the repeated phrases of Ravel's *Boléro* are growing more insistent. There is the steady beat of the snare drum as the rest of the orchestra grows louder and more discordant. The conductor, a young Gustavo Dudamel, smiles as he leads the players toward the inevitable conclusion. But then, just before the climax, the music stops. After sharing so much of themselves and their love in these letters, Ruth and Bert will consummate their love in privacy.

From time to time, as I've been reading and writing about these letters, I have asked myself if my parents would feel violated, disturbed, as if I had betrayed their secrets. So I was consoled to hear Bert saying in one of his letters:

> It <u>is</u> interesting to wonder what our children might think to read the letters that we are writing. Perhaps they <u>will</u> read them some day. I am saving the ones I get from you, and I am getting quite a collection.

Indeed, the collection kept growing and growing over the years, a testament to two souls drawn together by the mysterious force we call love.

During the summer, there is a sacred silence as Bert and Ruth began their married life in Bloomington. But three months after the wedding, the letters resumed. Bert's search for a job closer to Ruth had not been successful, so they are still living and working in different parts of the state. Reading the letters from this period, I once again hear music in the background, but instead of the pulsating rhythms of Ravel's *Boléro*, the melodious strains of a Chopin nocturne play softly in the background.

The marriage has been consummated, the tension has been released, and they are more sure than ever of their love.

Bert reminisces about a summer night when they went up to the terrace, the place where their love began, but now as a married couple. As they sat on a stone bench, Ruth was so happy she just "sang and sang" as he sat marveling at the beauty of her voice. She reflects that in the early days of their marriage, the simplest things were special when they were doing them together: "washing dishes, studying, eating, loving, talking, or just sitting quietly next to each other."

Their happiness knew no bounds. Bert writes:

> Truly there is no sensation in this physical world to compare with the wonderful thrill of being close to your beautiful body. But even that is only part of the glory of this great love that includes the spiritual and intellectual life we have in common.

Ruth's life, too, has been transformed:

> When I walk down the street at night, I tell the stars how much I adore you. When I am weary or discouraged, I remind myself of your love, and I take new strength, new hope. Your spirit abides with me always and life is richer, sweeter by far because I have you.

If possible, the letters from the fall of 1936 are even more romantic than the ones they wrote before their marriage—a lifeline drawing them close until the next reunion. As Ruth writes on November 22, she is preparing to spend Thanksgiving with Bert at the family farm in New Pennington. She ends with a pledge of her eternal love: "Everything in life revolves around you. You are my life—you're all in all to me and I am yours completely forever and ever. Ruth."

The next day, Bert replies. He has been trying to find a certain football game on the radio. Spinning the dial, he suddenly hears a beautiful piece of music.

> It struck a chord in my soul. I realized that the feeling incited within me by the music was exactly comparable to the feeling I experienced this morning when I read your letter. You have the power of lifting my soul out of the commonplace into realms of harmony.

As I nestle these letters back into the thick folder labeled "1936," the Chopin nocturne ends on a note of peace and contentment.

23

The Burden Marriage Bears

CHOOSING A LETTER at random from the stack on the table, I pick up one my mother wrote at the end of 1939, three and a half years into her marriage. Ruth and Bert were still living more than two hundred miles apart. After spending Thanksgiving with her husband, Ruth had just arrived back home in Evansville. Sorting through the mail, she picked up the latest issue of the *Readers Digest*. A piece entitled "The Burden Marriage Bears" caught her attention, and she sat down to read it. Its author, Harvey Zorbaugh, professor of education at New York University and director of the Clinic for Social Adjustment, argued that people's expectations of marriage had become unrealistic, "more than any one human relationship can fairly be expected to yield," especially considering that every marriage involves "two very different personalities." This resonated with Ruth, and she sat down at her new desk, a gift from Bert, and started a letter.

Bert had tried to convince her that their natures were much the same, but she was aware of their differences. "I enjoy the stimulation of people and gaiety while you seem to prefer a quiet evening at home. We have compromised somewhat but there's still room for a better adjustment."

Having recently turned thirty, her desire to have a child had become an obsession. Thinking strategically, she tells Bert that if only she had a couple of children to care for, she could "sublimate the need" to share a more active social life with him. "I don't think our adjustment is perfect as yet, but if you could get a good steady job and we could have a home and children, I see no reason why ours shouldn't be a highly successful marriage."

I'm shocked to hear my mother admitting their marriage is not yet up to her high standards. During my childhood and adolescence, she always portrayed her union with my father as the ideal against which all other marriages should be measured. And now, having read so many of their letters, her admission of problems in the marriage comes as a surprise.

"I know there are times when you think I am over-critical," she writes. "I wish I weren't so much that way, but I come of a critical family, and it seems to be almost in-born. You may not believe it, but I am even more critical of myself. It's all tied up with this philosophy of mine about personal growth."

As she ends this letter, squeezing her words in at the bottom of the page, she reveals that things are currently far from ideal:

> I realize, dear, that I am a bit difficult to live with. You expect so very much from marriage, and I always hate myself when I feel that I have disappointed you. I get a bit discouraged sometimes and then I say cruel things I don't mean. Forgive me, Bert!

How could Ruth be so discontented just a few years into her marriage? They had so much going for them—a great love for each other, shared values and intellectual interests, and a mutually satisfying sex life. I can't help wondering what caused this strain and conflict.

To answer this question, I need to read the letters that came before. Breathing a sigh, I walk over to the filing cabinet and pull out a thick folder labeled "1937."

~

THE BURDEN MARRIAGE BEARS

Right from the start, my parents faced burdens that would have challenged any new marriage—a continuing Depression and an impending world war. They also experienced more personal problems. In 1936, they spent their first Christmas as a married couple in Evansville. Ruth was still living in the cramped and uncomfortable house on East Tennessee Street with her mother and brothers. I wonder how she and Bert found any privacy at all to express their passionate love, but somehow they managed. Then, early in January, when Bert was back in New Pennington, Ruth's period was late. Both of them feared that the "cundrum," as Ruth still spelled it, had failed them.

They were worried sick about the possibility of having a child before they were emotionally and financially prepared. Finally, on January 7, 1937, Ruth was able to write, "At last I started menstruating today and what a relief!" If her period hadn't started by Saturday, she confides to Bert, she would have gone to her gynecologist to discuss having an abortion. She doubts that he would have done the procedure since he was "such an upright man," and she isn't sure she would have had the nerve to go through with it as she has always been "afraid of abortions." Despite her lifelong desire to have children, when faced with a possible pregnancy so early in her marriage, she felt totally unprepared to have a baby. "I don't even know how to cook yet. My poor family would suffer terribly at my inexperienced hands." It's hard for me to imagine my competent mother ever feeling so insecure about her abilities as a homemaker, but I now understand that she was the scholar of the family. Her own mother, my granny, was the cook, housekeeper, and nanny if a baby should arrive unexpectedly. Ruth knew how to teach a class and chair a meeting, but she had no idea how to change a diaper.

In replying to this letter, Bert confesses that his fear of an unplanned pregnancy put a severe strain on his nervous system. "At times I felt as if something within me were going to snap." Like Ruth, he doubts that

Dr. Ehrich would have agreed "to stop the development of an embryo," even at such an early stage. He had decided the best solution would be for Ruth to have the baby and for them to "make the best of it next fall," finding somewhere to live away from their relatives. "It really would be wonderful to live with you and our own child off somewhere where we would have no other relationships to consider." Now that they're sure Ruth is not pregnant, however, he feels "it is still infinitely better to know that we won't have a child until we are ready." For her part, Ruth lost no time in scheduling an appointment with Dr. Ehrich to be fitted for a diaphragm, the device he had recommended before they were married.

The first time I read about this pregnancy scare I was so stunned that I called my sister to see if she had ever heard about it. She was just as shocked as I had been. Although Mother often talked about the miscarriage she had a couple of years after I was born, she had never mentioned to either one of us the time, early in her marriage, when she had considered seeking an abortion. Our father's reaction also came as a surprise. Though he was a man who revered life in all its forms, he seemed to understand why Ruth was thinking about ending the pregnancy. Fortunately, they didn't have to make that decision.

Soon they were faced with a real catastrophe. Interspersed among all the romantic musings in their letters of early 1937 were regular reports about the weather. On January 13, Bert writes:

> I wonder if it is as damp and foggy in Evansville as it is here. The sun hasn't shown for a week. I notice by the paper that the Ohio River is up down there. Be sure that you don't float away.

Ruth joked in her reply:

> It's pouring rain outside and has been for several hours. I hope that if I do start floating, I'll land at your house.

> Think you could give me shelter for the night? I always feel so snug and comfy when I lie beside you and listen to the rain.

A few days later, Ruth described the weather in Evansville: "It's a gloomy old afternoon and pouring down rain as usual. I sometimes wonder if it will ever stop. The river is already at flood stage."

Later that same day, Bert reported on the situation in New Pennington: "It is a dark and stormy night and raining very hard. That means more high water. I certainly hope that highways between here and Evansville stay open."

Despite the high water, Ruth planned to take the bus to meet Bert on Friday, but the next day she wrote again—in a state of panic. The roads were under water, and no buses were running.

> I know I'm making a perfect fool of myself but I'm nearly frantic. I'll die if I don't get to see you this weekend. Even the fear of pregnancy did not upset me half so much as this. I don't know what to do or which way to turn.

I don't recognize the woman in this letter. During my father's illness and in the years after his death, my mother was the rock that held our family together. I never saw her out of control like this. Re-reading this letter, I realize the tremendous strain she was under because of not being able to communicate with Bert directly. Today we can just pick up our phones and contact anyone in the world instantly. But Ruth and Bert were completely dependent on letters. With the waters rising, Ruth considered indulging in the luxury of a long-distance phone call, but the telephone exchange in Bert's village had shut down an hour earlier, at 9 p.m. The only thing she could think of was to send a telegram in the morning and hope that Bert would reply.

"Where there's a will there's a way" was one of the maxims my mother lived by. The next morning, she managed to get a telegram through to Bert and then boarded one of the last trains headed north to Indianapolis. He drove over to pick her up at the station. On the following day, January 23, martial law was declared in Evansville as the water rose to nineteen feet above flood stage. Everything in the city shut down, but Ruth was safe in Bert's arms in New Pennington, where she stayed warm and dry, waiting out the flood.

Three weeks passed without any letters as Ruth remained at the farm. By February 12, she was back in Evansville and writing to Bert. Everything, including the schools, had been closed while she was away. Their small rented home on Tennessee Street was not flooded, but many homes on the upscale East Side were devastated by the flood waters. A friend who had stayed in town said the best word to describe the flood was "relentless." It seemed that the water would never stop rising. Ruth and her mother, along with almost everyone in town, were getting a series of typhoid shots.

~

In what remained of 1937, Bert and Ruth managed to spend many weekends together, but on weekdays, a steady stream of letters flowed between Evansville and New Pennington. In these letters, they dream of creating a home of their own. Ruth begins to practice her sewing and cooking skills. And Bert imagines the home they will soon share, "a place where we can eat and sleep and love—where we can read and write and study as we please—where we may have children if and when we please and raise them as we please."

So far, there is no sign of their passions cooling. This line from one of Ruth's letters is typical of so many others: "To see you, to feel you, to kiss you, to love you is ecstasy." But another thing that hasn't changed is their precarious financial situation as the Depression persisted. Both of them are struggling to save every possible penny to pay off what they owe to their parents. They want to start life in their own home "without any big debt hanging over our heads." The reality of life in the Depression hits me when I learn of Bert's plan for a generous Christmas gift to his parents: "100 pounds of sugar."

Besides trying to cope with the Depression, they sense that another war is brewing. After reading *Idiot's Delight*, a play by Robert Sherwood in which a group of wealthy tourists are stranded in the Italian Alps at the beginning of another world war, Bert thinks about how he would react if war were to break out.

> It would be "hell" to leave you to the uncertain horrors of modern warfare (uncertain only in their nature—not in their reality because they would be inevitable). And I say it sincerely and mean it literally. "I'll be damned if I'd go!"

With his reverence for life, Bert is firm in his opposition to war.

"I couldn't bear the thought of letting you go if the U.S. should go to war. It's too horrible to even think of," Ruth replies. Later in the year, after listening to President Roosevelt's speech in Chicago on October 5, she agrees that something must be done "to halt the imperialistic designs of countries like Japan, Italy, and Germany. Isolationist neutrality is not the way out. To a certain extent the whole international moral order is at stake." A pacifist at heart like Bert, she is hoping that an economic boycott might help to avert war.

Some of her letters sound almost like campaign speeches, especially when she writes about her hero, Franklin Roosevelt. Her progressive politics were at odds with the views Bert had absorbed in his staunchly Republican farming community. In fact, he owed his teaching job in large part to his father's role as the elected township trustee. Trying to convert him to more enlightened views, Ruth declares in one of her letters, "You Decatur County farmers are like the Pharisees. You reject your own deliverers."

Listing all the ways Roosevelt has helped farmers, she goes on for five very convincing pages before she becomes more personal. "Forgive me, my dear, if I seem carried away. This letter has turned out to be largely a eulogy of the president." She hopes Bert will be "big enough to at least share in part my feelings on the subject." If she seems "a bit irrational," it may be partly due to her physical condition. She explains that her menstrual period started that day, "exactly on time," and it's making her feel "high strung." From letters written later, I know that Bert eventually came to share Ruth's admiration for Roosevelt. But I've never been exactly sure where he stood when he stepped into the voting booth.

Although Bert was well-informed about world and national affairs, he was more interested in exploring the ideas in his own mind. Writing in February, he says he plans to write a book building on the notebook he kept for a few weeks before he met Ruth—a book where he would explain his philosophy of life and love. Ruth is supportive, to an extent. "I've been waiting for this announcement for quite some time and hope you will carry out your plan. I really believe that you have a talent for writing." But she's also thinking practically. "Don't you really think, dear, that you ought to start on your master's degree this summer? I feel very strongly about the matter and hope you will think it over."

Bert the dreamer, Bert the poet, has a strong desire to write. Ruth, the realist, recognizes his talent and his desire to write but tries to steer him toward a more practical goal. She encourages him to get the credentials required for a better paying job so they can create the home they both are yearning for.

THE BURDEN MARRIAGE BEARS

Reflecting on her own career, Ruth feels she has reached a kind of peak with her teaching at the elementary school and needs to move on to something bigger.

> I seem to be standing on the threshold, all my past life sealed and almost forgotten, waiting expectantly to step over into a newer and even fuller existence as your wife. I seem to be marking time, waiting for that day when we can walk across our own doorsill and really start life together.

At least for the summer of 1937, they will actually be living together in an intellectually stimulating environment away from their families as they take courses at the university to bolster their teaching credentials. They can hardly wait.

~

When summer ends and they're once again back in their own towns teaching school, the letters resume. And some of them shed light on the burdens their marriage was being asked to bear.

Writing on a Monday evening in September, the day before her twenty-sixth birthday, Ruth hints that their summer together has not been as blissful as she had expected. "Unless I'm feeling a lot better, I'm not going to summer school in 1938. It's too stimulating. I enjoy it but I live too much in a whirl of excitement. I need to take life easy for a while." This doesn't sound like my mother at all. She thrived on excitement, and I never knew her to take it easy. What happened during the summer to cause such a shift in her feelings? Glancing at the stack of unread letters from 1937, I'm hoping to find some answers.

My eyes focus on an envelope stamped "Postage Due 1 cent" even though Ruth had attached two three-cent stamps. Maybe this one will contain some clues about what was going on.

It begins in a charming way: "This is the time of night that inspires confidences—it is 7 o'clock and the church bells are ringing. I should like to tell you the story of the girl you married." She goes on for pages about her childhood dreams and how Bert is part of the plan she imagined. She acknowledges that they have had a few arguments, "mostly about politics," but for the most part their relationship "was quite happy and satisfying."

She hadn't seen signs of "any serious maladjustment" until the past summer.

> If we had had a room that afforded more privacy and if I hadn't been so worn out and tired, we wouldn't have had any trouble. What is done can never be undone, but I don't intend for you to ever have to go through another summer like last one.

Coming from my mother, I know this is serious. She often ignored problems, shoving them under the rug, hoping they would go away if she just didn't mention them. But when she finally addressed a problem, she did not flinch.

She promises to make an appointment with Dr. Ehrich. "If anything can be done, I shall do it." It's not clear exactly what this problem might have been. But judging from what she said earlier about the lack of privacy combined with her exhaustion, their sex life during the summer must have been less than ideal—and upsetting for Bert. It was like Ruth to seek professional help, in this case from her gynecologist. But she believes the adjustment they need to make is more than just sexual. "That is the thing I tried to tell you about this morning." Oh—I realize—this letter must be the continuation of a face-to-face discussion they had been having earlier in the day. While she was writing, Bert was on the road, driving back to the farmhouse he shared with his family in New Pennington.

Ruth had a habit of reading everything she could find on the subject of personal growth and adjustment, and in this letter, she turns to her latest authority for support. This expert, a Mrs. Seabury, writes about perfectly matched partners "who discern the same horizon and in the search for beauty and truth lose themselves in a great togetherness." To me, this sounds more like Bert talking than Ruth.

Ruth struggles to explain what she feels is missing in their marriage. "I want with all my heart to know and understand you. If it is my fault, I hope you will forgive me for a tactless, blundering fool, but, dearest, please don't close the door. I'm so lonely outside."

She reminds him of the conversation they had the night he asked her to marry him, when they talked about holding the gate ajar. "We agreed that there would be no private worlds." Confessing her own faults, she admits:

> I know, Bert, that I have been intolerant and hypercritical. I have been cruel and cutting in my remarks. I wish it were more in my nature to always be tender and gentle and thoughtful. I'm afraid I'm more like an eagle than a dove. I am sorry for everything I ever said that caused you pain and unhappiness, but I am not sorry for having told you how I feel about our marriage.

Her letter continues for three and a half more pages as she struggles to express her feelings. "I refuse to let our relation become stagnant. It is that which I was crying out against this morning although I'm afraid I was tactless and cruel in my approach." Then she launches into a long quotation from Mrs. Seabury, the gist of which is that it takes effort from both partners to achieve an ideal marriage.

> I know, dear, that yours is a very sensitive soul and I have not had social imagination enough to withhold criticism, which has hurt you. Patience has never been one of my virtues, but it is one which I intend to cultivate.

After quoting two more authorities, she tells Bert she's proud to see all the ways he's been growing since they were married. "I've noticed a great many changes and all of them for the better." She even says that Bert has grown more than she has in the past three years. She has been "more than encouraged by your enthusiasm for your work this year," which she feels is "a very healthy sign."

Reading this, I feel my whole body tense up. She sounds like a teacher grading Bert on his improvement. I remember her sometimes treating me the same way as I was growing up. I was not her student needing to be graded, and I didn't like her patronizing judgments. I empathize with Bert as she assesses his personal growth.

Toward the bottom of page ten, Ruth's handwriting gets smaller and starts to slope upward on the page as she tries to end on a positive note:

> I believe that if from this day forward we take steps to bring it about, we can make our partnership a growing, expanding relation which will result in that merging of spirit in which we lose ourselves in a great togetherness.
> At least it's worth striving for, don't you think?

I wonder what Bert did think after this exhausting and emotionally wrenching day. I picture him driving north in the old Plymouth, hoping it wouldn't break down, leaving him stranded. Perhaps he had a similar fear about his marriage, which had brought him such joy and fulfillment but now seemed at risk. He had tried as hard as he could to make Ruth happy. What more did she want of him?

Only a few letters remain in the folder from 1937. I read them carefully, looking for some follow-up to Ruth's critique of their marriage. But there's not even a hint that these harsh words were ever spoken. Some letters have undoubtedly gone missing, too painful to keep perhaps. But the ones that still exist sound like all the ones that came before. Rapturous accounts of their love and happiness. Finally, I turn to the last letter in the pile. It's from Bert and postmarked December 20.

This one, like all the others, is a testament to his love for Ruth and his anticipation of spending the upcoming Christmas holiday with her. But sandwiched between his account of family life at the farm and his ever-growing love for Ruth is a hint of something he had referred to much earlier—the times in his life when he suffered intensely.

> For no real reasons at all, I have suffered enough mental anguish to drive an army of men to suicide—and almost enough to drive me "nuts" at times. I don't want to make myself out a martyr, or pose as an unusual sort of person, but I profess to have had some very deep and trying experiences. I would have come to them in that story of my life which I started in 1935 but haven't finished. Anyway the significant thing as far as we are concerned is that I have survived. These experiences have altered me in some ways, we hope for the better. And I still maintain the ability to alter myself when and as I please.

Oh, Bert! What was it that caused all this suffering? Was it why you dropped out of college after learning about Darwin's theories? Or something that came later? Was it one sustained period of distress or moods that came often and without warning? Is there anything Ruth can do to help as she so wants to?

In a way, he responds to this last question as he continues.

> But the <u>most</u> significant experience of my life turned out to be a happy one. It is the story of <u>our</u> chance meeting and spontaneous love. What we experienced then, and continue to experience, should make us free and happy forever.

This marriage had so many burdens to bear. Tucking the letter back into its torn envelope, I wipe away my tears. I wish I could reach back over all the years and tell them how much I love them.

24

Climbing Toward the Heights

IN THE FALL OF 1938, the unthinkable happened in Indiana's Saltcreek Township. A *Democrat* was elected township trustee, replacing Bert's father, a staunch Republican. Throughout the spring, as the Depression dragged on, Bert's future was uncertain. There was a distinct possibility that the new trustee might decide to appoint a nice Democratic boy to take over his job teaching English and mathematics at New Point High School.

Although Bert never actually mentions this possibility in his letters, it must have been a constant source of stress. But there was also something exciting about standing on the threshold, pondering what his future might hold. He would be thirty years old in March, still living with his parents in the small farmhouse where he had been born, teaching a few miles down the road at the tiny school he had attended as a boy. Perhaps it was time for a change.

During these months, he often reports feeling "mystical," caused in part by "an accumulating sexual energy" when he and Ruth have been apart for weeks. As he describes it, this "elevates my feeling and thinking and acting into a spiritual realm" in which he has "glimpses of the real truth that might materialize into works of art, creative writing, high living, deep loving. I feel a rising towards the beauty of your spirit, a desire and striving to be one with you."

My stomach tightens as I read these words. He seems to be entering another dimension, perhaps on the verge of losing his grip on reality. I thought I had worked through my fear of my father's mental illness, the dread that makes my muscles clench when I sense a warning sign. Reading this letter, I realize that his words still have the power to unsettle me. With trembling hands, I pick up the next letter in the stack.

Mailed on April 3, this letter was so long that Bert had to paste an extra three-cent stamp on the envelope. Written over several days, he covers a lot of ground and seems even more elevated than in the previous letter. He begins by summarizing two library books he has read in the past few days, reports on a family dinner-table conversation about the looming war in Europe, and responds to Ruth's recent letter in which she mentioned the possibility of writing a book about her teaching. Bert has another idea. He hopes that he and Ruth might collaborate on a book of their own. He knows his own perfectionistic tendencies might be a hindrance. "Damned self-conscious, introverted idealist that I am, I am ashamed to submit anything to you that I don't believe comes up to the standard of perfection of your love and beauty." But something about this idea has captured his imagination.

> Having thought of the miracle of our meeting and of the excitement and ecstasy of our romance and of the beauty and wonder of our love and realizing that the so-called disillusions of marriage have served only to make our love deeper and more secure, I am struck by the reality of facts stronger and more beautiful than any fiction I have ever read.

If the story "materializes," he says, it will probably include "the experiences of motherhood—and fatherhood." When they conceive a child, he believes their lives "will have joined to produce the physical, tangible life that will link us to the future and make us immortal. It's only the truth—still it's the mystery of survival."

As an experiment, he tells Ruth, he's going to attempt "a take-off," trying his hand at what he might write in the book he's proposing.

> Even though we are young and have each other and our love, we have known the feeling of terror, haven't we? And pain, surely. And bitter disappointment. It is the rule of life that we must learn from those stern teachers. It is in the struggling and climbing toward the heights and the light—it is when one senses and knows for sure that he is moving in the direction of the eternal truth that one experiences the ecstasy of life. Then pain and suffering count for nothing—they are hardly noticed—terror and <u>bitter</u> disappointment are hardly known when one is no longer concerned with his <u>individual</u> fate.

Fearing that Ruth may feel overwhelmed by the project he's proposing, he writes:

> I realize the magnitude of the task I'm asking you about. For me such a possibility adds glorification and enchantment to our present life. And if carried out, it will be a very fine source of enrichment in the future.

Behind all this philosophizing is a desire to overcome terror and disappointment, to find love and beauty and truth—in a woman, in the natural world, in the universe, in his concept of God. I have always admired my father for his deep thinking and idealism. This is the man I remember from trips to the greenhouse at the university, quiet walks at the Tanglewood nature preserve, even the disturbing visit to his lab at Oak Ridge in 1953. But I also remember the man who emerged in March of 1954, pacing around the house, smoking cigarettes, and speaking in a loud voice, the man who terrified me. As I put these pages back in their envelope, I fear this letter may be an omen of disturbing things to come. I wonder how my mother will respond.

Two days later, she writes back. She's intrigued by Bert's idea for a book but is careful to limit her own involvement. "You are the poet; you will have to be the one to write our book. I'd be glad to help furnish ideas, but when it comes to the actual writing, you'll have to be the one to do that." She suggests that they talk it over the next time they're together.

I breathe a sigh of relief. Ruth is a steadying influence on her volatile husband. Throughout my childhood, I always knew I could count on her calm strength in any situation. Although she, like Bert, was an idealist, her feet remained firmly planted on the ground.

In his next letter, Bert shares his thoughts about the ominous situation in Europe as the world teetered on the brink of war. Then he returns to his plans for their book. "The idea I am playing with is this—to spend the summer writing while you go to school." Like a lawyer arguing his case, he writes, "I feel that a creative work would go much farther towards recommending me for a better job than the few extra credits I could earn at the University this summer."

He reminds her that he first thought of writing a book in the winter and spring of 1935, just weeks before they met—another time when his future was looking uncertain. Now the "literary bug" has bitten him again. The biggest drawback, he feels, would be the cost of publication, which he estimates to be $800 to $1,000, an enormous amount in their Depression-era budget. He warns Ruth that whatever she thinks of this possibility, she will hear a lot more about it. "In fact, it is in danger of becoming my Magnificent Obsession."

Bert has given Ruth a lot to think about. The project he has in mind could consume both of them for years—years with no income except her salary, no home of their own, no baby.

Ruth is surprisingly temperate in her response, trying not to throw cold water on his dreams while also suggesting a more sensible plan for the summer. "I do want you to write a book, but you have plenty of time. I rather question the advisability of your not going to summer school." She suggests that they consider all the options in two weeks when they will be together for Easter vacation.

After spring break, Bert's ardor for his book has not cooled. He even has a title in mind: *The Spiritual Adventures of a Man and a Woman*. He explains to Ruth that "the man and the woman won't be exactly 'us.' They will rather be the 'we' that we may hope and strive to become." He wonders if the title is "too high toned," but considering the subject matter, he feels it's appropriate: "an attempt to realize in thought and expression the possibilities for the realization of wonderful love, for the recognition of glorious beauty, and so for the achievement of a much more perfect life."

Ruth jolts me back into reality with her letter of May 17, and I hope it had the same effect on Bert. "In case you don't get a job for next year, I very strongly recommend that you start work on an M.A. degree."

And that's exactly what happened. Despite his earnest efforts to get another teaching position, Bert found himself out of a job in the fall of 1939. Beginning in September, as Great Britain and France went to war against Germany, Bert too had made a decision. The return address on his letters to Ruth is "216 S. Indiana Street, Bloomington, Indiana." He had started work on a master's degree in botany at Indiana University. Nothing more is said about his book. It has become a luxury they cannot afford.

~

I would have expected a man as sensitive and self-critical as Bert to be devastated by losing his job—especially a job in his own small town where everyone knew what had happened. But judging from the letters he wrote that fall, he was not dejected. Freed from the farm and the family, worlds he both loved and felt constrained by, he reveled in being part of a world of books and writers and thinkers. He was growing into himself, gaining confidence and self-assurance. He felt at home in this world where he could be an insider, not an outsider.

In the letters written during this period, he often described himself as "in the heights." In October, he heard Alfred Kinsey, the famous sex researcher and a professor in IU's biology department at that time, give a lecture in which he stressed "the importance of frankness in the sexual relationship." Naturally, this reminded him of Ruth, who had always been so frank in discussing sex with him.

About a month later, he attended a talk by Albert Kohlmeier, a history professor, who had been born on a small Indiana farm but went on to get a PhD from Harvard. Bert says he was brought almost to tears by this philosophical yet practical talk, with its "delicate beauty." He wishes Ruth could have been there to hear it.

After attending a vespers service at the Methodist church one evening, he writes:

> I couldn't help thinking of you. You are so fine, so real, so true and honest, so frank and friendly. And you are beautiful with a beauty that is not only superficial but that is as deep as life and love itself.

The printed program for this service included a quotation from Kahlil Gibran, a writer Ruth admired: "All work is empty save when there is love. And when you work with love you bind yourself to yourself, and to one another, and to God." Bert, who had been working so hard on his studies, identified with Gibran's words. "You can't imagine the thrill (yes you can) that comes when one sees a part of the truth of life." Already, just a few months into his graduate work, he had identified the subject for his master's thesis, reporting that he has discovered "something in the structure of plants that no one else had seen before me." His advisor, Professor Paul Weatherwax, agreed. More than just providing a thesis topic, Bert explains:

> This work binds me closer to myself. I get to know myself better. And it brings me closer to you really because I am doing it for you, as well as for myself and for the love of it. And I know that it brings me closer to God. And what is God but love (at least in part)? And it brings me closer to truth.

In closing, he writes, "I love you more than ever, Dearest!"

I take a deep breath. My father has found a focus. Still climbing toward the heights, he has narrowed his search for life and truth and God to the tiny structures found in the roots of plants. I have a feeling of relief mixed with love and respect for this earnest man.

~

After Ruth and Bert spent the Christmas holiday together, their letters resumed. "You seem to be living on the heights these days," she writes in January 1940. War is raging in Europe, but the two of them seem far removed from the conflict. She's thrilled that he's doing so well in his studies and getting so much out of life.

Just a few days later, she's in a very different mood. "You seem a thousand miles away." She quickly comes to the point:

> As I lay in bed this morning, I thought about "us" and the future. I am convinced, Dear, that if I am to have any children, I must become pregnant this year. I'll be twenty-nine. We mustn't wait any longer, Bert.

Oh dear, I think as I read this letter. I've seen her getting wound up like this before. The more she writes, the more overwrought she becomes. "I think you know how deeply I feel on this subject—it is an obsession with me." She says she has dreamed of having children since she was a little girl playing with dolls. "If you love me, you must bend every effort to get a job that will enable us to start having a family." The letter goes on and on, getting more dramatic with every sentence. "Without children, I shall become embittered, lonely, empty. I shall die of a broken heart if this is denied me."

I wonder what Bert is thinking as he reads this. After all, he's doing what she had advised—working toward a master's degree to advance his career. Now she's encouraging him to get a job, any job.

Buttressing her case, she writes that her love of children is the secret of her success in teaching, but that is not enough for her. "I must have children of my own. It is my 'manifest destiny.'" She says she plans to make an appointment with J. Ralph Irons, the superintendent of schools, to let him know this will be her last year of teaching as she intends to start a family. His part in her plan is clear. "Remember to register with the employment bureau as soon as possible."

If Bert responded to this diatribe, his reply has been lost. About a week later, in writing to Ruth, he doesn't mention her desperate desire to have a baby. Instead, he talks about his own pent-up sexual energy, which he is redirecting into his work. He reports that he did better than anyone else on a recent exam, and he is "on the heights" again. "Work is interesting, life seems beautiful and significant—and largely because of you."

In the spring of 1940, Bert was exhilarated and full of hope for the future, while Ruth was feeling stuck in her job and frustrated about not having children. On March 1, 1940, a small tornado touched down in Evansville just two blocks from the house on Keck Avenue where Ruth and her mother were living with her brother Erv, his wife, Leola, and their little daughter, Patty. No one in their family was injured, but that may help to explain why she was thinking about death. She tells Bert that riding home on the bus the day the tornado struck, she wondered if she were to die in childbirth, who would take care of the baby and what would happen to her mother. He assures her that she's not likely to die in childbirth but then says, as if to console her, "Death is not so cruel as life. But I can't feel that even life is cruel anymore since I have you. You and your love and my work are certainly making life joyful for me." He returns to this subject in closing: "As you say, 'Life is so uncertain.' One never knows when, or how, or why the storms come—but they come."

Reading this makes me shiver although it's warm in the room. Bert has mentioned the wrenching storms he endured before he met Ruth. And then, in 1954, when things were going so well in his life, they struck again. He almost seems to know what lies ahead for him. It's just a question of when.

About a month later, Ruth writes that she is feeling depressed, partly because her menstrual period is about to start. Bert responds with understanding.

> I know just how you feel in your periods of depression. It seems to me that my thinking and feeling, too, continue in cycles that are just about as regular as your menstrual cycles. I too am feeling rather "low" right now. This cycle of depression and inspiration has been with me so long that I am finding different ways of counteracting the ill effects of such unwelcome moods.

He describes in some detail the coping strategies he has developed. For example, he often reminds himself that "when it gets dark enough, the stars come out." Another way of saying this, he writes, is to remember,

"The deeper one goes in depression, the higher one will subsequently rise in ecstasy."

Reading this, I realize that Bert is describing the mood swings that today we would be quick to diagnose as bipolar disorder, though the term didn't exist at that time. However, I see Bert's moods as more than just a symptom of a medical condition. They are also a key to his identity—a man who was always striving to be better, to be kinder, to be more perfect. This striving reflected the world of ideas in which he chose to live—the books he read, the movies he admired, the woman he fell in love with. The standards he set for himself were so high.

By the time he writes again, just three days later, he has risen to a state of ecstasy.

> My life seems to me to be made up of the craziest mixture of depression and elation that one can imagine. I'm not depressed today. Today I'm elevated! I am on mountain tops where the air is so rare that I can hardly breathe. I seem to be in heaven. I feel like a God. I love life as it is in plants—that is, botany. And I love life as it is in you. You are life to me. You are love to me.

Describing his mental state, he writes, "Everything that I think about seems vivid and clear and in its proper relationship." Ending this letter, he says he must go and apply some of this "lucidity" to writing his master's thesis.

Reading this letter, I have mixed feelings. I'm happy that Bert is feeling such joy and inspiration and relieved that his scientific work is providing a focus for his exhilaration. But what will happen when the darkness returns as he seems to know it will?

~

In 1940, Ruth was still living with her extended family in the house on Keck Avenue and teaching in the same elementary school where she began her career eleven years earlier. Writing to Bert as the school year winds down, her world seems to be shrinking as his is expanding.

She describes a recent hike with the Girl Reserves and her plans to take a group of fifth graders to see Walt Disney's *Pinocchio*. For a woman who had worked continuously ever since she completed her teacher training in 1930, to consider giving up her job is a major step, but she is ready to take it. She reassures Bert that he could handle the increased responsibility: "I know, Bert, that I am your severest critic, but I do believe in you; otherwise I wouldn't be willing to give up my own career. I'd be too afraid of the future."

I can almost hear my mother saying this. She had such a strong sense of responsibility for others. For years she had been the mainstay of her family, supporting them with her teacher's salary and, for the past year, also subsidizing Bert's graduate work. It must have been hard for her to even think of giving up her job, but as she approached thirty, her need to have a child was becoming urgent.

Writing from Bloomington a few days later, Bert is living in a different world. While Ruth is hiking with the Girl Guides and planning to take a bunch of kids to see a movie, he is putting the finishing touches on his master's thesis and has just attended a formal reception hosted by the university's president, Herman B. Wells. "I went just for the purpose of cultivating social poise—you know—shake hands with the president of the university with the proper smile on my face." He seems almost surprised to admit, "I'm getting so I enjoy that sort of 'acting.' It really isn't acting if one likes the people." And he liked these people very much. They included a young philosophy professor who had gotten his PhD from Yale and a recent immigrant from Prague who was teaching violin in the music department. He tells Ruth he dreams of getting a job in a university. "I feel that there is a place for me (for us). If there isn't a place, I can make one."

On June 3, 1940, Ruth sat in the audience in Bloomington as Bert received his master of arts degree in botany. President Wells personally signed his diploma and shook his hand as he walked across the stage. But if Bert was serious about getting a job in a university, more years of study would be required.

Although both Bert and Ruth are clear about their goals for the future, I feel worried for them. How will they manage financially if Bert begins doctoral work? How will Ruth react if she has to postpone her dream of having a child? To make things even more uncertain, the United States will soon be at war.

25

The Romance of Being a Student

IN JUNE OF 1940, with his diploma safely stowed in a suitcase, Bert said a fond farewell to the campus he loved as he and Ruth headed back to Evansville. He was used to spending weekends and holidays at the house on Keck Avenue. Now it would become his permanent home, assuming he could get a job teaching at a high school in Evansville for the fall. The house was full of Ruth's relatives—her brother Erv, who worked at a bank in town; his wife, Leola, who worked for Dr. Ira Faith, a local dentist; their little daughter, Patty; and Ruth's mother, who cooked, kept house, and cared for Patty while Leola was at work. Neither Bert nor Ruth was working that summer, and they spent lots of time reading to Patty and playing with her, becoming almost like second parents to this precocious two-year-old. When tempers flared or the house felt chaotic, Bert sometimes longed for his quiet room in Bloomington, but he consoled himself with thoughts of a wonderful trip coming up in August.

Dr. Faith, the dentist, and his wife, Kathryn, had invited Ruth and Bert to accompany them on a cross-country car trip. Ruth had gotten to know Mrs. Faith through her involvement in activities at the YWCA. The older woman soon became her role model and dear friend. After Ruth's marriage, Mrs. Faith (as Ruth always referred to her) also became very fond of Bert. As the Faiths planned this ambitious trip—their goal was to see as many natural wonders as possible in nineteen days—they decided to ask their young friends to go along. Bert could help with the driving, and Ruth would be such a pleasant companion, chatting away in the back seat.

At 8 a.m. on Sunday, August 11, they set out in Dr. Faith's new Buick. Fortunately, Bert recorded the details of this trip in his pocket diary for 1940. What an amazing journey it must have been!

Driving through Illinois and then Iowa, Bert noted the "wonderful corn crop." As they drove further west, the list of places they visited reads like a song of praise to the American West.

> *The Bad Lands, the Black Hills, and Granite Pass.*
> *Mount Rushmore, Big Horn Mountains, Shell Canyon.*
> *Yellowstone.*
> *And then Glacier.*

"Marvelous," Bert wrote in his little notebook.

On Saturday, August 17, six days into the trip, while driving further west to Spokane, Washington, they listened on the car radio to Wendell Wilkie's speech accepting the Republican nomination for the Presidency. A Hoosier by birth, Wilkie insisted on giving this speech in his hometown of Elwood, Indiana. He opened with a solemn pledge: "We are here today to represent a sacred cause—the preservation of American democracy." I wish I could have heard the conversation in the car after Wilkie ended his long speech. As a loyal supporter of Franklin Roosevelt, the Democratic candidate, Ruth wouldn't have hesitated to speak her mind. Bert might have been more favorably inclined toward Wilkie, who had grown up just thirty miles from New Pennington. Dr. and Mrs. Faith undoubtedly weighed in with their opinions as well.

The next day, they continued their journey, visiting the Grand Coulee Dam before camping for the night in Vancouver, Washington, then heading south to San Francisco and Yosemite National Park.

THE ROMANCE OF BEING A STUDENT

It's hard for me to imagine how my mother managed the rigors of this vacation. After a long day of touring, I know she would have preferred a hotel room with a warm, soft bed to a rugged campsite. But the Faiths were adventurers, and Bert loved nothing better than sleeping under the stars surrounded by the sounds and smells of nature.

Their next stop after leaving Yosemite was Los Angeles, where they got a taste of city life, visiting some friends of Dr. Faith and seeing two recently released movies—*Boom Town* with Clark Gable and *The Sea Hawk* with Errol Flynn.

Then, eager to see as much of the Western landscape as possible, they just kept going—through the Mojave Desert and on to Boulder Dam, Zion Canyon, Bryce Canyon, and the Grand Canyon (underlined by Bert for emphasis). After leaving the Grand Canyon, they must have driven through the night since Bert notes that they "entered the Petrified Forest in Arizona at 4:30 a.m." I hope they found a place to park the car and sleep for a few hours before they explored this "forest frozen in stone." In later years, my mother often told the story of her adventure in the Petrified Forest. All four of them got out of the car and wandered over the barren landscape admiring the colorful pieces of petrified wood scattered here and there. "What great souvenirs," Ruth thought, loading up the trunk of the car with some of her favorites. When they drove out of the park, the guard asked if they had taken anything. "Oh, yes," Ruth replied enthusiastically. "I got some beautiful specimens." Fortunately, the guard surmised that she was just a naïve tourist, not a hardened criminal trading in geological treasures. Sheepishly, they drove back into the park and returned all of Ruth's souvenirs, trying to replace them as accurately as possible.

On August 29, they set out for home, with Dr. Faith and Bert trading off at the wheel, as they drove through Texas, Oklahoma, Arkansas, Kansas, Tennessee, and Kentucky. Late on Friday, August 30, they arrived in Evansville—tired but thrilled as they thought about all they had seen and learned.

Despite the challenges of this outdoor odyssey, my mother often talked about what a wonderful trip it had been. Not only had she gotten to see so many natural wonders of the American West, but she also experienced another way of life. Dr. and Mrs. Faith had grown up in cultivated, upper-middle-class families. As youngsters, they studied music and read the classics. They spent evenings with friends discussing books and current affairs. For Ruth and Bert, these weeks with the older couple offered a glimpse into a world they both aspired to enter.

Bert took just one day to rest up from the Western trip before driving north to Bloomington in his own car, the trusty Plymouth. Despite his best efforts, he had not been able to get a teaching job in Evansville, and so, with Ruth's blessing, he went back to IU to begin work toward a PhD in botany. His professors had been so impressed with his master's thesis that they accepted him, without any formal application, to continue as a doctoral student. His old room at 216 S. Indiana Street was still available, and on that Sunday evening, as he walked into the small, familiar room, he could see his future unfolding before his eyes. There was no place he would rather be.

~

I like to picture Bert settling back into life at the university. He was thirty-one years old and a married man, but sometimes he felt as carefree as an undergraduate as he strolled around the campus between classes, grabbing a bite to eat at the Book Nook and then heading to the library or the botany lab to study. Often, there would be a lecture or a cultural event, and he would make it a point to attend.

In mid-October, he heard Norman Thomas, the Socialist Party's candidate for president, give a lecture in Alumni Hall. He could hardly wait to tell Ruth about it. "You would have <u>loved</u> him," he writes. "You may even vote for him." Then he adds, "Even I may vote for Norman Thomas—even I." In his speech, Thomas condemned the recently passed Selective Training and Service Act, which required all men between the ages of twenty-one and forty-five to register for the draft. He felt it "marked another step toward hatred, war, death, and aggressive military collectivism." Bert, a confirmed pacifist, must have been wondering and worrying about what he would do if he was called up for service, so it's not surprising that he found Thomas's ideas appealing. He was hoping that as more men entered the military, teaching jobs would be "growing on trees next year." His goal was to get a teaching position in 1941, so Ruth could quit her job. She would then become his dependent, which would probably be enough to exempt him from military service. Still, with the war intensifying, his future was uncertain.

Fortunately, in the much smaller world of his research, all was well. He proudly reported that his advisor, Dr. Paul Weatherwax, planned to feature some of his slides of the cross sections of root tips in the textbook he was writing. Even Dr. Ralph Cleland, the head of the botany department, announced in his cytology class that Bert's slides were "just as good as, if not better than, any he had ever seen."

"So you see why my stock is up," he tells Ruth. "The first thing you know I may even have a good opinion of myself." With this type of recognition, he feels certain he will get a position in a college or university. "Some of our dreams are definitely on the verge of coming true. I love you more all the time, Dearest. To live with you in a college atmosphere would be near enough heaven for me."

Whenever Bert left his room on Indiana Street, he was careful to put a little notebook, slightly smaller than an iPhone, in his shirt pocket. Turning the pages of his pocket diaries for 1940 and 1941 is like going through a door into his world as a first-year doctoral student.

Interspersed among notes about colloids and root tips and sieve tubes are quotations from Walt Whitman, Maurice Maeterlinck, Francis Bacon, and John Henry Newman. He also copied sentimental poems by some of his classmates: "The Trilliums" by Floyd S. and "Ultima Veritas" by W. Gladden.

In an entry dated February 26, he mentions attending a convocation talk entitled "The Romance of Being a Student." Bert notes that the speaker, Rollo Walter Brown, "was very good!" I'm not sure how many of today's scientists, working in their carefully demarcated specialties, would describe their student days as "a romance," but for Bert—with his love of literature and philosophy as well as science—being a student *was* romantic. He reveled in the life he was creating for himself on the beautiful Bloomington campus.

Toward the end of March, he had an opportunity to explore the world beyond the campus. His supervising professor, Dr. Paul Weatherwax, made it a practice to take students on collecting trips to Florida. On March 27, Bert was one of the lucky students. After driving through Kentucky, Tennessee, North Carolina, and Georgia, they reached Florida on the 29th. On April 2, he notes that he "swam in Atlantic Ocean in Miami Beach." Just four days later, they arrived back in Bloomington. Bert's concluding comment says it all: "End of a perfect trip."

Writing to Ruth on May 24, as the academic year was winding down, he says this will be his last letter "for some time" so he hopes his words will "make a lasting and beautiful impression." Partly through Ruth's connections with J. Ralph Irons, the superintendent of schools in Evansville, Bert had been offered a job teaching math and biology at Central High School (Ruth's alma mater), starting in the fall. True to her plan, Ruth resigned from her job at Daniel Wertz Elementary School, having worked there for eleven years. She hoped to become pregnant in the next year. Finally, six years after their marriage, Bert would be living in the same house with Ruth. Practical demands would soon fill his life. His romantic life as a student had ended.

Not wishing to abandon his dream altogether, he planned to continue his research at IU during summers and school vacations and earn his PhD within the next few years. His results from the past year were promising. He received an A on the final exam in Organic Chemistry and had done well in Plant Physiology, Morphology, and Biophysical Chemistry. After completing these challenging courses, he was finished with coursework and free to focus on his doctoral thesis. Of course, it was possible that he would be drafted before completing the doctorate. But if he was classified as I-A, he didn't think he would pass the physical.

As Bert was writing this "last letter" to Ruth, his lab mate, Marvin, came into the room and handed him a letter. After scanning the letter (it was from Ruth), he continued his own, almost as if Ruth herself had walked into the room. "Well, Well. 'You Old Sweet Thing.' I have to get that into my last letter." Responding to her question about whether he had seen *Penny Serenade*, a recently released movie starring Cary Grant and Irene Dunne, he replies:

> Yes, I have seen that show and liked it very much! I could hardly suppress the tears at times, especially during the scene where their little daughter performs in the school Christmas pageant. I was reminded of your love and desire for children and knew that you would appreciate it.

The confidential mood of Bert's letter was broken when the door to the lab suddenly opened again. "Of all things—one of the girl graduate students who was in the Plant Physiology class with me and Marvin just came in and wants to read poetry to us. Her office is next door to ours." Bert seemed to feel a bit left out, realizing that Marvin and the girl would probably go out to a movie in the evening to celebrate the end of classes. He tells Ruth. "I would love to celebrate with you—but we'll have to wait until next weekend. I can hardly wait to be with you again, Dearest." In their letters, my parents always seem to be biding their time, counting the hours until the next romantic reunion.

~

Two months later, in July 1941, Bert is living with Ruth and her family in the house on Keck Avenue, far from his lab at the university. The pages of his little memo book, which had been filled with poems and scientific notes, are now mostly blank.

But on August 16, he lists some major expenses: "Lamps $22.34. Bedroom Suite $142.30. Radio $79.95." I remember this radio. It was a Crosley in a dark wood console, taller than I was. And I can picture the beautiful art deco bedroom suite. It included a full-size bed frame with headboard and footboard, a tall chest of drawers, and a glamorous dressing table with a matching bench, so Ruth could sit there to check her hair and makeup in the mirror before going out. This bedroom suite moved with my parents from Indiana to Alabama, and then, after my father's death, back to Indiana, where Carol and I were thrilled to find the dresser and chest of drawers installed in the bedroom we shared at 2719 Short Marion. I clearly remember a day—I was about ten years old—when I etched my name in tiny letters on the dresser with the end of a safety pin. I have no idea why I did this. In my mind's eye, I can see those tiny letters spelling "Becky" scratched into the smooth mahogany veneer. Even today, I feel a sense of shame mixed with pride as I recall my small transgression.

On August 18, two days after buying the furniture, Bert records more expenses: "Water Meter deposit $5.00. Rent $28. Insurance $41.88. Magic Chef $100. Frigidaire $182.50. Telephone deposit $2.00. Month's rent of telephone $2.25." These financial details evoke a whole world for me—the life of a young couple in a country finally emerging from the Depression. For Bert, these were major expenditures, and he recorded them with the pride of being the wage earner. At last, he would be supporting Ruth—and her mother, who would also be living with them. Ruth, as the oldest of three children, felt it was her duty to care for her mother in her elder years. And Bert, who had a strong sense of devotion to his parents, understood and accepted this living arrangement. Ruth's mother was grateful to both of them and repaid their generosity by keeping the house spotless and cooking delicious meals.

As soon as the furniture, the stove, and the refrigerator were delivered, the three of them moved to their new home, 300 Herndon Drive. This attractive bungalow, built in 1917, was only about a mile from the house on Keck Avenue where Ruth had lived for the past three years with her mother, her brother, his wife, and their baby daughter. For Bert and Ruth, this must have felt like a new beginning, even if the house was a rental and even though her mother would be sleeping in the next room. The house was close to Garvin Park and had a concrete-lined fishpond in the back yard. They planned to stock it with goldfish and frogs—a little touch of nature in the midst of the city.

In September, Bert started his new job teaching mathematics and biology to teenagers at Central High School. He loved the students, and they came to love him. But his heart and mind were elsewhere, 120 miles to the north, in the botany department of Indiana University. From September through December, there was not a single entry in his pocket diary.

Meanwhile, Ruth, who had started teaching at age eighteen, now had to adjust to being a full-time wife and homemaker. It couldn't have been easy, with her mother right there, always ready to second-guess her efforts. However, before too many months went by, history intervened to change the course of her future.

~

On December 7, 1941, Japanese fighter planes attacked the U.S. naval base at Pearl Harbor. The next day, at President Roosevelt's request, the United States Congress declared war on Japan. Three days later, on December 11, they declared war on Germany and Italy.

Evansville, with its solid industrial base and prime location on the Ohio River, soon became a hub for the production of war materials. From 1940 to the middle of the war, the number of jobs in the city increased from eighteen thousand to sixty thousand. The overall population surged from about 100,00 in 1940 to 150,000 by the end of the war. By March 1944, companies in or near Evansville had received more than 600 million dollars in defense contracts. Many of the new workers were women, which caused an obvious problem. Who would take care of their children while the women worked long hours in factories?

Evansville desperately needed a comprehensive system of child care to enable these women to go to work. In the fall of 1942, social agencies in the city working with the Office of Civil Defense (OCD) conducted a survey to assess the situation. By the end of November, they had developed a six-point plan to care for the estimated 7,200 children needing care. Point two of the plan was to hire a qualified person to work full time developing and coordinating day care plans in the city and county. In February 1943, Evansville's superintendent of schools, J. Ralph Irons, chairman of the OCD Committee on Care of Children in Wartime, reported that he had requested federal aid to set up nursery schools to provide full-day programs for children two to five years old. He emphasized that a full-time director should be appointed as soon as possible, "a person with community organization experience and a clear understanding of the various phases of child care and training. He will serve as executive director of the entire program as it is developed." As it turned out, Mr. Irons knew just the man for the job.

Ruth, with her energy, organizational skills, civic mindedness, and devotion to children, was a natural to develop and coordinate this system. Mr. Irons was well acquainted with her many strengths. Reflecting on her life years later, she remembered "the day I was offered the position of director of Child Care Services during World War II" as one of her proudest moments.

No longer a lady of leisure, Ruth now had a big job to do—a job so important that she postponed her dream of having a child. Instead of having one baby to care for, she now had to think of the welfare of hundreds, perhaps even thousands of young children and their parents. Her country needed her, her city needed her, and she was never one to shrink from a challenge.

Surprisingly, for a woman who was so talkative, she never told my sister and me much about this part of her life. All we knew was that she organized a network of nursery schools where preschoolers could spend long hours in a safe, comfortable space, complete with educational activities and healthy meals. I'm sure her own childhood experience of being left home alone to care for her little brothers while her mother worked in a series of low-paying jobs motivated her to create the best possible environment for these children whose mothers were working to support the war effort.

Of course, the kind of comprehensive day care she had in mind was costly, but somehow the city managed to come up with the funds. In 1941, the federal government had passed the Defense Housing and Community Facilities and Services Act, usually referred to as the Lanham Act. On June 29, 1943, the Senate approved twenty million dollars under the terms of this act for the care of children of working mothers. Finally, in December, some of these funds were allocated to Evansville for play centers to serve children when schools were not in session. The charge for care was fifty cents a week with an extra dollar to cover hot lunches. The results of this program were impressive. Evansville historian, Harold Gourley, notes, "Thanks to the Lanham Act it was possible to have nursery schools in Evansville which provided food for some 700 grade school children and afforded great assistance to parents working in defense plants."

Trying to imagine how my mother spent her days, I picture her walking into her new office in the morning and hanging her jacket on a hook. Even before she sat down at her desk, the phone rang. When she accepted this job, she had been thrilled to learn that her office would have a telephone, but now she sometimes felt like ripping the cord out of the wall. There was no end to her responsibilities—talking with elected officials and school authorities, interviewing candidates to work as caregivers and dieticians, planning activities, conducting meetings and site visits, filling out endless government forms to get the money she desperately needed. Even for a woman of her prodigious energy, it was exhausting. By the end of the day, her feet were killing her. Before leaving her office, she would slip off her pumps, arrange the papers strewn all over the desk into a few neat piles, and just sit for a few minutes to collect her thoughts before heading out to catch the city bus.

Bert's days were also tiring. Examining his memo books, I notice that when school was in session at Central, his philosophical musings and scientific notes disappeared. Most of the pages are blank except for the occasional note concerning the mundane but time-consuming tasks required of a high school teacher, new to the team. He had been tasked with chairing the teachers' program committee as well as taking charge of the activity office, a tedious job that consisted of keeping meticulous records of all student fees collected for extracurricular activities, like

THE ROMANCE OF BEING A STUDENT

school plays and football games, throughout the entire school year. Often, after classes had ended for the day, there was a teachers' meeting to attend or paperwork related to the activity expenses.

When he was free to leave, he would drive back to the house on Herndon Drive. After taking off his coat and tie, he would go out to feed the fish in the backyard pond and then check with Ruth's mother (by this time, he called her Mom) to see if he could help with supper. As soon as Ruth got home, they would sit down to a hot meal in the small dining room. Mom was an expert at stretching a dollar, and she quickly mastered the system of wartime rationing. Still, there were occasional meatless meals, and the strict rationing of sugar interfered with her baking. Sometimes she worked out a deal with one of her sisters, trading a few coffee ration stamps in exchange for some extra sugar.

After dinner, Ruth and Bert would talk as they washed and dried the dishes, and then get back to work—Ruth filling out the government forms that had piled up during the day and Bert preparing his math and science lessons for the next day or grading student papers. By the time they walked into their bedroom and closed the door, Ruth hardly had the energy to pull back the covers and climb into bed. She was asleep almost before her head hit the pillow.

Unlike Ruth, Bert was a night owl. He lay awake thinking about their life and their love now that they were living together in the same house. Most nights Ruth was so tired by the time she got to bed that she wasn't interested in making love. He almost found himself missing those nights in Bloomington when he sat up late into the night in his rented room writing letters to Ruth, counting the hours until they would be together again.

Now they were living in the real world. Not the romantic, rarefied world of their letters but a world of children who needed care and teenagers who needed to learn basic math. When he and Ruth arrived home at the end of the day, there was Mom, a reminder that it wasn't just the two of them. And always, in the background, there was the inescapable news of the war. People were dying in Europe and North Africa and the Pacific. So many people were dying. Bert's brother Dwight, serving in Italy, was at risk. This news was especially demoralizing for Bert, whose hope that war could be averted through diplomacy had not been realized.

Lying there, trying to fall asleep, he remembered something he had written in a letter to Ruth in 1938 or 1939:

> Had we set up a home immediately and plunged into all the responsibilities and constant intimacy of such a life, much of the spiritual significance and beauty of the relationship might not have survived. Even ignoring the financial side of the question, I think we "builded much better than we knew" when we decided to work as we have been during the winters.

Bert yearned for a marriage full of beauty and spiritual significance. Now, faced with the realities of daily life, this ideal of perfect love was in peril.

~

On June 14, 1943, a note of hope appears in Bert's diary: "Start work at IU." A week later: "Pd. rent 2 wks. in advance." And then on Monday July 5, I imagine him recording with a sigh of relief: "Entered Bloomington." He would be spending the rest of the summer at the university continuing his doctoral research.

Soon the pages of his little book began to fill up again—notes on convocations, a book recommendation from Dr. Cleland, philosophical observations, data related to his thesis. Bert was spending long hours in the lab, and one of the girl graduate students always seemed to be there when he was. Maybe this was the same girl who had burst into the lab two years earlier, her head filled with poetry.

Back in Evansville, Ruth scarcely had time to breathe now that all the nursery schools were up and running. But she was proud to know she was doing her part to support the war effort by creating and sustaining programs to help working mothers and their children.

She missed Bert, but the summer seemed to be flying by. One Saturday in August, she took a Greyhound bus to Bloomington to spend a few days with him at the university. Soon after he met her at the bus station, he made an abrupt announcement. He had fallen in love with a girl who had an office near his. Her name was Mary. He wanted a divorce.

I was in my thirties when my mother told me about Bert's unexpected announcement, and even though many years had gone by, I could still hear the shock and anger in her voice. "This came as a complete surprise to me, and I was absolutely devastated." In the afternoon, she pulled herself together enough to accompany Bert to a picnic and field trip organized by the botany department. This was the first and only time she saw Mary. "Bert spent all his time fawning over that little girl. He completely ignored me. I have never felt so humiliated in my life!"

"What happened afterwards?" I asked. "How did you and Daddy work through the situation?"

Swallowing hard and looking straight into my eyes, she said in a steady voice, "I never mentioned it again. And neither did he."

I had had enough therapy by then to know this wasn't the ideal way to handle a marital crisis, and I was shocked to hear that a woman who had studied psychology and given public lectures on the subject chose to deal with this betrayal by just ignoring it. But then this was how she had always handled a difficult situation. Once Bert was back in Evansville in September, they went on as if nothing had happened. But something had happened, and their marriage was never quite the same.

~

Many years later, during the early days of the COVID-19 pandemic, I came across an intriguing photograph while paging through the scrapbook my mother made after my father died. A group of graduate students was standing in a meadow. Dr. Ralph Cleland, the head of the botany department, is on the right, and there is Bert—tall, young, and very handsome. Standing next to him is a plain-featured girl with a blank expression on her face. She wears a checked dress and a cardigan sweater. She looks so young and shy, as if she had just stepped off her parents' farm. Someone has marked a large X in ballpoint pen above her head in the picture. That someone must have been my mother because under the picture of that girl on the page where she had pasted the photo she wrote just one word: "Mary." So this was the woman who stole my father's heart in 1943.

That X speaks volumes. Thinking of my mother's hurt and shame, I remember a letter she wrote a few weeks before her wedding in 1936. Responding to Bert's fear that she might tire of him, she said it was more likely that a man who hadn't sown his wild oats before he married would do so afterward. Then she boldly proclaimed, "But I'm not losing any sleep over this. If I can't hold you, I can't blame you." But she did blame him for this infatuation, confirmed by the anger I heard in her voice when she told me so many years later. Nothing ever came of it. Mary ended up happily married to another graduate student who later became a successful professor.

There is no record of what happened during the rest of that summer. Ruth took the bus back to Evansville. And, a few weeks later, as Bert prepared to return to Herndon Drive to resume his teaching at Central, he entered a reminder to himself in his pocket diary: "Take Ruth a gift as I go home."

26

A Stake in the Future

"ALLIES LAND IN FRANCE: See Infantry Scramble Up Beaches." That was the headline on the evening paper waiting for Bert and Ruth when they got home on Tuesday, June 6, 1944. The Allied forces had pulled off a tremendous feat by landing thousands of soldiers in Nazi-occupied France. And Evansville had played a major role in this stunning success. The LSTs, (Landing Ship Tanks) and the P-47 Thunderbolt fighter planes, many of which were built in Evansville, were invaluable in pulling off this surprise invasion.

Ruth, Bert, and Mom spent the evening huddled around the big Crosley radio listening to President Roosevelt's address to the nation. Instead of his usual Fireside Chat, he spoke in the form of a long prayer, concluding with his hope that an Allied victory would lead to "a world unity that will spell a sure peace, a peace invulnerable to the schemings of unworthy men." I can imagine the three of them sitting there, riveted by these words, hoping that the terrible world war might be nearing its end and feeling proud that their city had played a major role in the success of the Normandy invasion.

There are no letters to reveal Bert's reactions to this news, so I pulled out his little memo book for 1944, hoping for some insights. But no, the few entries relate to mundane things like income tax payments—$206.83 on March 8—and filling up the gas tank on the Plymouth—$1.89 on March 14.

A STAKE IN THE FUTURE

Flipping through the pages, I notice that every few weeks, next to the date, Bert has written a capital M and circled it. It seems like some kind of secret code. Oh no, I think! Maybe he's still in touch with Mary. I'm surprised how much this upsets me. To calm myself, I make a list of all the dates he marked: Tuesday, March 14; Tuesday, April 11; Monday, May 8; Monday, June 5; Monday, July 3; Monday, August 1. I breathe a sigh of relief. This has nothing to do with Mary. He has been keeping track of Ruth's Menstrual cycles.

So far, Bert's plan for completing his PhD while also helping to support Ruth and her mother was working. From September through June, he taught at the high school in Evansville, contributing his salary to household expenses. Then, in the summers, he rented a room in Bloomington and continued doing research for his doctoral thesis. In his diary for May 1944, he was already writing entries about root tips, eager to get back to his work at the university. On June 16, he noted that he paid his tuition for the summer: $29.25. On June 25, he splurged on a pair of swimming trunks ("100% wool") from Sullivan's department store in Bloomington. They were expensive, costing $3.95, about as much as two tankfuls of gas. I have to laugh as I picture this frugal man so excited about his new trunks that he noted "must be kept in crystals over winter" to avoid moth damage.

The pages of his pocket diary for the rest of the summer are filled with information related to his research as well as an account of a bright but windy July day "just right for collecting butterflies." Near a flower bed of zinnias and phlox, he collected two swallowtails, two sulphurs, and a large fritillary. Then, on Sunday, September 3, squeezed into the margins around an entry about Dr. Cleland's Oenothera (evening primrose) seeds, is a personal note: "Ruth sick. Just 3 weeks after conception." The note is so tiny I almost missed it, but there it is. Ruth is pregnant! I was born exactly eight months later—on May 3, 1945.

FROM SEED TO TREE TO FRUIT

[Image of an open pocket diary showing handwritten notes for September 1944, with annotations including "just 3 wks. after conception," "Ruth sick," and various entries about visiting fields, museums, and Garfield Park in Chi.]

No letters exist to document the first months of Ruth's pregnancy because Bert was back in Evansville teaching at the high school. She was working too, continuing as director of child-care services. Bert's memo book for 1945 makes no mention of the impending birth. Instead, he uses every single page to honor his New Year's resolution of learning one new word each day, words such as "laconic," "lascivious," and "hegemony." This is so typical of the man I've come to know from reading his letters and pocket diaries. Bert was always learning, always growing, always expecting so much of himself.

In March, he resigned his job at Central High School and returned to the university, working long hours to complete his doctoral thesis. He hoped to have a first draft completed by the end of April. Finishing his PhD was now essential because he had accepted a position in the biology department at the University of Alabama in Tuscaloosa with a start date of June 1945. Once he was back in Bloomington, his letters to Ruth resumed. Sadly, Ruth's letters from this period have not survived.

Writing to Ruth on April 8, he begins on a joyous note: "Ah! This is the life. If I just had you here, it would be next door to heaven! How are you? Enjoying your new freedom?" With about a month to go before the baby's arrival, Ruth had stepped down from her job and had been attending a series of parties and showers in her honor. Bert understood that giving up her job was not an easy decision. "It would seem to me to require a great deal of courage (or something) for a woman to stop a career, as you have, after such an impressive start."

Even when writing to his own wife, his writing is so formal, almost as if he's composing an article for a professional journal, with phrases like "It would seem to me to require a great deal of courage."

Bert loved the written word and worked hard to develop the persona he projected in his writing. With his constant reading, his habit of copying passages he admired into his notebooks, and his determined efforts to increase his vocabulary, he hoped to create a distinctive voice as a writer.

This formal quality was also typical of his spoken conversation, something I imitated almost as soon as I could talk. My first word, as recorded in the baby book my mother kept, was "Da-Da." By the time I was three years old, I was speaking in complete sentences and using words like "represent." As a toddler, I was already starting to sound like my father.

In the spring of 1945, Bert was living in a rented room at the university, spending hours each day focused on his research and writing. When he needed a break, he would walk to the Student Union Building to read the daily newspapers. Writing on April 10, he asks Ruth, "What do you think of the war these days? Fast & furious, isn't it? I think VE day is going to be here before Junior is. Would you like to bet on that?"

Writing two days later, he says he has been "wondering what kind of a young woman our daughter will become. I do hope it is a girl. On the other hand, I suppose my masculine pride will be flattered if it turns out to be a boy."

Bert had already mailed this letter when he felt compelled to write again. He had been listening to the radio in the Union Building when he heard the news of President Roosevelt's death. "That is a blow to this country and, no doubt, to the entire democratic world. I know how much you liked Roosevelt and so I imagine this sad news almost brings you a personal feeling of loss." In the cafeteria as he was having supper, "you could literally see the news of his death spread by watching the appearance of shock and incredulity as it spread among the people with the knowledge of his passing."

Despite his own Republican upbringing, Bert had come to admire Roosevelt.

> I, too, consider him one of the great men of all time. When I think of his great courage in championing good causes, and of his attitude toward world peace, and of how well you liked him, it all seems to bring you so close that I had to write to you again. It makes me want to see you and talk to you again even more than ever.

Sitting here in Plainfield on a hot summer day, with the fan rustling the pages of Bert's letter, it's comforting for me to know that despite Ruth's intense focus on her nursery schools and Bert's infatuation with Mary, their marriage is on a solid foundation as they expect their first child. Not just a romantic fantasy, their love is based on common interests and mutual respect, all the things they have shared through their letters and conversations—thoughts about politics, science, philosophy, psychology, and, especially, their love for each other. The phrase "soul mates" has become a cliché, but after reading their letters, I can't think of a better way to describe my parents' love as it deepened over the years.

Always appreciative of Ruth's strengths, Bert writes, "Dearest, your fine attitude and high morale during these many months, and especially during these final weeks of preparation and waiting speak most eloquently of your great spirit." Apparently, Ruth's mother has been expressing anxiety about the birth, and Bert tries to reassure her: "At the very last, the matter is really out of your hands, so all you need to do is let nature (and the Dr.) take its course."

In another letter from this period, he writes with the poetic flare that was always just below the surface for this scientist. "You are repeating the miracle of the ages, the renewal of life, the propagation of the species. You are about to become the complete woman. Our child will be lucky to have such a mother."

Reading this in the twenty-first century, it seems so dated, as if only through having a child could a woman's life become complete. But I know that my mother accepted this version of reality as well. Although she had worked full time since she was eighteen years old and had established herself as a competent professional in a world dominated by powerful men, she wrote in some of her most emotional letters that her life would not be complete without having children of her own. As if she were giving a campaign speech, she proclaimed in more than one letter to Bert that having children was her "Manifest Destiny." Now, at age thirty-three, time was running out. With the war winding down, she was happy to give up her job as Evansville's director of child-care services as she prepared to become a full-time wife and mother. Fortunately, it didn't take long for this dream to come true.

In another letter written in April, Bert discloses an important date.

> I shall always remember August 12. That we should effect
> conception the very first time is little short of a miracle.
> We started something that night that will affect the whole
> course of our lives. If all continues to go well, we will have
> a stake in the future and more than ever to live for.

Reading this eighty years later, I realize he's talking about me. Is there anything this note-taking scientist doesn't record in minute detail? My parents documented everything in their letters, right down to the exact date of my conception. It's as if they were writing history while also living it.

Bert sometimes seemed to enjoy writing to Ruth even more than living in the same house with her, as he had done for the past three years. Now that he was back at the university, he savored the chance to communicate with her through letters once again.

> I think I like to write to you even better than I like to
> write on the thesis. Too bad one can't earn a PhD writing
> love letters to his wife. You are my inspiration, Dearest. If
> my work is any good, it should be dedicated to you.

This comment reveals so much about Bert. He misses the sex, something he mentions often in these letters. This snippet from April 17 is typical:

> Right now I am more jealous of that little junior who
> is occupying your beautiful body so completely and so
> long and so definitely at my expense. I am having some
> difficulty, at the present time, utilizing my surplus sexual
> energy.

He seems to be channeling some of this excess sexual energy into writing all these letters. In a way, he seems to prefer loving Ruth from a distance. Perhaps when he expresses his love in writing, it seems more real to him, more profound. Some would see this as a form of distancing himself from the real embodied woman he has married. And I suppose it is. But I understand what he is saying since I, too, sometimes experience my emotions most deeply only after writing about them. So often, reading these letters, I remember what my mother told me when I was in my mid-forties: "You're more like your father, and Carol is more like me." Now I understand what she meant.

About a month before the due date, he asked Ruth to be sure to have someone call him at the lab as soon as labor began.

> I would like to be there when the baby comes—not in the delivery room perhaps—or not because I think you will need me, but I would feel much better just to be closer to you at that time.

But as the birth grew nearer, he seemed to withdraw this offer. Suddenly, helping his youngest brother Denzil on the family farm became his priority. He explained to Ruth that with his father getting too old to do heavy work and his brother Dwight in the army in Italy, there was no one to do anything around the farm except Denzil. "My heart goes out to him." He proposed a plan. He would come to Evansville and spend about a week, "perhaps less," when the baby was born and then travel back to Bloomington to work on his thesis for about three more weeks. After wrapping up his work at the university, he would go to the farm to help Denzil "build fence" for four days before finally returning to Evansville.

> Those few days at home will mean an awfully lot to Dad and Denzil, and among other things will give me a chance to get brown and tough for the summer. Once I get back

to Evansville, we will have four or five days to get ready to leave for Alabama.

I don't know how my mother responded to Bert's plan, but it makes me furious. Why is building fences on the farm more important than helping Ruth care for their new baby? And who needs help more? His strong young brother or his wife, recovering from childbirth, and her elderly mother? The two women will have to care for a newborn while packing up an entire house to move to a new home more than three hundred miles away? I realize that in those days, most fathers were less involved in caring for their babies than they are today, but still, he seems to be abandoning Ruth when she needs him most. I think there is something deeper going on here as well. For Bert, who prefers to live in the heights, the thought of an actual birth—a messy process just about as real as it gets—and caring for a crying newborn is just too much reality for him to face. He certainly knew what it would be like since all five of his younger siblings were born at home as he had been.

As Ruth was about to give birth, the war in Europe was also drawing to a close. It was hard to know which would come sooner—the baby or the Allied victory. On April 24, Bert writes, "Hitler says he's 'in Berlin to win or die.' That's a good one, isn't it?"

By April 25, Bert had completed a draft of his thesis, "Origin of Tissues of the Root and Structure of the Meristematic Root Tip of Vascular Plants," and handed it over to the typist. Ruth had been to see her obstetrician, Dr. Victor Huggins, who predicted that the baby would be born on May 5 or 6. Writing on May 2, Bert said he planned to drive to Evansville in a few days so he could take Ruth to the hospital and be near her at the time of birth.

In 1945, fathers did not attend childbirth classes with their wives as Frank and I did thirty years later. But I see from his letters that

A STAKE IN THE FUTURE

Bert was preparing for the birth in his own way. After reading about human embryology in the biology library, he shares some of his newly acquired knowledge with Ruth, explaining how a "cervical plug" is formed soon after fertilization so that nothing can pass from the uterus during the entire period of pregnancy. "Just before birth, the cervical opening enlarges, the plug is released, and you will notice the so-called 'bleeding' that signals the actual onset of birth."

When his roommate at the university asked if he was beginning to get nervous about the birth, he replied that he was not at all worried. Reporting on this conversation, he assures Ruth:

> The human body is such a wonderful mechanism. Your endocrine glands secrete hormones and other substances which enable the female organism to give birth involuntarily and naturally at exactly the right time. Confidence, then, in the human body to react naturally, plus confidence in the modern doctor, with all his scientific knowledge and equipment, should remove all doubt and fear from the mind of the modern intelligent woman.

I bristle while reading this. What about the woman herself? Doesn't she have a role in this process? Or is she just a passive vessel at the mercy of natural forces and the doctor's expertise?

I wonder how my mother felt when she read this letter. Rather than having her husband pontificating from afar, she might have preferred having him next to her holding her hand. But that was not to be. I arrived on May 3, a few days earlier than expected—a forceps delivery, perhaps because Ruth was completely anesthetized. Bert didn't make it to Evansville until May 6, when he visited Ruth and met his new daughter, Rebecca Kay, at Deaconess Hospital. After a stay of only two days, he drove back to the university, so that he could revise his thesis after receiving feedback from Dr. Cleland, the chair of the botany department. Reading this, my muscles tighten and I realize I'm still angry with Bert for leaving Ruth alone at a time when she needed him by her side.

Speaking as a mother myself, I regret that he didn't remain in Evansville with his wife and baby during their ten-day stay in the hospital. But I have to admit that I treasure the letters he wrote once he was back at the university, letters revealing thoughts and feelings that would have been lost to me if he had stayed in Evansville. In a letter written hours after he arrived back at his room in Bloomington, he is overflowing with love and delight. "You certainly are the sweetest young mother I have ever seen or can even imagine! I can't begin to tell you how much I love you—even more than ever!"

He doesn't get around to mentioning what's happening in the wider world until page two.

> Say, Kid! What are you doing to celebrate V-E Day? Isn't that great? Kay was four days old on V-E Day. I think I will call her "Kay." What will you call her? She is the Sweetest Little thing.

As a new father, Bert no longer seems compelled to use impressive vocabulary words to describe his feelings. "Sweet" is now his adjective of choice. He plans to return to Evansville on May 12, when Ruth and Rebecca will be discharged from the hospital. He feels he may be more attuned to the significance of birth since he is "a biologist who thinks about life and reproduction from a scientific point of view." But he is feeling more like a poet or philosopher than a scientist. "The birth of a baby is a wonderful miracle, and the fundamental power of life is still a mystery to science."

He remembers the baby as "very calm and peaceful and sleepy—altogether unconscious of the fact that she is the center of a great attraction." It will be a privilege, he says, "to watch her and to help her grow and gain self-consciousness. We are two lucky people, Dearest—and now I should say three. Isn't it wonderful?"

He realizes there will be sleepless nights, childhood illnesses, and other prices to pay. "But she is precious, she is invaluable. She is our future. We will give her to tomorrow for a better world. If we make her better by loving her more, she, in turn, will be better for the world." It gives me chills to read these words. I hope he would not feel disappointed if he could look back on the life I have lived.

"Well, you old sweet things!" he signs off. "I'll be glad when Saturday comes. Can she smile yet?"

On May 12, things went smoothly as Bert checked Ruth and Becky out of the hospital, paid the hospital and doctor's bill ($160), and brought them home to Herndon Drive to settle in with help from Ruth's mother.

He must have stayed there for about ten days since his next letter is postmarked May 21.

He sat down to write just minutes after walking into his room in Bloomington. While he was away, a letter had arrived from his brother Dwight. Writing on May 6, Dwight reports that he "weathered the storm without a scratch" though he doesn't know how he managed to be so lucky. He tells Bert that he "advanced with a tank unit and saw some serious action." As they moved through occupied territory in Italy, the people were thrilled to be liberated by the American troops. He expects to be home in Indiana by August or September, which will be a huge relief for the whole family—especially for his wife, Ercil, and his mother, my Grandma Williams.

The next day, Bert was making some edits to the introduction and bibliography of his thesis but took time out to write a letter to Ruth.

"How is everything by now? Does Becky wake you up at night? Do smiles still flicker across her face when she is asleep? I think I first noticed those fleeting smiles when she was ten days old."

His letter is short but full of love.

> For those pessimists who maintain that life is just a thorny pathway full of aches and pains and sorrow from the cradle to the grave, we could point out that Becky rests peacefully and beautifully and smiles more than she frowns. She may make a terrible fuss when she is hungry and have the tummy ache sometimes, but those reactions are only incidental to the real joy of being alive.

I remember having similar feelings of joy after the birth of my own two children. How strange—and how wonderful—to hear my father putting these feelings into words as he watches his infant daughter, as he watches me.

On May 24, he was thinking about the future. "Living with you and Becky and teaching on a university faculty in an atmosphere of learning and research is truly a dream coming true for me." He asks Ruth to "give Becky another kiss for me. I love that baby—and you too—you sweet thing, you."

I treasure a photograph of the three of us taken when I was about two years old. My mother looks so happy, her dream of having a child of her own has finally come true. My father is holding me and smiling down with such tenderness and pride, not looking sad as he does in many photos.

A STAKE IN THE FUTURE

The letters arranged on the table in front of me are starting to show their age. Some of the envelopes are fraying at the edges, and a few pages have split along the lines where they have been folded and refolded so many times. Saved in shoeboxes, stored in filing cabinets, moved from state to state, these letters have come to have a life of their own, and they have given me a precious gift as I have come to know my parents in new and unexpected ways.

In my younger years, I often felt overwhelmed by my effusive and extroverted mother. Through the letters, I have gotten to know her as Ruth—a dedicated young teacher, a courageous advocate for social justice, an efficient and effective chief executive, a stabilizing force for her beloved Bert, and my amazing mother.

Bert's letters meant so much to her. She first read them a day or two after they were written, when she was young and in love. As a woman in her sixties and retired from her job as a high school history teacher, she read them again. Finally able to grieve her loss, she cried as she read Bert's letters, using a red pencil to mark her favorite parts, the words that told the story of their great love. Then more than twenty years later, as a woman slipping into dementia, she read them once again. She couldn't hold his words in her mind for more than a second, so she copied them out in her own flowing script on the covers of manila folders, reminding herself of how she had once been loved.

Now it's my turn. Reading these letters, written in the tiny, neat handwriting of a scientist, I am searching for my father. No longer just the Daddy of my childhood memories, the kind and gentle father who took me for walks in the woods or the scary man he became in the spring of 1954, I have come to know him as Bert—a thinker, a writer, a lover, a teacher, a scientist, and the man I am proud to call my father. Finally, after all the years of struggle, searching everywhere for clues as to who he really was, I feel a peace and contentment I have never known before.

Maybe that's why, after finishing the final revisions of this chapter, I decided to tackle a daunting project I had been putting off for years—cleaning the attic. Frank and I bought the Plainfield house in 1972. When our children, Susanna and Alex, were young, we spent every summer there. The kids never wanted to go to sleep-away camp. Plainfield was their camp as they roamed the fields, swam in the pond, built a treehouse, and spent lazy evenings reading and playing games. Over all these years, it was good to have an attic to store things we weren't quite ready to part with. Now that our kids have kids of their own, the attic has become a major attraction of their summer visits. The grandchildren disappear up the staircase and come down with items I haven't seen for years—stuffed animals that were once beloved, the remnants of curtains long since replaced, models of tanks and airplanes that Alex crafted from tiny pieces of plastic during his boyhood.

But after their most recent visit, I realized the attic was more than just a treasure house. It was a dangerous fire trap. Something had to be done, and with my feeling of satisfaction after finishing this chapter, I felt equal to the task. Deciding to skip my Friday exercise class, I climbed the stairs to the attic, the air growing hotter and heavier with every step.

Anticipating this project, I had purchased a large supply of heavy-duty garbage bags. It wasn't hard to fill them. So many things we once had treasured had outgrown their usefulness. Quickly sorting through the piles of junk, I set aside items to recycle or drop off at the town swap shop. Opening a small cardboard box, I found it filled with photo envelopes, the kind I used to pick up at the local pharmacy about a week after taking a roll of film to be developed. Tucked among all the fading photos of our family life in the 1970s and 1980s was a single postcard. On the front was a picture of the Smoky Mountains swathed in mist. Turning it over, I saw that it was addressed to "Miss Rebecca Kay Williams, 89 Cedar Crest, Tuscaloosa, Ala" and postmarked "Oak Ridge, Tenn, July 16, 1953."

> Dearest Becky,
>
> How is our sweet little 8 year old? Is she sweet to the sweet little 5 year old? I was so happy to find such a beautiful letter from you when I got back to my room in Oak Ridge on Monday. Write again when you have time.
>
> All my love, Daddy

How strange that I should happen to find this postcard from my father in a box with photos from a much later era—and just after finishing a chapter about my own birth. I saw it as a sign that he wanted to send me a message of his love and support, perhaps to express his appreciation for the book I've worked so hard to complete, a dream he never got to fulfill himself.

As I put the card back in the box, I saw a typed letter nestled between two of the photo envelopes. Dated June 15, 1986, it was from my mother, age seventy-four at the time, writing to her middle-aged daughter. "Dearest Rebecca," the letter begins:

> Today is Father's Day! No daughter ever had a better father. Your Daddy loved you two little girls with all his heart. He had the perfect role model. Grandpa Williams was the sweetest, kindest man I ever knew. He used to say, "Let me nuss you a while." He truly loved little children, and so did your Dad.

This brings back so many memories of my father and also my grandfather. I can picture Grandpa sitting in the big rocker on his front porch, holding me on his lap, gently rocking back and forth, nursing his little granddaughter. No wonder I remember that porch with such fondness.

Setting the letter aside, I kept sifting through the box and found one more envelope among all the photos. Postmarked "September 13, 1986," it held a single sheet of bright yellow stationery—a note from my father's youngest sister, my Aunt Lois. Reading her words, I began to accept what my grandchildren have always believed. The attic is a magical place. Lois wrote this from her home in Indianapolis after having attended the family reunion in Greensburg earlier in the summer, where we saw her for the first time in many years. She had enclosed a copy of her favorite photograph of her brother Bert and explained:

> Your father was such a very special, special person to me, and I've always felt that you and Carol were very special too! I hope this picture gives you as much pleasure as mine does for me.

A STAKE IN THE FUTURE

The photo disappeared long ago, but my aunt's memories of her very special brother, my father, give me great pleasure today as I write the final words of this chapter.

27

From Seed to Tree to Fruit

MY FATHER LOVED being a teacher. "Really, many of my happiest hours are in the classroom," he once said in a letter to my mother. "It seems that there I can get out of myself—away from myself—above myself. You know what I mean because you, too, have experienced it. To express myself creatively and originally is a glorious release and relief."

In the fall of 1937, teaching at New Point High School, the small school he had attended as a boy, he had a special group of students in his sophomore English class. "It really does a teacher good to see how interested they become in all things deep and significant. It seems to be a matter of kindred spirits. I can talk about anything in that class and they will understand. One can literally see right into their souls, and some of them are very beautiful."

The subject matter he was exposing these fifteen-year-olds to was challenging by today's standards. On Fridays, he usually read aloud to them from something he found especially worthwhile. His selections included poems by Shelley and Emily Dickinson, a short story by John Steinbeck, and writings from his own notebooks. The class had been studying the Greek philosophers in history, so he chose to read an excerpt from Socrates. He felt there were several students in that class "who can meet me as a student on common ground."

Writing to Ruth about a week later, he described a memorable class session with this special group of students:

FROM SEED TO TREE TO FRUIT

I had occasion in the sophomore English class to trace the development of a papaw from seed to tree to fruit. (The sophomores are composing personal essays now.) I began by telling how well Mr. Zetterberg [the school principal] and I like papaws—that he had several in his desk at various times this fall—that he gave me one occasionally—that one day he gave me an especially fine one. It was so good, the seeds were so beautiful, so well developed, and apparently so full of life that I saved them—there were ten. I planted them carefully in a large flower pot. I watched hopefully for signs of life. (The class was enthralled. I have never seen such eager attention.)

The other evening I came home after having been gone for four days. One of the seeds had germinated and was up about an inch. It grows about half an inch each day. And now here is a peculiar thing about that beautiful, delicate little plant. It is about three inches tall now, very slender with two small leaves at the top. It is sitting on a stand in front of the window. There is a lamp on the stand in such a position that the plant is directly between the window and the lamp. Each evening after dark the lamp is lit for two or three hours. This is the peculiar thing that the little plant does. It turns obviously and definitely and rather quickly (about 90 degrees in one hour) toward the sunlight in the daytime and the lamplight at night.

The plant is alive as we are but can't think as we do. However, it acts as though it knew that the light was good and necessary to its natural and beautiful development. Just so, the human mind turns toward the light of truth,

> beauty, and love. Even though we can't define life, love, truth, or beauty we can detect their presence and turn toward them when we recognize or feel them.
>
> I doubt if the little plant survives the winter. I'm going to care for it as well as possible. If it is still alive in the spring, I will transplant it to the big out-of-doors. There it will live, and when you come to visit me years hence in the autumn, and I give you a nice papaw from my tree, you are to remember the one Mr. Zetterberg gave me, for the one I give you will have in it something from the one he gave me. Life! Isn't it true? And they say, "Sure!"

Reading this, I almost feel that I too am present in that little classroom. I can picture the students, all twelve of them, sitting at their wooden desks, leaning forward, listening with rapt attention to their teacher as he says, "Life! Isn't it true?"

And they respond in unison, "Sure!"

For Bert, teaching was more than just a job. It was "a privilege," as he once wrote, "and a divine responsibility." And teaching wasn't limited to what happened in a classroom. Three weeks after I was born in 1945, he wrote to my mother:

> My mind already jumps ahead to Becky's high school and college days, partly because I am a teacher. But we'll have our best chance to do our best teaching before she even gets into grade school. It is a great opportunity as well as a responsibility. I guess we will have to be careful not to love her too much. I have had so many students that I have liked so well. Now that I have one of my very own flesh and blood and of yours too, I'll have to be careful not to go overboard too far.

FROM SEED TO TREE TO FRUIT

Thinking of my father as a teacher, I realize part of his secret was that he didn't just teach a subject. He got to know each one of his students and supported their interests. When he took me for a walk in the woods, if I was curious about something, that was what he would explain. When I asked him about what he did all summer at Oak Ridge, he didn't launch into a long explanation. He took me to visit his lab.

I remember with special tenderness something that happened when I was about six years old. It was a lazy Sunday afternoon, and I was sitting in the living room. Suddenly, coming from our huge Crosley radio was the most beautiful music I had ever heard. The melody echoed in my mind for the rest of the day. I told Daddy how much I had loved this music. Not knowing the name of the piece himself, he called the radio station to find out. A few weeks later, he handed me a large, flat package. Inside was a recording of Variation 18 of Rachmaninoff's Rhapsody on a Theme of Paganini. I played it over and over. Even today, when I hear this hauntingly beautiful piece, it reminds me of my father.

I was nine years old when he died. I felt so lost without him. And then I learned I was going to lose my home as well when Mother decided we should move to Indiana. Maybe she just wanted to escape from a place that held so many memories of happier times. But she didn't mention this to me and Carol. Instead, she explained that she would earn a lot more money teaching in Indiana, and she wanted to be closer to her relatives, all those aunts who had been almost like mothers to her. I understood that her plan made sense, but it meant leaving behind precious memories of my father that were tied to this place. When I went out in the back yard, I could picture him mowing the grass, trimming the hedge, teaching me the names of all the trees and flowers.

Around the beginning of March, I had an idea. All through the spring I collected leaves and seeds from the trees and plants in our yard. Daddy had taught me how to press a plant specimen and then mount it on heavy paper with glue. I did everything just the way he showed me. I already knew most of the names, but Mother had to help me with a few. About a week before we moved, I punched holes in all the pages and put them into a big notebook. This was my way of saying goodbye to the plants Daddy had taught me to love. Deep down, I knew I was saying goodbye to him as well.

~

Before I was born, my father—and my mother—were important teachers and role models for their little niece, Patty. At the time, Ruth was living in the house on Keck Avenue in Evansville with her mother as well as her brother Erv; his wife, Leola; and then, in October 1938, their infant daughter, Patty. Ruth and Bert adored this blonde, curly-haired baby and spent many hours with her.

My cousin Pat, now in her mid-eighties, remembers Bert as her first and, perhaps, her most influential teacher. "He was tall, very gentle, with a soft voice, so soft you had to listen carefully to hear what he said. He used to take me out for long walks in the woods. Those walks were an education. He invited me to think much more deeply than a child normally would." She missed him and Ruth deeply after her family moved to Illinois when she was seven years old. For young Patty, losing contact with Bert and Ruth "was like taking part of my core away from me. They were so influential in my development, possibly more than my own parents. We connected differently."

I didn't get to know and appreciate Pat until I was well into adulthood. When she came to visit us in Tuscaloosa, I was about seven years old. I sensed her special relationship with my parents, and I was terribly jealous. Seven years older than me, she was already a teenager and seemed so sophisticated with her northern ways. It didn't help that I often heard my mother say, with a touch of pride, "Patty is more like me than either you or Carol." I never understood what my parents saw in her. It wasn't until many years later, when Mother was in the early stages of dementia, that I got to know Pat through long phone conversations. As we shared memories of my parents, I came to understand why they had loved her so much. Today I consider her one of my dearest friends and most trusted confidantes.

In a recent conversation, Pat recalled, "Bert loved to teach and he loved to learn. He was a very sensitive man, and he allowed me to develop my sensitivities as I never would have with my own parents." She described a time when she was four or five years old, and Bert let her use his microscope. He taught her how to prepare a slide, putting the fragile cover slip on it to protect the sample, and then peer into the microscope looking for things so small they were not visible to the naked eye. "Later, when I got to school, I was so disappointed. I remember thinking, 'This is science?'"

~

In 1946, when Bert was in his second year of teaching at the University of Alabama, another young person benefitted from his mentorship, a first-year student who planned to major in entomology. When the student walked into an office in Nott Hall seeking advice about his future career, Dr. J. Henry Walker, chairman of the biology department, welcomed him warmly and admired his ant collection, which the young man had brought along. Then he made a telephone call and walked the student upstairs to Bert Williams's office. This is how that student later described the meeting that followed:

> Williams, a tall gangling man in his thirties with a slight stoop and Lincolnesque face, greeted me warmly without hesitation, as though I were a fellow academic on sabbatical leave. After we talked ants, natural history,

and botany for a while, he took me to a table space in his laboratory where, he suggested, I might wish to conduct my research. His largess knew no bounds thereafter. He lent me a dissecting microscope, glassware, and alcohol. He offered to take me along on future field trips. Later in the year he gave me a part-time research assistantship, tracing radioactive phosphorus through the roots of plants. Perhaps because Williams had no other research students at the time, and certainly in part because he was by nature a modest and caring man, he treated me as though I were a graduate student or postdoctoral fellow. I even came to feel as though I had joined his wife and infant daughter as part of the family, like a favored nephew. I have known no kinder or more effective mentor. Forty-seven years later, in 1993, I had the great pleasure of welcoming his granddaughter to her freshman year at Harvard University and offering her my assistance.

That young man's name was Ed Wilson. He went on to become one of the most famous biologists of the twentieth century, known as "a modern Charles Darwin for his influence as both a close observer and a unifying theorist." But when he walked into Bert's office in 1946, he was just a seventeen-year-old boy planning to major in entomology. Even in that first meeting, my father recognized Wilson as a kindred spirit. For Bert, it didn't matter whether he was talking to his four-year-old niece, a group of sophomores at a small high school in Indiana, or a freshman newly arrived at the University of Alabama. He valued their curiosity and encouraged their explorations. He didn't have to think twice before offering Wilson a space in his own lab to pursue his many interests.

A few months later, when Bert was awarded research funding to use radioactive phosphorus, acquired from the Oak Ridge Institute for Nuclear Studies, as a "tracer" in the study of the differentiation of tissues in the root tips of plants, he chose Ed Wilson, still an undergraduate, as his senior research assistant. I recently discovered a photo in the 1949 *Corolla*, the University of Alabama's yearbook, with the caption "Using Gadgets to Study Biology." My father is using a Geiger counter to check root samples for radioactivity. A student stands behind him, his hand resting on the machine.

Staring at the young man's face, I wondered, "Could it be?" I immediately called my sister, and we began searching for photos of Wilson online, comparing them with the picture in the yearbook. Soon it was clear beyond a doubt. The student standing behind our father was the young man who later became known as E.O. Wilson.

Bert and his most famous student shared important similarities. Both were dedicated field biologists who shared a reverence for life on earth. Like Bert, Wilson's interests extended far beyond his chosen specialty, the study of ants. He founded the fields of sociobiology and island biogeography. Toward the end of his forty-six-year-long career at Harvard and after his official retirement in 1996, he became a tireless crusader for preserving biodiversity and saving the planet. He was also a gifted and prolific writer, winning two Pulitzer Prizes. By the time of his death at age ninety-two, Wilson had published more than forty books, including a novel, *Anthill*, and a memoir, *Naturalist*, the book in which he described his first meeting with Bert. Thinking about Wilson's stunning output, I feel sure that my father, who never achieved his own dream of writing a book, would have been immensely proud of his student's accomplishments.

Bert truly cared about all his students—those he taught in and outside of classrooms. And they responded by caring about him. When he was hospitalized after his breakdown in 1954, many of his biology students at the university sent cards and letters of encouragement. One of the most touching is a telegram my mother pasted onto one of the pages of her big scrapbook. It was sent on Monday, March 29, only two days after he was taken to the hospital. Headed "WESTERN UNION" in a large font, the message was typed in all caps on ticker tape paper, with each line separately pasted onto the page. It is addressed to "Dr. Bert Williams (PATIENT) Jefferson-Hillman Hospital Birmingham ALA."

> WE WORRIED SATURDAY THINKING YOU
> MIGHT BE SICK BUT NEVER A COMPLAINT
> FROM YOU. ALL LAST WEEK WE WANTED
> TO TELL YOU THAT YOU ARE THE BEST
> TEACHER ANY CLASS COULD EVER HAVE.
> DIDN'T MEAN TO WAIT UNTIL YOU WERE
> SICK TO TELL YOU. WE MISSED YOU AT THE
> LAB THIS AFTERNOON. EACH MEMBER

FROM SEED TO TREE TO FRUIT

LOVES YOU DEARLY AND WISHES FOR YOU A SPEEDY RECOVERY.

YOUR MONDAY AFTERNOON
LAB STUDENTS

I find the students' love for their professor and concern for his well-being so touching. As a teacher myself, I understand the close connections that often develop between teachers and their students. But this telegram speaks of a deeper level of devotion. Dr. Williams was different from other professors.

In May, a representative from this class wrote again:

> Things are not the same with you away. The worms look horrible, the photosynthesis is losing its chlorophyll, and the fleas have quit hopping! We would have shouted for joy had you been in your place yesterday in zoology. We believe the class would have gone into an uproar. Even the President wouldn't suffice in your place.

Reading this, I smile, knowing how much my father would have appreciated this playful message.

When he died in July, the students were away for the summer. They didn't get the news until later. But many colleagues from the university community sent messages of sympathy within days of his death, including this note from one of the librarians: "I shall miss seeing Dr. Williams in the library. He often read periodicals at a table near my desk. He meant a lot to all who knew him and will be greatly missed." Dr. Williams was a still, quiet presence, creating a kind of aura as he sat there reading.

When classes resumed in the fall, the faculty of the College of Arts and Sciences composed a memorial tribute. Besides mentioning his academic accomplishments, the statement noted that he was "an inspiring teacher" who had guided hundreds of students and directed more than twenty master's theses and supervised two doctoral dissertations. While upholding "the highest standards of scholarship," he also earned his students' "affection and genuine admiration" and the respect of his colleagues. "His record shows that he was a man of wide human interests and broad human sympathies," admired for his "gentility of manner" and "high character." I know that it is standard practice for university committees to write a tribute when a faculty member dies, but this statement is more than a pro forma acknowledgment of loss. Whoever drafted it—I'm guessing it was Dr. Henry Walker, the biology department chairman—knew and appreciated Bert for the special gifts he brought to his teaching and research.

~

Thinking about what teaching meant to my father—and my mother—it's no wonder that I too became a teacher. After college, I worked for five years as an editor but found the jobs unfulfilling. Instead of just working on manuscripts, I wanted to work with writers face to face. I wanted to be a teacher. In 1974, I heard from a friend that Brooklyn College was hiring people with master's degrees in English to work as writing tutors for students who were being admitted under the university's new Open Admissions policy. I mailed in my résumé, got an interview, and started work the next day.

After a few days in this experimental program for students considered unprepared for college work, I knew I had found my calling. These students, who came from the barrios and ghettoes of New York City and spoke other languages or dialects, had so much to say. I loved getting to know them through their writing. In 1975, I was asked to start teaching writing classes for this same population—the beginning of a career in the City University of New York (CUNY) that lasted until my retirement in 2011. Like my parents before me, I regarded teaching as more than just a job. For me, as for them, it was a privilege and a responsibility. Even now, years after my retirement, when I am filling out a form that asks for my profession, I write in one word: "teacher." Like my father, I am happiest in a classroom or in my office talking with a student. This is the work that feeds my soul.

28

Everything Endures

SITTING HERE, trying to think of a way to begin this final chapter, I look out the window toward the western horizon. It's August, but already there's a chill in the air. Yellow leaves from the crabapple tree are swirling about in the breeze before settling onto the lawn. Four and a half years have passed since I started to write this book. Isolated at home in the early months of the COVID-19 pandemic, I had so much time to think, so much still to learn, so much fear and grief to experience.

Hoping for inspiration, I pick up the scrapbook my mother created after my father's death—the book I opened with so much trepidation in 2020. I used to feel the book's heaviness was more metaphorical than physical, but on a whim, I decide to weigh it on my kitchen scales. It *is* heavy—more than six and a half pounds. Supporting the book on my lap, I find myself thinking about the words from Rebecca Solnit that I chose as the epigraph for this part of the book: "There is closure and reopening and sometimes something reopens because you can bring something new to it, repair it in a new way, by understanding it in a new way." This is what has happened for me. I now understand my father's life in a new way. The healing hasn't been quick or complete, but it is real. I know how far I have come as I open the scrapbook. No longer afraid of what I might find inside, I welcome it as I would an old friend who shares memories from long ago.

When I was young, these memories of my father's illness and death were just too frightening for me to face. If I started to read a magazine article about mental illness, my whole body would tense up, and I would turn the page. I wasn't ready to think about these things. Not wanting to stir up memories of my father, I hadn't visited relatives on his side of the family in years.

Finally, in midlife, my desire to know more overcame my fears of what I might find. I had begun seeing my previous therapist and progressed to the point where I was ready to begin the search. In response to my questions about my father, Mother mailed me some of his letters. As I started to get a sense of the kind of man he was, I decided it was time to take a road trip into the past.

~

On a hot day in July 1986, we set out from the family home on Short Marion. Carol was the designated driver, with Mother in the passenger seat. I folded myself into the tiny back seat along with my two children, Alex (age seven) and Susanna (age ten). The weather was torrid—about 100 degrees Fahrenheit and very humid—but Mother's little Nissan Sentra was air conditioned so we didn't mind being crammed in so close together.

We spent the first night in Bloomington, the site of Indiana University, where my mother and father had met in 1935 and where Carol had married her first husband, Joe, in 1968. The university was just as beautiful as we remembered, with its limestone buildings and small stream meandering through the campus.

The next morning, we stopped at Greencastle to see DePauw University, where I tried to imagine my father as a shy eighteen-year-old. By lunch time, we had reached West Lafayette, where I had my first taste of independence as a freshman at Purdue in 1963 and where I met Frank, my husband-to-be, in 1966.

As we drove on, the land got flatter and the soil blacker, and by late afternoon, we had reached Pontiac, Illinois, a small town south of Chicago, where Mother's two brothers had spent their adult lives. Roy still lived there. Erv had died in 1956, but his wife, Leola, also lived in Pontiac, and their daughter, my cousin Pat, lived on a farm in Odell, just a few miles away.

That first night, we met at Leola's house to share stories about the past. She was getting up in years, but if I looked closely, I could still see the beautiful Aunt Ola I remembered from childhood. Roy looked older too and had recently gone through treatment for colon cancer. Carol and I used to be afraid of Uncle Roy. When he visited us in Tuscaloosa, he drank beer and talked in a loud voice. He was so different from our father. But seeing him here in Ola's living room, I could understand why my mother loved him. He was a wonderful storyteller, and his mannerisms reminded me of my granny, who had died in 1983 at age ninety-seven.

The next night, we gathered at a country inn near Pontiac to celebrate Mother's seventy-fifth birthday a few months early. She had always looked years younger than her actual age, but that night she had a special glow, surrounded by the people she loved most in the world. At seventy-five, she was still in her prime. I couldn't imagine she would ever grow old.

The next morning, she looked radiant as she said to Carol and me, "I can't believe they said all those nice things about me." Mother always seemed so confident, but under that brave façade, she still sometimes doubted her own self-worth.

We didn't linger over breakfast because we had to be in Greensburg by lunch time. In the past, I found excuses not to attend the annual reunions of the Williams family, knowing that seeing these people would remind me of my father and might trigger fears that what happened to him could also happen to me. But this year, I was in a different place. Forty-one years old, in a happy marriage with a job I loved and two wonderful children, I felt ready to reconnect.

When we arrived at the city park, Aunt Goldia welcomed us with the same special smile I remembered from childhood visits to the Miller farm. Her daughter, our cousin Arlene, looked and acted so much like her mother. She took us over to the food table, explaining that she had brought extra so we wouldn't have to feel guilty about not contributing to the potluck. Frank had flown to Indianapolis earlier that day so he could attend the reunion. He had never met my father or any of these relatives, but they welcomed him like just another cousin. Soon he was joking with Dyar about his career as a Major League baseball player and coach and consulting Doug about farm equipment.

Looking over at Mother sitting between Uncle Carl and Aunt Lois, laughing and reminiscing, I could tell she was having a wonderful time. I hadn't thought of it this way before, but these weren't just my father's family members but hers as well. She had spent so much time with them when they were young, and they shared precious memories. No one else had known Bert as well as they had.

There were lots of kids at the reunion, and soon Susie and Alex were playing horseshoes and swinging on the swings with all the others. Carol and I got to catch up with cousins we hadn't seen since childhood. We had been especially close to our cousin, Peggy, Goldia's daughter. We asked her if she still remembered the time when Grandma Williams had stomped up the stairs to yell at us. "Oh yes," she said. "I'll never forget it." Carol and Peggy had been on the bed in an upstairs bedroom telling embarrassing stories about me when I sneaked up and scared them. They jumped so high that the bed came crashing to the floor. The next thing we heard was Grandma climbing the stairs one step at a time. Now we could laugh about it, but at the time all three of us were paralyzed with fear.

All too soon, people began to pack up their picnic baskets and fold the lawn chairs. Arlene knew we were interested in family history, so she had arranged for us to go out to New Pennington to see the old farmhouse. Grandma and Grandpa Williams had died in the 1960s, but the house was still in the family.

Leaving the highway to turn onto that country road felt like traveling into another era. We recognized the house at once, with its yellow brick columns, big front porch, and gazing globe, still sitting there on its pedestal in the front yard. Inside, the house was smaller than we remembered but otherwise much the same. Carol and I asked if we could go upstairs to the bedroom where we always slept on visits to the farm. It smelled exactly as we remembered. Carol, Frank, and I took the children and walked down the road to the old quarry pond. The path was overgrown with weeds, but we finally found it. Looking out over the still water, I pictured my father rowing me around the small lake in a wooden boat when I was very young.

~

While we were planning this trip, Mother told Carol and me that if we really wanted to understand our father, we needed to meet Ebert Whipple, and she had arranged for us to visit him on our way back to Evansville. Now retired from his job as superintendent of schools, Ebert was standing on his front porch to greet us when we drove up in front of his house in Salem, Indiana. He had met Bert in 1927 when they were both traveling by train to Greencastle to begin their studies at DePauw. They soon became good friends and roommates. Ebert served as best man at Bert's wedding, and after our family's move to Alabama, they stayed in touch through letters and visits.

Ebert shook our hands and led us inside, where his wife, Louise, was waiting with iced tea and home-baked cookies. Ebert was a big talker (he had been a devoted member of the Toastmasters Club), and he regaled us with some old-fashioned jokes he must have memorized for the occasion. Not finding the jokes terribly funny, Mother shifted the conversation. "The girls were very young when Bert died. You knew him so well. How would you describe their father?"

He paused for a moment. "I never knew Bert to get angry, and I never had a real argument with him. There was something about him that set him apart from other people. I think of Abraham Lincoln. He was different from the rest of us."

After waving goodbye to Ebert and Louise, I kept thinking about what he had said about my father. That he was different from the other students, that he reminded him of Lincoln. As we rode along the two-lane highway with corn plants on either side of the road shimmering in the sunlight, I pictured my father walking through fields like this as a young boy, just as Abe Lincoln had done before him. Both of them were strong and worked hard on their father's farms, but there was something different about them. Unlike most other Indiana farm boys, they were voracious readers and deep thinkers. Both of them were eloquent speakers and writers, realizing the value of language to shape perception, to record transient things. Their eyes were fixed on a world beyond the neatly delineated fields of their fathers' farms, a world that no one else could see.

Pulling into the familiar driveway at 2719 Short Marion five days after we set out, it felt like a door that had been closed for a long time had been opened. I still hadn't faced what frightened me most, everything surrounding my father's illness and death, but I had made a start, revisiting the scenes of his youth and reconnecting with the people who knew and loved him before he got sick.

~

Thirty-six years later, in the summer of 2022, I was well along on my journey. Using Mother's scrapbook as a guide, I had traced every clue related to my father's illness and hospitalization. I had forced myself to read the letters he wrote while he was in the hospital and the notes about his breakdown and treatment. Reading these things, I was terrified. I felt it physically. But as I continued to read and write, I began to see much more than just my fears. I recalled a childhood surrounded by true friends and loving family members. I remembered the anxious months after my father's death, but I also began to understand how we made it through.

Although it wasn't my intention, as I looked back at my father's life, I was looking back on my own life too. Understanding him helped me to understand myself better as well—my love of reading and writing and reflecting, my reticence in social situations, and my appreciation of nature. Now, when I walk along a country lane or a path through a forest of old-growth trees, I can imagine my father just a few steps behind me, following along in my footsteps.

When I started reading all the letters my parents had exchanged over the years, I got to know both of them in ways I never would have thought possible. I discovered the complex marriage that led to my own birth, and I began to see my father as someone much larger than just the Daddy of my childhood. For me, there was sadness in learning about his lifelong struggle with mental illness but also a newly found acceptance as he told me, in his own words, about all the joy he had experienced. This acceptance could never have come without the searching.

The more I read and wrote and learned about my father, the more I realized that I never got to say goodbye. I felt cheated that I had not been allowed to attend his funeral in 1954, and by 2022, I needed to share my grief and my love with others through some sort of ritual. I talked with Carol about having a small family ceremony, a celebration of life as we now call it, even though our father had been dead for almost seventy years. Planning the service together was part of the healing, drawing my sister and me even closer as we talked about how to convey our father's essence to family members who had never met him.

On July 1, 2022, we gathered on the porch in Plainfield. I began by explaining why Carol and I had decided to have this ceremony. Then Susanna, a biologist by training, read Bert's reflection about the papaw seedling he had nurtured so carefully. Our oldest granddaughter, Liberty, read an excerpt from our cousin Pat's recollections of her Uncle Bert. Carol's husband, Bob, a retired history professor, read from the letter where Bert described meeting Ruth in a history class at IU in the summer of 1935. Frank read the passage from E.O. Wilson's memoir about his relationship with Dr. Williams. Carol talked about her memories of the quiet, gentle father who sat on her bed every night reading her stories before she fell asleep.

The love of music is one of many gifts Carol and I received from our parents, so we decided to include a song, the same one we had used in the fall of 2003, when Mother's ashes were buried next to our father's grave in Greensburg. Entitled "Blessed" and composed by Lui Collins, a singer and songwriter from Western Massachusetts, this song seemed perfect to express the gratitude we feel for what our parents have given us. The second verse spoke to us especially:

> *Rain so gently falls to soak the earth, life bursts forth from the seed*
> *Roots go stretching down to draw their strength from the soil*

FROM SEED TO TREE TO FRUIT

Upward grows the plant always reaching toward the hot, beating sun
Oh blessed are we this day.

As the last strains of the chorus faded out, Carol looked around at our loved ones gathered there on the porch and asked, "After all these years, what do we still have that Bert, our father, your grandfather or great-grandfather, left behind?"

There was a long pause. And then Stella, Alex and Sarah's daughter, nine years old at the time, spoke up as if it were obvious.

"His soul."

~

While planning the service, Carol and I agreed that we wanted to include something that the younger children would remember, so we asked Alex's wife, Sarah, for advice. An art therapist with lots of experience working with children, she said, "If you want to connect with the kids, you should include fire in the ceremony." Of course! So while we were gathered there on the porch, we asked everyone to write or draw a message they would like to send to Bert. Then we went into the back yard and lit a fire in the outdoor fireplace. As golden sparks started flying up into the cool air of evening, each of us went over and dropped our paper into the fire. The younger children were so excited that they couldn't contain themselves any longer and began to chase one another around the yard, shrieking with delight. Finally, as they began to run out of steam, we called them back to the patio.

Alex led us in singing one of Daddy's favorite songs, "Cool Water," composed by Bob Nolan in 1936. The rest of us sang along to Hank Williams's iconic recording of this country music classic. Even then, just two years ago, I didn't fully understand what it was about this song that spoke so deeply to my father. But now, after reading so many of his letters, I know why this poignant ballad meant so much to him, the tale of a lonely cowboy traveling through a dry prairie with his horse, both of them so thirsty they keep seeing mirages of green trees and springs of cool, clear water. The song ends with the cowboy imagining that his horse is longing for "just one thing more than water."

> *Like me, I guess, he'd like to rest,*
> *Where there's no quest for water,*
> *Cool, clear water.*

I recently found a photograph of my father that I had never seen before. It was not framed, and there's no notation on the back indicating when it was taken. It speaks to me louder than all the words in all his letters.

Throughout his life, Bert struggled toward the light, but darkness always lurked just a few steps behind. Looking into his eyes, I remember the words my mother copied into her scrapbook for 1954, an excerpt from a letter Bert wrote to his beloved Aunt Lydia after her husband died in 1937:

FROM SEED TO TREE TO FRUIT

> The anticipation of my own inevitable death is not unpleasant when I reflect that I will then be with God, at peace spiritually and alive physically in the beautiful plants which I love. In some very real senses, life is harder than death. Yet life can be very beautiful.

In this picture, Bert looks like the tired cowboy in the song he loved, yearning for that place where he could rest at last, no longer searching for that cool, clear water always just a few steps beyond his reach.

After the song finished playing, Carol shared a quotation she had found in our father's pocket diary from 1950. After seeing a movie entitled *The Earth's Rocky Crust*, he questioned the film's ending, which declared, "Nothing endures." Looking around at all of us gathered there in his honor, my sister read in her strong, clear voice:

> Nothing endures?
>
> The land erodes, the mountains crumble away. Nothing endures?
>
> Everything endures!

Holding back her tears, she continued.

> The water, the rocks, the soil may change places, may change form, may even be converted to energy.
>
> But everything endures.

Sitting there on the patio, looking out at the green hillsides in the distance, there was an unplanned moment of silence.

~

It has been hard for me to write this last chapter. I knew what I wanted to say, but I kept finding reasons not to sit down and actually put my thoughts into words. It was as if after waiting so long to find my father,

I didn't want to let him go. But today, looking out at the hills beyond my window, colored with the muted greens and golds of autumn, I realize that I don't have to let him go. I will see him when I pick a persimmon from the tree he planted on his father's farm. I will feel his embrace when I hug my grandchildren. I will hear his voice in a bird's song. I will experience his love when I look into the eyes of a newborn baby. He is there.

Epilogue

Child of the equinox,
holy and pure—
teeter-tottering on the universe.

Boy,
country boy, quiet boy.
At home in the fields,
at home in the trees.
Boy with fevered heart.

Man,
turbulent as magma under the calm.
Loving with a passion never imagined.
Climbing toward the heights
afraid to look down.

You,
standing firm, standing strong.
Your head bloody, your head unbowed.
Chasing the mirage that promised cool water,
that promised clear water.

You knew what the geologist said.
Mountains explode, mountains crumble, stone turns to sand.
The river cuts, relentlessly, snaking to the sea.
"Dust to dust," they said.

EPILOGUE

They tried to contain you—
in sterile rooms
where machines drummed out the wind.
Your spirit roiling under the surface like waves at sea.
The wheels of time grind slowly, they said, and they grind exceeding fine.

But time stands still.
"Seven lonely days make one lonely year," your daughter said.

And though the current pulled you under,
and the shock machine exploded your mind,
the supernova of your soul illumines the half-life of our memories.
Nothing endures?

Everything endures.
Love endures.

—Carol June Williams
"Poem on Your Birthday," March 20, 2025

Acknowledgments

Writing this book has been a long, difficult, and rewarding process. I would like to express my gratitude to the people who supported me along the way.

A big thank you to Lynn Gentry, a street poet who had set up his typewriter on a corner in my Brooklyn neighborhood. After talking with me for just a few minutes, he sensed my need to revisit my Southern childhood and wrote a beautiful poem expressing that idea. This book began on that day. It was my seventy-third birthday.

Toward the end of 2019, I told my friend Jack (N. John Hall, a distinguished scholar and prolific writer) that I was thinking of writing a memoir centered on the trauma of my father's mental illness and death, but I wasn't sure I could do it. His response was clear and concise: "You have to do it, Rebecca." I knew he was right.

Early in 2020, I realized that in order to get started, I needed to be in a writing group. Searching the web, I found Mindy Lewis, author of *Life Inside*, a compelling memoir about her experiences in a psychiatric facility as a teenager. Mindy, who has been facilitating groups for aspiring memoir writers for years, turned out to be exactly the person I needed. For the next five years, I attended her regular online groups, benefitting tremendously from her sensitive and astute responses to my work. Thank you, Mindy, for giving me the time and space to explore a new kind of writing as this book gradually emerged.

Other members of the group offered inspiration, encouragement, and insightful feedback. Special thanks to Theoni Angelopoulos, Ruth Ferris, Mike Higgins, Susan Kellermann, Stu Morden, John Munnelly, Julia Newman, Heather Potts, Rosemarie Ross, and Nina Simon.

I was also helped by attending two online writing workshops led by Joe Wilkins, the poet, novelist, and author of the memoir *The Mountain and the Fathers*. Thank you, Joe, for sharing your wisdom as a writer and a teacher.

Of course, the thinking that went into this memoir began many years before I sat down at the computer. Without the gentle support and understanding of three outstanding therapists I worked with at different times of my life, I never could have written so frankly about my father's illness and the impact it had on my life. To them, I am eternally grateful.

My desire to revisit the past has led to rewarding new connections with relatives and childhood friends. What a joy it was for my sister and me to reunite via Zoom with the twins—Judy Nisbet Caldwell and Jean Nisbet Cates, our neighbors and best friends on Cedar Crest in Tuscaloosa. Talking with Patty (Patricia Connelly Besch), my best friend from the Evansville days, led both of us to reflect on that time from a new perspective. Long conversations with Pat Stamps Madson, a treasured cousin on my mother's side of the family, yielded critical insights into the past and a deeper understanding of my parents and grandmother. In 2024, cousins on the Williams side welcomed my sister and me to the Miller farmhouse in Indiana (now beautifully restored) and provided vivid details about our childhood visits to the family farms. A big thank you to Arlene Miller Parker, Dyar and Bertha Miller, Peggy and Joseph Weil, Doug and Beth Ann Miller, Susan and Dan Hahn, John and Bonnie Williams, and Michael and Chloe Williams.

Hoping to recover memories of the Alabama landscape of my childhood, I watched many episodes of *Discovering Alabama*, an award-winning public television series developed and hosted by environmentalist and educator Doug Phillips. In April 2024, when I traveled back to Alabama for the first time since 1956, accompanied by my sister, Carol, and my daughter, Susanna, Dr. Doug welcomed us to his office in the

ACKNOWLEDGMENTS

Alabama Museum of Natural History and spent an hour sharing his enthusiasm for the natural wonders of his state.

The next day we joined a wildflower walk at the University of Alabama's arboretum, led by Dr. Michael McKain, professor of botany and curator of the university's herbarium. I was thrilled when he pointed out a young papaw tree, the same species referenced in the title of this book. Two days later, Dr. McKain welcomed us to the university's herbarium. He located several botanical specimens collected by our father and also showed us the herpetology collection. The snakes were stored in large glass jars filled with that same yellow fluid I remembered from childhood visits to my father's lab. Some of the most impressive specimens had been collected by my father's colleague in the biology department, Dr. Ralph Chermock. Thank you, Dr. McKain, for helping us to understand why our father loved his job so much.

A poignant part of our time in Tuscaloosa was a visit to Bryce Hospital. In 2010, the University of Alabama purchased the property and restored the main building to its original splendor. It now houses the university's glitzy new Randall Welcome Center. The second floor has been transformed into the Bryce Mental Health Museum, a moving reminder of the place where our father spent the last days of his life.

Driving south from Tuscaloosa, we visited Selma, where we met an amazing man named Columbus Mitchell. Thank you, Mr. Mitchell, for helping visitors understand the role of your city and your family in the civil rights struggles of the 1950s and 1960s.

In Montgomery, we spent a day of sober reflection at the Legacy Museum created by the Equal Justice Initiative (https://legacysites.eji.org/about/museum/) and the National Memorial for Peace and Justice, dedicated to honoring thousands of lynching victims across the United States. I would like to thank Bryan Stevenson for his tireless efforts to increase our understanding of the history and legacy of slavery in America.

Oak Ridge was the last stop on our Southern odyssey. We enjoyed lunch with Delonda Anderson, the chief editor of *Appalachia Bare*, a blog that published my piece about Oak Ridge in 2023. Her father worked for many years as a security inspector at the Oak Ridge National Laboratory, where my father spent several summers doing research. Thank you, Delonda, for your enthusiastic support of my project.

After my retirement from full-time work as a professor of composition and rhetoric at the City University of New York (CUNY), I was fortunate to serve in a part-time capacity as faculty consultant for the CUNY Pipeline Program for Careers in College Teaching and Research, administered by the Graduate Center's Office of Educational Opportunity and Diversity. Working for this program from 2010 to 2023 was one of the highlights of my career. My dedication to the program's mission was informed by childhood memories of the injustices endured by people of color in the segregated South. I would like to thank the three distinguished scholars who oversaw the program during my time there: Anthropologist Donald Robotham, Historian Herman Bennett, and Psychologist Martin Ruck. I offer my heartfelt thanks as well to Assistant Program Officer John Eric Frankson, who works ceaselessly for the good of students from diverse backgrounds. During my years with this program, I was endlessly impressed by the doctoral students, many now college professors, who served as my colleagues and as mentors for the undergraduate Pipeline fellows.

Three of them deserve special thanks. Dr. Brian P. Jones is the inaugural director of the New York Public Library's Center for Educators and Schools and the author of *The Tuskeegee Student Uprising: A History* (2022) and *Black History Is for Everyone* (2025). Dr. Robert P. Robinson is a professor of Africana Studies at CUNY's John Jay College, a member

ACKNOWLEDGMENTS

of the doctoral faculty at the CUNY Graduate Center, and the author of *Stealin' the Meetin': Black Education History & the Black Panther Party's Oakland Community School* (2025). Sharifa Hampton, a CUNY adjunct faculty member and former Pipeline fellow, is a doctoral candidate in English at the Graduate Center, where she is writing a dissertation on the editing and curation of groundbreaking Black feminist anthologies. Thanks to all three for reading a draft of my chapter entitled "Waiting for Justice." They offered honest, insightful responses, which I greatly appreciated and tried to take into account when revising.

Thanks to Laurie Hefner for sharing memories of growing up in Alabama and for taking the author photo included in this book. I also wish to thank singer and songwriter Lui Collins for permission to quote the lyrics of her beautiful song "Blessed." I am grateful to Island Press for waiving the fee to quote E.O. Wilson's recollection of my father, included in his memoir, *Naturalist*. Staff at the University of Alabama Libraries were extremely helpful as I researched my father's years at the university. I am especially grateful to Alex Boucher, Reference and Instruction Librarian of Special Collections, for his generous assistance. I would also like to express my gratitude to James William Oakley, Jr., a student at the university, who took a series of gripping photographs of the protests spurred by Autherine Lucy's attempt to enroll in February 1956, one of which is included in this book. Thanks are due as well to two librarians at the David L. Rice Library at the University of Southern Indiana. Mona Meyer, Metadata Librarian in the University Archives Special Collections, and Jennifer Greene, University Archivist and Associate Professor of Library Science, searched the local newspapers for information related to my mother's role as Evansville's director of child care services during World War II.

Norbert Elliot, my colleague, friend, and editor at Purple Breeze Press, believed in this book even before I did. He has read every word of every chapter multiple times, offering unstinting praise and posing open-ended questions that led to further thought and revision. As the book progressed over several years, he promptly replied to every email, helped me through technical glitches, shared thoughts about his own memoir in progress, and calmed me down when I felt discouraged. For me, Norbert is the editor every writer dreams of finding.

Thanks also to Frances Ward, Norbert's wife, the president and co-founder of Purple Breeze Press, for her hard work and efficiency in handling all the business aspects of running an independent press. I am deeply grateful to Meg Vezzu, the press's extraordinary copy editor and book designer. Thank you, Meg, for the skill, flexibility, and love you devoted to my book and all the others published by PBP. I'm especially grateful for her role in designing the book's cover. Wanting to convey the botanical theme of the book for the background, she selected a photo of a persimmon tree my father planted from seed many years ago. It was loaded with persimmons in September 2024, when I took this photo, a beautiful illustration of the book's title.

The most important gift I received from writing this book is a deeper understanding and appreciation of my parents. My mother, Ruth, blessed me with her exuberant love of life. Over many years, she always found a way to turn challenges into opportunities. When I think of her now, I see her smiling and declaring in a strong voice: "My cup runneth over!" My father, Bert, died when I was still a child, but he passed along his quiet thoughtfulness and reverence for life in all its forms. I will be forever grateful to both of them for the love they shared with me and Carol. Before we were born, they expressed their innermost thoughts in letters to each other, carefully preserving them in the hope that someday we would come to value them as much as they did. That day has come.

My husband, Frank, never met my father, but he has always felt a special connection with the quiet and thoughtful man he came to

ACKNOWLEDGMENTS

know as I shared my memories. Never once has he complained about all the hours I spent "working on the book." His love and patience have sustained me through this long and all-consuming process.

My adult children motivated me with their love and support. Alex always wanted to know more about the grandfather he never met. I felt I owed it to him to write this book. Thank you, Alex, for inspiring me to keep going when the going was hard. Susanna decided to become a biologist after finding Grandpa Bert's insect collection in the attic when she was a child. She chose her field of cell biology in part due to an experience during a high school biology lab: peering through the microscope, she was awestruck by the beautiful geometry of plant cells arranged in concentric rings. As a graduate student, she read her grandfather's scientific publications and was surprised to learn that his research focused on microscopic sections of plant root tips just like the one she had seen in that high school biology lab. Thank you, Susanna, for your encouragement, your editorial feedback, and your beautiful drawing of a papaw seedling, used as a motif in the book's design.

Frank and I are blessed to have six wonderful grandchildren ranging in age from seven to sixteen. Susanna and Bill Evans are the parents of Liberty, Naomi, Everett, and Raina. Alex and Sarah Mlynarczyk are the parents of Stella and Malcolm (a.k.a. Max). My hope is that each of them will read this book, in their own time, when they want to learn more about the generations that came before them.

Carol's husband, Bob Asher, a professor of history, supported the idea of this book from the beginning and offered feedback on a near-final draft. Carol and I acquired two new sisters when our mother remarried in 1960. Glenna Fowler, an avid reader, listened patiently as I shared progress reports about "the book" in our frequent phone conversations. Anne Nellis, a dedicated elementary school teacher with a passionate interest in Indiana history, died, much too soon, in 2006. Though she never got to read this book, I like to think she would have appreciated its contribution to understanding family life in Indiana during the 1930s and 1940s.

Finally, I offer my deepest thanks to my sister, Carol June Williams, who has shared the journey with me every step of the way. This book is dedicated to her with love, respect, and gratitude.

Notes

1. Another World

This was the biology department: Nott Hall housed the biology department during my father's years at the University of Alabama. In this photo, taken in 1948, he is the tall man standing second from the left. The building was named in honor of physician and scientist Josiah C. Nott (1804–1873) in 1922. Nearly a hundred years later, in 2020, after student protests that Nott espoused racist theories, the building was renamed Honors Hall and now houses the university's Honors College. Used courtesy of the University of Alabama Libraries Special Collections.

3. The Spotted Men

A newspaper report: Cited in Kelly Kazek, "Alabama's Deadliest Train Wrecks, Plus a Brief History of Deadliest Train Accidents," AL.com, January 15, 2015. Web.

"a ray of sunlight": Shannon Holland, "November 25, 1951, 17 Killed, Woodstock, Tuscaloosa County, Alabama," Alabama Pioneers. Web.

5. Tanglewood

Dr. Chermock had a huge collection: Though he was an entomologist, Ralph Chermock was also very interested in herpetology and had a collection of 15,000 snake specimens, which were stored at the University of Alabama. John V. Calhoun, "Long-Lost Holotypes and Other Forgotten Treasures in the Ralph L. Chermock Collection, with Biographical Notes," *News of the Lepidopterists' Society* 57, no. 2 (2015): 80–85. Web.

"**investments in humanity**": DePauw University, "The Rector Scholarship." Web.

6. Waiting for Justice

The bond issue was passed: "Grand Reunion Keeps Spirit of Druid High School Alive," *Tuscaloosa News*, July 3, 2011. Web.

a big dog sleeping on another porch: This photograph, taken in 1956 by my parents' close friend Dr. Roland Harper, shows the neighborhood I remember seeing when my father drove Pinkie home in the early 1950s. Used by courtesy of the University of Alabama Libraries Special Collections.

Ku Klux Klan members in full regalia: This photograph of a group of robed Ku Klux Klan members during a protest against the enrollment of Autherine Lucy was taken on February 2, 1956. James William Oakley, Jr., collection. Used by courtesy of the University of Alabama Libraries Special Collections.

The court battles continued: Harrison Smith, "Autherine Lucy Foster, First Black Student at University of Alabama, Dies at 92," *The Washington Post*, March 2, 2022. Web.

It took reinforcements: Claude Sitton, "Alabama Admits Negro Students; Wallace Bows to Federal Force; Kennedy Sees 'Moral Crisis' in U.S.," *New York Times*, June 12, 1963. Web.

"It felt somewhat like you were not really a human being": Richard Goldstein, "Autherine Lucy Foster, First Black Student at University of Alabama, Dies at 92," *New York Times*, March 2, 2022. Web.

NOTES

It had previously been known as: J. Wayne Flynt, "David Bibb Graves (1927-31, 1935-39")," *Encyclopedia of Alabama*. Web.

"If I am a master teacher": "Autherine Lucy Foster Made History in 1956 by Integrating the University of Alabama," *Tuscaloosa News*, January 31, 2025. Web.

8. Oak Ridge

"where the radioactivity has traveled inside the root": For more information on the role of radioactive phosphorous in studying the development of root tips, see R. Boggie, R. F. Hunter, and A. H. Knight, "Studies of the Root Development of Plants in the Field Using Radioactive Tracers," *Journal of Ecology* 46, no. 3 (1958): 621–39. Web.

Many didn't receive any payment: Atomic Heritage Foundation, "Civilian Displacement: Oak Ridge, TN," July 17, 2017. Web.

9. The Half-Life of Memory

my fear of the mysterious machine: See Louise Atkinson, "For Years Doctors Prescribed It for Everything from Sore Throats to Childhood Acne: How 'Sunray Therapy' with Ultra Violet Lamps Has Put a Generation at Risk of Cancer," *Daily Mail*, May 21, 2014. Web.

endangering the children they were supposed to be protecting: See Matthew Underwood, "What is a shoe-fitting fluoroscope?" Oak Ridge Associated Universities Blog, July 7, 2024. Web.

pre-history of my own elementary school: Tuscaloosa Area Virtual Museum, "Northington General Hospital Property, Circa 2000." Web.

He died at age fifty-three: Ben Windham, "Southern Lights: Northington: A Big Blast from the Past," *Tuscaloosa News*, August 20, 2016. Web.

state-of-the-art facility: Tuscaloosa Area Virtual Museum, "Northington General." Web.

The University of Alabama gained control: There is a dramatic coda to the strange story of Northington General Hospital. Although the brick buildings look sturdy in photographs, they were built in a great hurry and never intended to be permanent. Over the years, various buildings on the site were razed. And then, in 1978, a few of the remaining buildings along with two towering brick smokestacks were blown up in the final chase scene of the action film *Hooper*, starring Burt Reynolds and Sally Field. See "Best Car Action of *Hooper*," YouTube, AutoMojo (2019). Web.

12. Unanswered Questions

a graceful arc like a bride's veil: The beautiful house on Forest Lake Drive that belonged to Dr. and Mrs. Auddis Walker, Judy and Jean Nisbet's grandparents, as well as our own modest homes on Cedar Crest were destroyed by the tornado that tore through Tuscaloosa on April 27, 2011.

17. 2719 Short Marion

She was also very kind: My cousin, Pat Stamps Madson, remembers standing next to Caroline during the small graveside service for our grandmother. Granny died on February 12, 1983, at age ninety-seven, the last survivor of her many siblings. "Caroline cried bitterly all through the service," Pat told me. "Now she was all alone. I didn't know what to say. I just held her." Caroline, Granny's niece, died a year and a half later at age eighty-seven. She is buried next to my grandmother in the

NOTES

Lutheran Cemetery in Darmstadt, Indiana. Two brave single women who lived to serve their families.

18. Opening the Book of the Past

a book about his experiences at Bryce: Otis Daniel Thomas, *Through These Eyes: My Ministry to the Mentally Ill* (Best of Times, 1996).

Mother and Freeman slept down there: Freeman died on March 18, 1990, at the age of seventy-eight. He and my mother had been married for nearly thirty years.

the hospital was not touched: Bryce Hospital was closed to patients in 1995 and allowed to deteriorate. Teenagers used to go there at night as a test of nerves. In 2010, the hospital and grounds were acquired by the University of Alabama. In January 2024, Bryce Main opened as the university's new Randall Welcome Center for prospective students and their parents, billed as "the country's premier welcome center." The second story was converted into a museum highlighting the history of mental health in Alabama. In April 2024, I visited the campus with my sister and daughter, and we toured the museum. "New Randall Welcome Center Showcases Alabama Experience," UA News Center, January 19, 2024. Web. See also Ava Morthland and Gabriella Puccio-Johnson, "The Hidden History behind Bryce Hospital," *The Crimson White*, November 1, 2023. Web.

The doctor surmised: Otis Daniel Thomas, *Through These Eyes: My Ministry to the Mentally Ill* (Best of Times, 1996), 8–9.

"I remembered the ugly walls": Thomas, 117.

"to love our enemies": Thomas, 2.

"where God wanted me to be": Thomas, 201.

"haunting fears and guilt feelings": Thomas, 76.

"I have loved the stars too truly to be fearful of the night": Sarah Williams, "The Old Astronomer to His Pupil," AllPoetry.com. Web.

"We are alone in death—we often find God in death": Lawrence K. Shook, "Etienne Gilson in Bloomington," *Speculum* 60 no. 4 (1985): 789-99.

19. Letters from the Psych Ward

Dr. James William MacQueen died: "Dr. James W. MacQueen Dies after Heart Attack," *The Birmingham News*, September 8, 1954, 29, Newspapers.com. Web.

he had also published: "Dr. James W. MacQueen," *New York Daily News*, September 10, 1954. Reproduced in GenealogyBuff.com (Miscellaneous New York Obituaries). Web. See also "McQueen [sic], James William, 1900–1954," *Alabama Authors*, The University of Alabama Libraries. Web.

20. Double Vision

he was publicly humiliated: For more about Oppenheimer's career, see Kai Bird and Martin J. Sherwin, *American Prometheus: The Triumph and Tragedy of J. Robert Oppenheimer* (Knopf, 2005).

22. This Force We Call Love

Ravel's *Boléro* plays silently: While drafting the first part of this chapter, the music I imagined was Ravel's *Boléro*. This is the version I played while writing: "Wiener Philharmoniker – Maurice Ravel – Bolero

– Regente Gustavo Dudamel, Lucerne Festival," 2010, YouTube. Web.

the melodious strains of a Chopin nocturne: As I read my parents' letters from the early days of their marriage, I imagined this music playing in the background: "Chopin's Nocturne no. 8 in D flat, opus 27, number 2, Maurizio Pollini," 2005, YouTube. Web.

23. The Burden Marriage Bears

The December 1939 issue: Harvey Zorbaugh, "The Burden Marriage Bears," *Readers Digest* 32, no. 212 (1939): 41–43.

25. The Romance of Being a Student

"We are here today to represent a sacred cause": Wendell Wilkie, "Address Accepting the Presidential Nomination in Elwood, Indiana," The Presidency Project, University of California Santa Barbara, undated. Web.

Professor Paul Weatherwax: For a description of the career of Bert's advisor in the botany department, see "Paul Weatherwax (botanist)," Wikipedia. Web.

Dr. Ralph Cleland: For a description of the career of Dr. Cleland, the chair of the botany department, see "Dr. Ralph Cleland Dies at 78; Botanist Taught at Indiana U," *New York Times*, June 12, 1971. Web.

The speaker was Rollo Walter Brown: "Rollo Walter Brown," Wikipedia, undated. Web.

His supervising professor: See Charles B. Heiser, Jr., "Memorial Resolution: Paul Weatherwax (1888-1976)," Historical Materials, Biology, Indiana University. Web.

From 1940 to the middle of the war: Thalia Ertman, "The Lanham Act and Universal Child Care During World War II," Friends of the National WWII Memorial, June 27, 2019. Web.

By March 1944: Mona Meyer, Archives and Special Collections Metadata Librarian, David L. Rice Library, University of Southern Indiana, "Living 'La Vida Local' (Evansville in WWII, part 4)," August 16, (2023). Web.

In the fall of 1942: "Day Care for 3200 Children Needed as Evansville Mothers Plan for War Jobs," *The Sunday Courier and Press–Evansville, Indiana*, October 25, 1942, 45. Web.

By the end of November: "Six-Point Child Care Plan Set Up to Aid 7,200," *The Evansville Courier*, November 24, 1942, 1. Web.

In February 1943: "Ask 10 Day Care Centers in City," *The Evansville Press*, February 9, 1943, 26. Web.

He emphasized that: "Plan to Establish Day Nurseries Here for Children of Mothers Working in War Plants," *The Sunday Courier and Press–Evansville, Indiana*, February 28, 1943, 4. Web.

In 1941, the federal government: Ertman, "The Lanham Act." Web.

Finally, in December: Meyer, "'Living 'La Vida Local.'" Web.

Evansville historian, Harold Gourley: Harold E. Gourley, *Shipyard Work Force: World's Champion LST Builders on the Beautiful Ohio* (Wiedrich Publishing, 2000), 55. Quoted in Meyer. Web.

NOTES

26. A Stake in the Future

The LSTs (Landing Ship Tanks) and the P-47 Thunderbolt: Harold B. Morgan, *Home Town Warriors: Building the P-47 Thunderbolt and the LST Warship in Evansville, Indiana During World War II* (M. T. Publishing, 2016). Web.

I was born: Bert, always the note taker, made this entry in his small pocket diary on September 3, 1944.

27. From Seed to Tree to Fruit

Rachmaninoff's Rhapsody: This recording comes the closest to the sound I remember hearing in 1951. The part I especially loved is Variation 18, which comes at 14:44 in this recording: "Rhapsody on a theme by Paganini," op. 43 by Sergei Rachmaninoff. Performed by Gary Graffman, piano, Leonard Bernstein, conductor, and the New York Philharmonic. Posted 2015. YouTube. You can listen to this 1964 performance on Spotify.

"Williams, a tall gangling man": Edward O. Wilson, *Naturalist* (Island Press, 1994), 103–104.

awarded research funding: "Dr. Williams Plans Plant Invasion Via Project 153," *Tuscaloosa News*, July 6, 1948.

The student standing behind our father: This photograph of the young Ed Wilson, senior research assistant to our father, appeared in the 1949 *Corolla*, the University of Alabama yearbook. Used by courtesy of the University of Alabama Libraries Special Collections.

"a modern Charles Darwin": Georgina Ferry, "Edward O Wilson Obituary," *The Guardian*, January 6, 2022. Web.

Wilson's interests extended: For more about E.O. Wilson, see "Remembering Professor Wilson: A Tribute to E.O. Wilson from Gorongosa National Park," Gorongosa National Park, Mozambique. Web; Carl Zimmer, "E.O. Wilson, a Pioneer of Evolutionary Biology, Dies at 92," *New York Times*, December 27, 2021; Paula J. Ehrlich, "E.O. Wilson, 'Darwin's Natural Heir,' Has Passed away at 92," E.O. Wilson Biodiversity Foundation, December 27, 2021. Web.

"His record shows": "A Memorial Tribute to the Late Dr. Bert C. Williams," Adopted by the Faculty of the College of Arts and Science, September 15, 1954, University of Alabama, Tuscaloosa.

28. Everything Endures

Entitled "Blessed": Lui Collins, "Blessed" (Live), *Alive at Home*, 2021, YouTube, CD Baby. Web.

Hank Williams's iconic recording: Hank Williams, "Cool Water" (2019 Remaster), YouTube, BMG Rights Management. Web.

Photo Credits

All personal photos are from the author's collection. Additional photos are listed in order of appearance.

Chapter 1. Another World

Group posing in front of the Biology Department, then housed in Nott Hall, University of Alabama, Tuscaloosa, 1948. Courtesy of The University of Alabama Libraries Special Collections.

Chapter 6. Waiting for Justice

African American neighborhood in Tuscaloosa, mid-1950s. Roland Harper collection. Courtesy of The University of Alabama Libraries Special Collections.

Group of robed Ku Klux Klan members during a protest against Autherine Lucy's enrollment, February 6, 1956. James William Oakley, Jr., collection. Courtesy of The University of Alabama Libraries Special Collections.

Chapter 8. Oak Ridge

Aerial view of Oak Ridge National Laboratory, 1948. Photo by Ed Westcott. Wikimedia Commons. https://commons.wikimedia.org/wiki/File:Oak_Ridge_National_Lab._(7584965750).jpg

Chapter 9. The Half-Life of Memory

Alabama Insane Hospital (later renamed Bryce Hospital), Tuscaloosa, 1907. Wikimedia Commons. https://commons.wikimedia.org/wiki/File:Alabama_Insane_Hospital_front_1907.jpg

Chapter 27. From Seed to Tree to Fruit

Dr. Bert Williams using radioactive phosphorus as a tracer to study the development of root tips. Pictured with his chief research assistant, E.O. Wilson, then an undergraduate at the University of Alabama. The Corolla collection. *Corolla*, Vol. 57, 1945. Courtesy of The University of Alabama Libraries Special Collections.

About the Author

Born in southern Indiana, Rebecca Williams Mlynarczyk spent her early childhood in Tuscaloosa, Alabama. A Professor Emerita of Composition and Rhetoric at the City University of New York, she now divides her time between Brooklyn, New York, and Plainfield, Massachusetts. She is the author of *Conversations of the Mind: The Uses of Journal Writing for Second-Language Learners* and the co-author of *In Our Own Words* (with Steven B. Haber) and *Basic Writing* (with George Otte). *From Seed to Tree to Fruit* is her first memoir.

www.ingramcontent.com/pod-product-compliance
Lightning Source LLC
Chambersburg PA
CBHW020922090426
42736CB00010B/997